Identifying
Poets

Identifying Poets

Self and Territory in Twentieth-Century Poetry

ROBERT CRAWFORD

Edinburgh University Press

© Robert Crawford, 1993

Edinburgh University Press Ltd
22 George Square, Edinburgh

Typeset in Linotron Galliard
by Koinonia Ltd, Bury, and
printed and bound in Great Britain
by The University Press, Cambridge

A CIP record for this book is available
from the British Library

ISBN 0 7486 0409 X

The Publishers wish to acknowledge
subsidy from the Scottish Arts Council
towards the publication of this volume.

Contents

To my co-editors of *Verse*
with gratitude

Acknowledgements

MANY PEOPLE have played a part in the writing of this book. I would like to thank in particular my fellow editors of the magazine *Verse*, to whom *Identifying Poets* is dedicated. Since founding *Verse* in 1984 with Henry Hart and David Kinloch, I have enjoyed participating at first-hand in the dissemination of work by some of the poets discussed here; with its Scottish-international outlook, *Verse* has also made me think all the harder about territory and poetic identity and has helped me maintain connections between my work as poet, critic and editor. So I am aware of the considerable debt I owe to Henry Hart, to David Kinloch, to Richard Price, who became an editor of the magazine in 1990, and to my St Andrews colleague Nicholas Roe, who was a co-editor in 1990 and 1991. For information and sometimes argument in conversation and letters I wish to thank John Ashbery, John Burnside, Douglas Dunn, W. N. Herbert, Frank Kuppner, Somhairle MacGill-Eain, Edwin Morgan, and Les Murray, particularly the last named who has been unstintingly generous in letting me see the work of other Australian poets. Earlier versions of some parts of this book appeared in *Cencrastus, Journal of American Studies, London Review of Books, Poetry Review*, and *Scottish Literary Journal*. I record my gratitude to the editors of all those periodicals, especially Peter Forbes and Karl Miller, as well as to the universities of Dundee, London and Wales, the British Association for Australian Studies and the Fourth International Conference on the Literature of Region and Nation, to all of whom various earlier versions of chapters were given as lectures. My own colleagues and students in the Department of English at the University of St Andrews, particularly those involved with the St Andrews Poetry Festival, have helped provide an open and stimulating atmosphere in which to work. Thanks are due also to the Principal and Fellows of St Hugh's College, Oxford, for electing me to the Elizabeth Wordsworth Junior Research Fellowship there from 1984–7; and to the British Academy for the award of a Postdoctoral

Fellowship which I enjoyed holding in the Department of English Literature at Glasgow University between 1987 and 1989 when I took up my present post as Lecturer in Modern Scottish Literature at St Andrews.

The sources of copyright materials quoted in this volume are acknowledged in detail in the endnotes to this book (which should be seen, like this page, as an extension of the copyright page of the present volume), but I would like to thank in particular Georges Borchardt, Inc., and Carcanet Press for permission to quote from John Ashbery's *As We Know* (published in USA by Viking Penguin), *Selected Poems* (published in USA by Viking Penguin) and *Self-Portrait in a Convex Mirror* (published in USA by Viking Penguin), John Burnside's *The Hoop*, Frank Kuppner's *A Bad Day for the Sung Dynasty*, Les Murray's *The Boys Who Stole the Funeral* (published in Australia by Angus & Robertson and in USA by Farrar, Straus & Giroux, Inc.), *Collected Poems* (published by permission of Persea Books in USA by Farrar, Straus & Giroux, Inc.), and *Dog Fox Field* (published in Australia by Angus & Robertson and in USA by Farrar, Straus & Giroux, Inc.), and from Judith Wright's *A Human Pattern: Selected Poems* (published in Australia by Angus & Robertson); to Secker and Chatto & Windus for permission to quote from Peter Reading's *3 in 1*; to Faber and Faber for permission to quote from T. S. Eliot's *Collected Poems 1909–1962* (published in USA by Harcourt Brace Jovanovich, Inc.); to Galloping Dog Press and Tom Leonard for permission to quote from *Intimate Voices: Selected Work 1965–1983*; to Michael Grieve and Carcanet Press Ltd for permission to quote from Hugh MacDiarmid's *Collected Poems*.

The typescript of this book was prepared by the secretaries at the Department of English, University of St Andrews – Dorothy Black, Helen Kay and Frances Mullan; Judy Moir copy-edited it; J. C. Bittenbender helped in its proofreading (though errors remain my own); and Dr Robyn Marsack compiled the index. I would like to thank all these people, along with Penny Clarke and the staff of Edinburgh University Press.

Most of all I would like to thank my wife for her love and patience while I was pondering and writing what follows.

R.C.
St Andrews, 1993

Introduction
Bakhtin and the Identifying Poet

THIS BOOK deals with the way twentieth-century poets construct for themselves an identity which allows them to identify with or to be identified with a particular territory. *Identifying Poets* has a Scottish accent, but covers an international range of writers; cumulatively, the following individual studies aim to suggest that the 'identifying poet' is crucial to modern verse. An awareness of this lets us see Scottish poetry (in English, Gaelic and Scots) as essential rather than peripheral to the development of poetry in the century now ending. It is not difficult to think of twentieth-century poets who have made for themselves identities which let them be identified with, re-state, and even renovate the identity of a particular territory – Yeats, Williams and Curnow spring immediately to mind. At the same time, there are other poets – David Gascoyne, Elizabeth Jennings, perhaps T. S. Eliot – whose work would seem to deflect such an 'identifying' reading.

Good poetry resists pigeonholing. So although this introductory chapter proposes ways in which literary theory may suggest models useful for interpreting the work of 'identifying poets', I intend these to be suggestions only. Paradigms and labels are of limited use in the interpretation of poetry, though they can be helpful. The increasing professonalization of literary studies has led in many cases to a sometimes acrimonious split between critics (including theorists) and poets within academia, where theory and criticism is often presented as one institutional department, and creative writing as another. In a wider context, there is growing suspicion which divides writers, journalists and others outside academia from those who do at least some of their work in an institutional academic framework. International signs of this suspicion have crystallized recently in such pieces as Les Murray's essay 'The Suspect Captivity of the Fisher King' and Dana Gioia's controversial attacks on creative writing programmes as expressed in his contributions to *The Atlantic Monthly*, *Poetry Review*, and *Verse*.[1] Between some of the poets discussed in this book there are obvious connections; between others the differences are as striking. I would be doing both the poets and my argument a disservice if I made their poetries sound the same. Sorley MacLean and John Ashbery are writers who have engaged with non-native traditions and made out of that engagement a voice which articulates the culture of the place which is their home; beyond that they have virtually nothing in common. In stressing the importance of what links them I do not intend to betray their difference.

Identity (and so difference) is one of the central modern obsessions. The self-image is as important in the boardroom as the pub. In literature, as in other areas of human activity, questions of the self and of identity have come to be more discussed and more problematic as the twentieth century developed from Robert Musil to Roland Barthes and beyond. The 'death of the author' and the 'decentring of the subject' have made critics and writers more and more aware of the self as a synthetic construct, and of the problem of what one recent reviewer called 'Finding one's self in a self-less world.'[2] Postmodernity appears to offer us a shopping arcade of selves from which we may pick one or several, ready to wear, ready for modification, and frequently ready also for obsolescence in the face of next year's fashions.

Our obsession with the instability of the self has grown since the Enlightenment; it was fuelled particularly by the thought of the Scot David Hume, whose philosophical work on the flux of identity is contemporary with the work of the Scottish 'identifying poet' James Macpherson. Through his Ossianic 'translations', Macpherson sought to give his country a Gaelic identity. Yet in this identity the genuine and the fictional were so shifting, unstable and closely bonded that readers still argue over its precise nature. After Macpherson came the quintessential 'identifying poet' Burns, who was adopted as Scotland's national bard, and after Burns came Wordsworth of the Lakes. One might assume that the age of Romantic nationalism was the great age of the 'identifying poet', and that the twentieth century with its supposedly cosmopolitan modernism and postmodernism brought poets of a very different, delocalized emphasis.

Even if one goes along with such an assumption, there are exceptions, such as Yeats; and Robert Frost; and MacDiarmid; and Auden with his 'English Study'; and W. C. Williams; and Charles Olson; and R. S. Thomas; and Judith Wright; and Derek Walcott; and Les Murray; and Seamus Heaney, Tony Harrison, and Edwin Morgan and the Douglas Dunn who aims to 'reconstruct a self...'. Looking over the course of modern verse, the more one thinks – so this book argues – the more such 'exceptions' become the norm. The 'identifying poet' is not someone to be discussed in the terms of metropolitan cultural imperialism as 'regional' or 'provincial', but to be seen as central to and typical of the poetry of the twentieth century. Accompanying such a realization is the appreciation that the concerns of those poets who construct poetic selves that may be identified with particular territories are bound up with the shifting and constructed selves which lie at the heart of the Enlightenment itself and at the heart of post-Enlightenment Romantic poetry.

> Forlorn! the very word is like a bell
> To toll me back from thee to my sole self!

When was the modern literary self ever 'sole'? Certainly not in these lines from Keats's 'Ode to a Nightingale' where the 'me' is travelling a distance to rejoin the 'self'. Certainly not in *The Prelude* where, for all the illusion of intimate access to 'The Growth of a Poet's Mind', readers are aware of a host of selves: the 'I' who is appearing to author the poem sometimes joins with the reader in a convivial or authorial 'we', or moves away from the reader to become a 'he' – The Poet – or another past 'I' who is distanced from the 'present' authorial 'I' – a removed self. Such a process of self-distancing can be observed in a few randomly chosen lines from Book X of *The Prelude*.

> Why should I not confess that earth was then
> To me what an inheritance new-fallen
> Seems, when the first time visited, to one
> Who thither comes to find in it his home?
> He walks about and looks upon the place
> With cordial transport, moulds it, and remoulds,
> And is half pleased with things that are amiss,
> 'Twill be such joy to see them disappear.
>
> (X, 145–52)

In this passage about the bonding of an individual to a territory there is a movement from 'I' through 'one' to 'he', so that when the next verse-paragraph opens with the lines 'An active partisan, I thus convoked / From every object pleasant circumstance / To suit my ends', we are aware that these lines about the formation of a self are about the formation of an 'I' which is at some remove from the 'I' of the authorial producer of *The Prelude*.[3] That 'Growth of a Poet's Mind' is in part at least about the transformation of one self into another.

If we allow ourselves recourse to modern biographies of the historical William Wordsworth, we realise also that much of the apparent intimacy with 'a poet's mind' which *The Prelude* grants us is itself an illusion. The act of self-distancing which produces 'Vaudracour and Julia' is at one with the repression of Annette Vallon. *The Prelude*, in whatever version, is an act of shielding as well as one of revelation. It is not a piece of individual soul-bearing so much as the creation of a textual self, that textual self which more than all others allows us to see less a historical individual than the reader's constructed 'Wordsworth'.

Behind Keats and Wordsworth lies the Robert Burns whose work both later poets admired and learned from. Burns is one of the archetypal modern poets in his formation of a multiple self or selves – earthy, urbane, pious, libertine, demotic, high-literary. These selves simultaneously won for the literary entity 'Robert Burns' an identification with the territory of Scotland and its folk, and an ability to be claimed as universal – by men at least – since 'A man's a man for a' that'. Burns worked on his image, created his public and his literary self, at least as carefully as would Wordsworth. René Wellek reminds us of Wordsworth's interest in the way in which Burns had, in Wordsworth's own words, 'constructed a poetic self'.[4] Burns was the poet as amazing and erotic public star, precursor of Byron, ultimately unknowable as an individual and compelling as a text.

The example of Burns, in whom we see less a self-made man than a man-made self or selves, is but one of many reminders that our contemporary preoccupation with 'self-fashioning', with an unstable synthetic 'subject', and with constructed identities is simply an outgrowth of earlier cultural concerns. *'Je suis un autre'* wrote Rimbaud to Paul Demeny in 1871, punning perhaps on *Je suis un auteur*.[5] An increasing awareness of the otherness of textuality is clear in the work of the Italian Futurists and in the Apollinaire of *Calligrammes*, who prefaces that volume with a poem ('Liens') which, according to one modern editor, raises 'self-division to the rank of the major theme around which the whole modernist section of the volume is constructed'.[6] Self-division could hardly go further than it did in the case(s) of Portugal's Fernando Pessoa whose work appeared under the names of four poets, each with a distinct literary character and style.[7]

Such creative divisions made possible by the generation of textual selves are at one, surely, with the tradition of the *doppelgänger*, with Freud's divisions of the psyche, and with the twentieth-century's growing emphases on relativity and relativism: different perceptions produce altered or mobile selves. The text, however, may also unite different selves. An interest in self, other, and textual identity is clear in Stevenson's 1886 *The Strange Case of Dr Jekyll and Mr Hyde* whose concern is patently psychological, rather than simply depending on the physical advances of chemistry. 'I stood already committed to a profound duplicity of life', writes Henry Jekyll of his earlier self before he ever became Mr Hyde.[8] Yet writing, textuality, is also of great importance in *Jekyll and Hyde*, a story which must be pieced together from documents. The final document has been given the title 'Henry Jekyll's Full Statement of the Case', but this is an 'editorial title', like the titles of such earlier bits of the tale as 'Story of the Door' and 'Incident of the Letter'. The identity of the assumed author of the final section of the story is to a degree deliberately blurred since it has become clear that Jekyll and Hyde share the same handwriting. In some ways these opposing selves – or self and other – are textually united, as the shifting pronouns and referents indicate: 'I saw for the first time the appearance of Edward Hyde... This, too, was myself... I had supplied my double with a signature... I could write my own hand.... He, I say – I cannot say, I.'⁹ As this narrative nears its conclusion it is noticeable that its writer presents both 'Hyde' and 'Jekyll' in the third person yet continues to use the pronoun 'I'. This 'I' is a purely textual self, distanced now from either the atrocities of Hyde or the impotence of Jekyll, yet horrified because it is not fully independent. The two selves, Jekyll and Hyde, interfere with each other through the medium of the text, yet the ultimate, textual 'I' belongs to neither. It is that 'I' with which the story leaves us. *Je suis un autre.*

With its fascinating destabilization of identity and its culminating sentence, 'Here, then, as I lay down the pen, and proceed to seal up my confession, I bring the life of that unhappy Henry Jekyll to an end', we could read *Jekyll and Hyde* as dealing with the death of the author and the birth of the text.¹⁰ Such a reading could be limiting but useful – useful not least because Scottish literature has been ghettoized recently in part at any rate by the refusal of most of its critics to engage with international developments in literary theory. Perhaps if Scottish critics were less conservative, they would be better attuned to their own often experimental literature. However, my invoking of *Jekyll and Hyde* here is designed not to link it to Barthes or beyond, but to set it, along with the exploration of self and other in Wilde's *The Picture of Dorian Gray*, Laforgue's *dédoublement*, Pessoa's work and Freud's, along with Yeats's self and anti-self and MacDiarmid's Caledonian Antisyzygy, as part of the European context of that fascination with self and other in which we may view the work of the literary theorist who seems to me to have most to offer to those interested not just in Scottish writing but in the construction of regional and national territorial voices in literature. That theorist is Mikhail Bakhtin.

In the English-speaking world the contextualizing and historicizing of Bakhtin's work are only now getting under way. David Danow points out, for instance, that Bakhtin's emphasis on dialogue is paralleled in the work of the American semiotician C. S. Peirce who maintained in 1933 that 'thinking always proceeds in the form of a dialogue – a dialogue between different phases of the ego.'[11] Other points of contact between Bakhtin and familiar Anglo-American thought are likely to emerge and be developed. For instance, the impact made on Bakhtin by the neo-Kantian Marburg School around the time of the Russian Revolution may put us in mind of the graduate student T. S. Eliot who chose to study philosophy at Marburg in 1914, but had to depart hastily as the First World War got under way.[12] In relation to Bakhtin's early writing on 'Author and Hero in Aesthetic Activity' we may consider not only Jekyll and Hyde but also the obsessively self-conscious J. Alfred Prufrock:

> A man who has grown accustomed to dreaming about himself in concrete terms – a man who strives to visualize the external image of himself, who is morbidly sensitive about the outward impression he produces and yet is insecure about that impression and easily wounded in his pride – such a man loses the proper, purely inner stance in relation to his own body. He becomes awkward, 'unwieldy,' and does not know what to do with his hands and feet. This occurs because an indeterminate *other* intrudes upon his movements and gestures and a second principle of axiological comportment toward himself arises for him: the context of his *self-*consciousness is muddled by the context of the *other's* consciousness of him, and his inner body is confronted by an outer body that is divorced from him – an outer body living in the eyes of the *other*.[13]

This surely explains to us the Prufrock paralysed and formulated by his own supposed impression on others: '(They will say: "But how his arms and legs are thin!")', and it is striking that behind Prufrock is Bakhtin's revered Dostoevsky, author of *Crime and Punishment* and *The Double*.[14] The more we read Bakhtin, the more familiar he becomes. Though I write neither as a philosopher nor as a literary theorist, I suggest that Bakhtin may appeal strongly to the culture which produced Adam Smith's *Theory of Moral Sentiments* and the Burns who wrote 'O wad some Pow'r the giftie gie us / *To see oursels as others see us!*'[15]

Certainly Bakhtin's notion of heteroglossia – 'other tonguedness' or linguistic division – is surely valuable in a Scottish context, as in many other settings. The sociologist David McCrone, writing on 'The Sociology of a Stateless Nation', has argued that 'Scotland stands at the forefront of sociological concerns in the late twentieth century. Rather than being an awkward, ill-fitting case, it is at the centre of the discipline's postmodern dilemma.'[16] In *Devolving English Literature* and elsewhere I have been concerned to demonstrate that Scottish culture not only shaped crucially the university subject of 'English Literature', but also produced heteroglot and multicultural kinds of writing which form not a peripheral exception to but a model for international writing in the English-speaking world in the nineteenth and twentieth centuries.[17] Bakhtin's thinking on heteroglossia may provide a useful intellectual framework in which to view these contentions, for if language is normally made up of languages – if discourse is always a blend of discourses (scientific, demotic, jargons, dialects) – then, like Caribbean or Australian writing, Scottish writing, in which this blending is frequently explicit, becomes typical rather than eccentric.

Since the majority of its potential and actual readers are users of a form of English , one may consider writing in Scots as having the effect of what Bakhtin calls 'dialogized heteroglossia', that is, utterance or writing in which there is clear friction or 'argument' between different discourses. An example may demonstrate this most clearly. In MacDiarmid's famous first line of 'The Bonnie Broukit Bairn' – 'Mars is braw in cramassy' – the words 'Mars', 'is', and 'in' must be recognized by most readers as 'Standard English'; yet when such words appear in the context of a Scots poem, they appear to be 'quoted' or recontextualized in the zone of Scots and are turned back on their more familiar indentity. They become double-voiced, acting out a dialogue between Scots and English. Scots language purists will argue that such words are 'guid Scots words' which happen to be shared with modern English. Yet it would be hard to argue today that these words were not most familiar as English and that Scots is likely to strike the majority of international readers as a deliberate variation on English, which frequently quotes, re-accents, and realigns elements of English vocabulary, mixing them in a rich impurity with alien elements (in the same way that some 'Black English' works). Such Scots is a form of 'dialogized heteroglossia,' which is why the use of it affects not only Scottish but English identity, in much the same way as does the superbly impure language of James Joyce and the other Modernists. Recent studies have begun to see *Ulysses* and *The Waste Land*, for instance, in terms of Bakhtinian heteroglossia, but the process will extend much further, encompassing the work of MacDiarmid, Morgan, and other Scottish writers.[18] Certainly the thought of the Bakhtin who contended that 'one language can, after all, see itself in the light of another language'[19] will provide a strong theoretical context for the reading of such contemporary Scottish poets as the W. N. Herbert who contends that 'For one English reader to understand one of MacDiarmid's synthetic lyrics is qualitatively more important than the publication of any number of wee bardies who never stray from 'normal' Scots in vocabulary or idea. Because it suggests to that English reader what the wee bardies cannot, that Scots is a language capable of doing more than English, capable of doing something different from English that criticises and, finally, extends English. That is the spirit on which I write Scots poetry.'[20]

With Herbert's position towards contemporary Scots and English we may provocatively align Bakhtin's description of the relationship between Latin and Greek: 'From its very first steps the Latin literary word viewed itself in the light of the Greek word, *through the eyes* of the Greek word; it was from the very beginning a word "with a sideways glance", a stylized word enclosing itself, as it were, in its own piously stylized quotation marks.'[21] Tzvetan Todorov cites Bakhtin's remark that 'Verbal and ideological decentering occurs only when a national culture sheds its closure and its self-sufficiency, when it becomes conscious of itself as only *one* among other cultures and languages.'[22] That remark is fruitful for the consideration of both Scots and English in all their international varieties.

Yet if Bakhtinian heteroglossia and dialogized heteroglossia are potently attractive for all interested in dialect, regional voices and the articulation of particular cultural identities – for all of us who know that 'one's own language is never a single language' – it is as well to bear in mind that recent commentary is valuable not least because it problematizes the applicability of Bakhtin's work.[23] One might wish to use in Scottish, Australian, Irish, or innumerable other contexts Bakhtin's idea that, as Tony Crowley summarizes, 'all forms of discourse – from the smallest units to the national language and beyond – are shot through with social and historical conflict'.[24] One might wish to contend, for example, that Scots writing carnivalizes and subverts the authority of standard English. Yet Crowley points out that we need to historicize Bakhtin and recognize that many of his ideas may have evolved as covert strategies for dealing with the monologic authoritarianism of Stalinist Russia. In such circumstances, heteroglossia may promise liberty; in other circumstances it may not.

So Crowley aligns and contrasts the attitudes to language held by Antonio Gramsci and Bakhtin, pointing out that 'For Gramsci, unlike Bakhtin, it is the historical situation which will enable the cultural activist to evaluate which are to be the required forms of discourse and language.'[25] At one historical moment (as in contemporary Britain) it may be that centralizing tendencies are to be resisted by heteroglossia and dialogism; at another historical moment, circumstances may require different strategies. As Crowley indicates, 'The fate of nations which have managed to escape from colonial rule and the historical complexities involved in such processes serve as further counter-examples to Bakhtin's preferences and again stress the need for historical specificity in the analysis of such situations. The preference for pluralism and difference may well be a laudable one: but history demonstrates that forms of unity and organization may be a prerequisite before such an achievement can be attained.'[26]

This is a salutary emphasis. Particularly for those who are much concerned with writing outside the English metropolitan or cultural centre, the stress on the centrifugal as opposed to the centripetal which Bakhtin's writing encourages, may be readily attractive. Lest it be too easily attractive, it is as well to be aware that some of Crowley's cautions can be seen as implicit in the writing of Bakhtin himself:

> Alongside the centripetal forces, the centrifugal forces of language carry on their uninterrupted work; alongside verbal-ideological centralization and unification, the uninterrupted processes of decentralization and disunification go foward.
>
> Every concrete utterance of a speaking subject serves as a point where centrifugal as well as centripetal forces are brought to bear. The processes of centralization and decentralization, of unification and disunification, intersect in the utterance…. Every utterance participates in the 'unitary language' (in its centripetal forces and tendencies) and at the same time partakes of social and historical heteroglossia (the centrifugal, stratifying forces).[27]

To all of us who are interested in the articulation of cultural difference and the construction of territorial voices within the English-speaking world, Bakhtin has much to offer. I predict that the thinker who spent his boyhood in Vilnius, that 'realized example of heteroglossia', and whose own biography relates so arrestingly to his theories, will become the dominant, certainly the most attractive literary theorist of the 1990s.[28] Moreover, Bakhtin's work is likely to appeal not least to those constituencies which have been most ignored by the mid-century growth of literary theory, marginalized groups which include the heterochronous Scotland and Wales. Among the texts available in English which are most likely to appeal to those constituencies are the essays on 'Art and Answerability' (in the book of that title), 'From the Prehistory of Novelistic Discourse' (in *The Dialogic Imagination*), 'Response to a Question from the *Novy Mir* Editorial Staff' (in *Speech Genres & Other Late Essays*), and *Rabelais and his World*.[29] Arguably the best introduction remains the 1984 *Mikhail Bakhtin* by Katerina Clark and Michael Holquist, though the opening sections of David K. Danow's *The Thought of Mikhail Bakhtin* offer a shorter, accessible approach, as do some of the essays in David Lodge's *After Bakhtin*.[30]

Lodge's book is one of a number of indications that Bakhtin's work may be attractive to writers as well as to critics. Though Bakhtin exalts his concept of the 'novel', his treatment of Pushkin's *Eugene Onegin* as 'a living mix of varied and opposing voices' and 'a self-critique of the literary language of the era, a product of this language's various strata (generic, everyday, "currently fashionable")' mutually illuminating one another', invites consideration of both *Don Juan* and the different poetries of MacDiarmid and Ashbery.[31] Significantly, of the very few writers who have been involved in the application of Bakhtin's work to modern poetry, two are poets – the American 'Language' poet Michael Palmer, and the Welsh-based English poet Ian Gregson.[32] Though he has not written about Bakhtin, Edwin Morgan has recalled that he was attracted to Bakhtin's ideas when he read them 'a considerable time ago'. Such profoundly dialogic poems as 'The First Men on Mercury' would suggest something of the nature of Bakhtin's attraction for Morgan.[33] For all their awkwardnesses, Bakhtin's ideas are writer-friendly.

Bakhtin's work is also a textual minefield, pitted with revisions, lost works, disputed translations and illegibilities. As befits a thinker so enthusiastic about dialogue and co-authoring, there remains a virulent argument about the disputed authorship of several Bakhtin-influenced texts attributed to Bakhtin by Michael Holquist and others. As an outsider who does not read Russian, I find it difficult to counter the objections to Bakhtin's authorship of the disputed texts which have been raised by Morson and Emerson, whose *Mikhail Bakhtin: Creation of a Prosaics* is a useful if heavy supplement to the Clark-Holquist study.[34] Understandably, critics appropriate Bakhtin for their own ends. The pioneering introductory work by Julia Kristeva and Tzvetan Todorov tended to reduce Bakhtin's emphasis on the dialogic to mere 'intertextuality'.[35] More recently, Don H. Bialostosky in *Wordsworth, Dialogics, and the Practice of Criticism*, despite some stimulating material, seems to me to use Bakhtin as part of a too narrowly 'professional' academicism which would confirm John Carey's worst fears about literary theory's 'anti-popular status'.[36]

Bakhtin's terminology is often awkward and apparently inconsistent; his commentators are united in emphasizing that we cannot simply adopt his work but, in keeping with its thrust, we must enter into dialogue with it. The Bakhtin who loved the liberating interpretative 'loophole' which makes possible future new meaning, who linked the religious to the literary, and the literary to the dynamic, prosaic everyday world which we inhabit, this Bakhtin who lectured to packed audiences of 700 electrical workers at a light bulb factory in the late 1950s is far removed from the gurus of the French *grandes écoles*.[37] It is this Bakhtin, eager to see language and writing as grounded in the actual, and fascinated by the authoring of a self, who has so much to suggest to us about the construction of a poetic identity linked with a particular territory, not through any simple local chauvinism but through the optimal use of the available language or languages.

For Bakhtin, as for the thinkers of the Scottish Enlightenment, people are fundamentally *social* beings. The self exists, not in isolation, but in society; self and society interact in a dialogic process. Just as every act of utterance anticipates a possible answer, so every self is open to the dialogic process. This is not the same, though, as saying that the self is submerged in the multiple 'other' of society. Rather, as Morson and Emerson point out,

> Bakhtin warns us, however, that neither individuals nor any other social entities are locked within their boundaries. They are extraterritorial, partially 'located outside' themselves. Thus, Bakhtin refers to the "nonself-sufficiency" of the self [TRDB, p. 287]. 'To be means to be for another, and through the other for oneself. A person has no sovereign internal territory, he is wholly and always on the boundary; looking inside himself, he looks *into the eyes of another* or *with the eyes of another*. [ibid.]'[38]

Identity then (including, I would contend, the poetic identity which allows a poet to identify with a particular territory) always lives through and is determined by a 'debatable land', a shifting, dynamic border territory. Though Bakhtin is using the terms 'territory' and 'boundary' metaphorically as part of a discussion of culture, these metaphors are surely richly suggestive. In *Problems of Dostoevsky's Poetics*, discussing cultural entities, Bakhtin maintains that they are, in effect, made up entirely of boundaries: 'One must not, however, imagine the realm of culture as some sort of spatial whole, having boundaries but also having internal territory. The realm of culture has no internal territory: it is entirely distributed along the boundaries, boundaries pass everywhere, through its every aspect.... Every cultural act lives essentially on the boundaries: in this is its seriousness and significance; abstracted from boundaries it loses its soil, it becomes empty, arrogant, it degenerates and dies.'[39]

Taking such metaphors rather literally helps me to explain my own excitement as a critic at the crossings of territorial and linguistic boundaries in the work of Scott, Fenimore Cooper, Carlyle, the Modernists, and the other nineteenth and twentieth-century writers I discussed in *Devolving English Literature*. It also provides theoretical support for my contention in the final chapter of this book that it is an enriching position for the writer in Scotland to 'live between and across languages'. But much more important than these personal satisfactions, and arguably more important than the support which Bakhtin may offer as a potential saint of Scottish writing, is what Bakhtin has to offer all those around the world who are interested in the formation of an individual poetic identity, that construction of a particular literary self which allows a writer to identify with a particular territory, be the writer Robert Frost or Les Murray, Sorley MacLean or Derek Walcott. For Bakhtin reminds us that the creation of a vital cultural identity, like that of individual and personal literary identity, depends less on a looking in than on a looking out. It is the outward-looking, expansive gaze which makes possible the interaction with a 'significant other', a foreign culture in which gifts for the future of one's own culture may be located, and in which an illuminating reflection of one's own identity (or desired identity) may be glimpsed. That foreign culture may be geographically or linguistically or temporally 'other', or a combination of these.

Towards the end of that remarkably rich short essay which deserves to become a key text in modern criticism, the 'Response to a Question from the *Novy Mir* Editorial Staff,' Bakhtin writes two paragraphs that are exuberantly fruitful for any consideration of 'identifying poets':

> There exists a very strong, but one-sided and thus untrustworthy idea that in order better to understand a foreign culture, one must enter into it, forgetting one's own, and view the world through the eyes of this foreign culture. The idea, as I said, is one-sided. Of course, a certain entry as a living being into a foreign culture, the possibility of seeing the world through its eyes, is a necessary part of the process of understanding it; but if this were the only aspect of this understanding, it would merely be duplication and would not entail anything new or enriching. *Creative understanding* does not renounce itself, its own place in time, its own culture; and it forgets nothing. In order to understand, it is immensely important for the person who understands to be *located outside* the object of his or her creative understanding – in time, in space, in culture. For one cannot even really see one's own exterior and comprehend it as a whole, and no mirrors or photographs can help; our real exterior can be seen and understood only by another people, because they are located outside us in space and because they are *others*.
>
> In the realm of culture, outsideness is a most powerful factor in understanding. It is only in the eyes of *another culture* that foreign culture reveals itself fully and profoundly (but not maximally fully, because there will be cultures that see and understand even more). A meaning only reveals its depths since it has encountered and come into contact with another, foreign meaning: they engage in a kind of dialogue, which surmounts the closedness and one-sidedness of these particular meanings, these cultures. We raise new questions for a foreign culture, ones that it did not raise itself; we seek answers to our own questions in it; and the foreign culture responds to us by revealing to us its new aspects and new semantic depths. Without *one's own* questions one cannot creatively understand anything other or foreign (but, of course, the questions must be serious and

sincere). Such a dialogic encounter of two cultures does not result in merging or mixing. Each retains its own unity and *open* totality, but they are mutually enriched.'[40]

These two paragraphs, oriented towards both anthropology and literature, provoke in me a sense of immediate revelation and excited recognition, as if they came out of my own personal circumstances. They do not, but they help explain me to myself and they help me to perceive my culture in a new way. The application of Bakhtin's words will be manifold. One might, for instance, consider the past of one's culture as an 'other' culture which the present confronts, questions, and is interrogated by. Certainly these paragraphs from the *Novy Mir* response explain the way in which the American Robert Frost travelled to Britain to construct for himself his New England self; and why Sorley MacLean's engagements with English-language Modernism and with the North African desert were crucial to his developing a poetic identity which helped him identify with and recreate a mid-twentieth-century Gaelic self. Parallel cases are numerous – Ashbery in France or in the nineteenth century, Murray in Scotland or in Australia's Aboriginal culture, MacDiarmid in Salonika, Marseilles or London – these are but a few instances of identifying poets who develop an identity with and for their own culture through a fructifying engagement with another culture and literature.

There is a tendency, particularly when considering so-called 'regional' and 'provincial' literatures, that we concentrate too much on a writer's relationship with precedents and antecedents in his or her own culture. One consequence of this is that we place too much emphasis on the apparently unchanging elements of a culture, tending towards an essentialist position which assumes some sort of unaltering Scotland or Wales or Canada. In practice, though, such a community or tradition would be dead. It is only by remaining dynamic, by evolving, that a culture or a literary tradition continues to live. It is its loopholes, its openness to the 'other' or 'others' which allows it to re-view and develop itself. In literature and in poetry it is those writers who look abroad who are often its most valuable territorial voices. Bakhtin's interactive model of the self and the other allows us to appreciate that vital to Robert Frost's constructed New England identity may be aspects of his Scottishness and that the most valuably 'Scottish' writers of this century may be those most open to international modernism. Kafka was not opposed to Muir's Scottishness, but was part of it. In examining 'identifying poets' it is the living borders that matter, the transforming open-ness to the other. Without such openness these poets can only stultify; they cannot recreate and revoice an identity for their territory or communities. For regional and national identities are never fixed, but are fluid, part of an ongoing

dialogic process whose every articulation is open to a different and trans-
forming response. This means that there is no one essential, unchanging
Scotland, England, America, Australia, or New Zealand. Instead, there are
Scotlands, Englands, Australias, Americas, New Zealands. For identity is
dynamic, it alters; and the 'identifying poets' who come to be taken as
spokespeople for these territories evolve for themselves voices which may
often appear dynamically different from those of their local predecessors.

Identifying Poets does not aim to be comprehensive in the poets it
examines. Rather, it presents a number of studies of individual writers
whose work marks them out as 'identifying poets'. All these poets come
from geographical areas normally thought of as lying within the 'English-
speaking world'; all are or were speakers of English. Yet as befits a book in
which heteroglossia is an important underlying theme, not all of these
poets write in English. Some of the poets considered are widely regarded
as important writers; others are not. Some are, some are not fashionable.
Since my aim is to demonstrate the wide applicability of the term
'identifying poet', this is all to the good. I have included recent as well as
established writing because it is essential for the reader and for the writer
of modern poetry to be aware of contemporary developments. Only then
may readers and writers avoid simply repeating or being completely
trapped by what their contemporaries are producing; and only then may
readers and writers be fully alert to the contemporary literary idiom as well
as to ways in which it is revoicing or reinterpreting the literature of the
past, for good and for ill. I am aware that almost all the poets discussed in
this book are male, and I suggest in the last chapter that the prime
identifying gestures of female poets, especially as the century ends, may
relate to gender rather than to territory. Nonetheless, the instance of
poets such as Liz Lochhead and Judith Wright indicates that gender and
territory are not necessarily mutually exclusive. No critic can pretend to
produce a definitive reading of contemporary poetry; at the same time, for
critics to avoid engagement with a wide range of contemporary material
seems an abnegation of reponsibility. I am tempted to say that for critics
interested in localities the fault is all the worse, since there is great danger
in the reader who is interested *only* in Scottish or English or Australian
material, or who thinks that Frost or MacDiarmid is a contemporary poet.

The chapters which follow discuss a number of individual 'identifying
poets', including Robert Frost, Hugh MacDiarmid, Sorley MacLean, Les
Murray, John Ashbery and Frank Kuppner. In the final chapter, 'Home', a
variety of poets is considered in order to demonstrate that the theme of
'home, crucial for the 'identifying poet', is one of the great themes,
perhaps the major theme of late twentieth-century poetry in the English-
speaking world – using that last, problematic term only to fracture and

problematize it by paying close attention to the world of poets who write in Scots. In the postmodern world, home has no one, pure language; its language is heteroglot, richly impure. Writers who delight in this seem to me more authentically 'identifying poets' than those who would contend that home and its language are pure and undefiled. Just as the earlier chapters of *Idenfifying Poets* are selective, focusing on Frost rather than on Yeats, on Ashbery rather than on O'Hara, so even the last chapter might have been expanded endlessly to include a far greater range and variety of contemporary poets, from Iain Crichton Smith to Dave Smith and from R. S. Thomas to Andrew Greig. If readers are left thinking of more and more modern poets whose work would merit inclusion, that can only reinforce the contention of this book: we have lived and are living, particularly in the late twentieth century, in an age of 'identifying poets'.

1

Robert Frosts

Chicken farmer, shoe-worker, bobbin-boy, messenger, teacher, journalist, leather-worker, poet, student, cultural ambassador, berry-picker, lecturer. Few poets have more selves than Robert Frost, and such a list does not even exhaust Frost's occupations, let alone his ambitions. In fact, when he writes in 'Two Tramps in Mud Time' that

> My object in living is to unite
> My avocation and my vocation
> As my two eyes make one in sight

it is tempting to see here a sly joke at his own expense. For Frost had so many vocations and avocations that they are well-nigh impossible to combine in any clear-sighted unity. 'No poet in this century has written more poems involving more different kinds of work than Frost,' writes William H. Pritchard, before going on to list some of the jobs which Frost found and abandoned between 1885 and 1892.[1] Even the many jobs he did do were insufficient to content him. 'I should have been an archaeologist', he wrote to A. J. Armstrong in 1943 and though Frost as an extremely successful poet might allow himself that ironic wistfulness, he was not being merely whimsical.[2] If some of his family were drawn into the darker sides of his poetry, then they also enacted a few of his brighter dreams. Welcoming Willard E. Fraser as a new son-in-law in 1932, Frost proposes not one but four desired careers: 'I am particularly glad you are bringing archaeology into the family. Archaeology is one of the four things I wanted most to go into in life, archaeology, astronomy, farming, and teaching Latin. When I saw I wasn't going to be able to go into them all, I began to hope my four children would go into them for me, each taking up one, or in the case of the girls, marrying into it. Carol is in farming. Marj marries into archaeology. Lesley almost went into Latin.' (*SL*, 384–85)

This passage makes plain something of Frost's attitude towards women, as well as the power he exercised over his family. His wife had written poetry and criticism; when she married Frost, though, that stopped; she had married into poetry. But the letter also reveals further aspects of a Frost here seen looking in four directions. The idea of his standing where only two roads divide in a yellow wood seems a dramatic over-simplification. It would be more accurate to envisage a major inter-section where Frost takes one route, but keeps close track of the others. One of the many deft peculiarities of 'The Road Not Taken' is the speaker's being sorry that he 'could not travel both / And be one traveler.' Those last words are not just a 'poetic' embellishment, but the regret of a poet who so readily split into multiple selves. It is typical of Frost's 'Scotch-Yankee calculation' (*SL*, 201) that the lyric 'I', the self of his poem, stood at the divergence of the two roads, 'And looked down one as far as I could', before taking the other. I hope to show in this chapter that Frost made a point of maintaining contact with roads which, on the surface of things, he did not take. 'Oh, I kept the first for another day!' he exclaims with a calculated mischievous regret in the 'Oh', but given the way paths in a wood not only diverge but often re-join and criss-cross, it is quite possible that the poem's walker might find himself again on his path, perhaps even without being aware of it. The device of projecting forward into a supposed distant future is a preferred Georgian one (seen at its most striking in James Elroy Flecker's 'To a Poet a Thousand Years Hence'). Frost's self-aware use of the poeticism 'with a sigh' signals that irony is present in 'The Road Not Taken' as he antici-pates his later career as a raconteur; so does the faintly pompous repetition of 'I'. Taken quite straight, the poem's punchline ('And that has made all the difference') *is* a punchline, concluding with an effective clarity. If we take it ironically, it is also successful: the envisaged self-important dramati-zation of an insignificant turn in a wood is a send-up of conventional homely wisdom. But between these two diverging paths of interpretation are other tracks, most interesting of which is the idea that the choice between the two roads is neither definitive nor simple, since the possibility remains that the roads may join up or cross again 'as way leads on to way.'

Certainly, in the course of Frost's poetry such intersections between selves, or between parts of what his close friend Sidney Cox called Frost's 'flexible firmness of form', occur frequently.[3] The Latinist, astronomer, and archaeologist are all brought into the poetry, though not always into the best-known poems. There is a danger that, despite recent scholarship and his own intermittent notes of caution, Frost is still frozen in the guise of (albeit dark and ironic) New England farmer-sage. Of course there are complications, some of which this slippery 'identifying poet' pointed out at the end of 'New Hampshire' where, again, we may note that clear reluctance to be one traveller.

> Well, if I have to choose one or the other,
> I choose to be a plain New Hampshire farmer
> With an income in cash of, say, a thousand
> (From, say, a publisher in New York City).
> It's restful to arrive at a decision,
> And restful just to think about New Hampshire.
> At present I am living in Vermont.

These paradoxes are too simple. Frost was not merely a poet-farmer or a New Hampshire-Vermonter, and part of the effective irony here comes from its being so doubtful if he ever did arrive at a decision between his different selves. It was the way his various facets intersected and tugged at each other that enriched his poetry in its ironic and other aspects.

Studies such as John C. Kemp's *Robert Frost and New England, The Poet as Regionalist* have increased our awareness of Frost as his own public-relations man, determined to create what was, in part at least, an artificial image of himself. So successful was he that, as Kemp points out, early reviewers 'were soon sighing over his life on a "lonely farm in a forest clearing", despite the absence of any such farm in *A Boy's Will*.'[4] This was just after Frost had returned from the cosmopolitan literary life of England, determined to 'get Yankier and Yankier'. (*SL*, 103) Though he sometimes worried that he had been too successful in encouraging this public image, Frost clearly found it irresistible. So far did he like to push it that by 1942 even his time in England could seem an agricultural as well as literary interlude, with Frost speaking of being 'in Beaconsfield and in Ryton, England, where I farmed, or rather gardened in a very small way from 1912 to 1915'. (*SL*, 105) It is amusing to see Frost barely managing to qualify the farm by reducing it to a garden, just as it is fascinating to watch his construction of a farmer-self, venturing out occasionally from his New England fastness. Frost appears to be living up to a dream proposed not in England in 1913 when he determined to 'get Yankier and Yankier' but dreamed thirty years before that in San Francisco where he produced his first literary work, a piece detailed most fully by Lawrance Thompson.

> The details of it had all come to him in one of his own dreams. Alone, after running away from home and after having become lost in the mountains, he had followed a scarcely visible trail which led him through a cleft between two mountaintop cliffs. The trail led him down, down, down into a beautiful green valley, where he was welcomed and honored as a hero by a tribe of Indians who were the

only inhabitants of the secret valley. The Indians themselves had escaped from their enemies by retreating through the narrow pass into this valley, where life was always serene. Occasionally, their braves made sorties back through the secret pass in order to make surprise attacks against their enemies. But these braves always returned victoriously to their happy valley.[5]

Thompson quotes Munson's remark that this was a 'master-image, one that constantly recurs in Frost's life', and notes that Frost sometimes put himself to sleep by dreaming of it. (*EY*, 496) It offered protection, like the tribal land of Pamir reached through a Vale in 'The Bearer of Evil Tidings'. The sleep-inducing power of the dream is corroborated by Newdick who speaks of the adult Frost dreaming of these Indians and relates his dreams to the minister's philosophizing in 'The Black Cottage' where 'The speaker wishes for an isolated, uncoveted place where ideas could be held and not assailed by aggressive intruders.'[6] This may be so, but the fantasy is surely most important as foreshadowing the later life of a Frost who became on various occasions a runaway, but became, too, Frost the Californian who settled in his own New England mountain 'interval' (a gap in the mountains) and in a New England identity. This Frost, though, was not just the protected refugee; he had also incorporated into himself those Indians who sallied forth victoriously (uniting like his childhood hero, Natty Bumppo, white and Indian traits), whether to defeat his literary or his political enemies, darting from behind the figure of the farmer. Such a Frost, so unwilling to be found out, ventured abroad in various disguises, each of which was based upon a part of his genuine nature. It is two of these partly fabricated selves which I wish to examine here, showing how each could play its part in the conduct of Frost's life and in the growth of his work, and how each, in turn, intersected with the others in his development as an 'identifying poet'.

II

Robert Burns, rather than Robert Frost, must rank as the world's best-known farmer-poet, and from early boyhood Frost was well aware that Burns was part of his literary heritage. His Scottish mother read Burns's poems to him as a child.[7] Typically two-edged, Frost emphasized at once that mother's foreignness ('...my mother was an immigrant. She came to these shores from Edinburgh...') and her Americanness – a quality which, while Frost's New England father took it for granted in himself, 'meant something live and real and virile to her' (*Interviews*, 50–1). Certainly William Prescott Frost, Jr had no doubts about the Scottish side of Isabelle Moodie when, proposing marriage to her, he began his successful letter by quoting a stanza by James Graham, Marquis of Montrose. (*SL*, 5)

Frost's mother had left Scotland at the age of twelve, but her heritage was of great importance to her and she was determined to pass it on to her family. Frost's sister, Jeanie, bore her mother's cousin's name – that of the heroine in Scott's *Heart of Midlothian* – and given the strong character of his mother it is unlikely that the baby Robert was so christened solely because of his father's copperhead sympathies. The added middle name 'Lee' made Robert Frost's nationality clear, but his mother must have approved of the happy coming together of American and Scottish ideals of liberty in the forename 'Robert'. She educated the boy in Scottish heroic folktales such as those found in the ballads, in Scott's *Tales of a Grandfather*, and in the stories of Ossian. Robert enjoyed the Caledonia Club and, aged thirteen, was pleased to speak of his Scottish background and would be well aware of the career of Robert the Bruce from *Tales of a Grandfather*. It is significant that the first book which the boy read was Jane Porter's *The Scottish Chiefs*, an account of Bruce and Wallace. (*EY*, 69–72) He had to 'start that several times before I went on to the end, for I saw Wallace's execution coming and I couldn't endure it'. (*Interviews*, 218) But Frost did endure it, and as a writer-strategist he took to himself his own version of one of the most famous episodes in the career of his early namesake-hero Robert Bruce: 'I always have something back when I go to press so I wont feel too cleaned out or drawn down. I once saw a spider like Robert the Bruce. Only my spider came half way down from the roof of a church and there he had to stop and secrete some more web before he could let himself down the rest of the way to the floor and the lesson he taught was different from the lesson the spider taught Robert the Bruce. Dont attempt any more than you have secretions for! And some to share.' (*Cox*, 216)

This is more than an example of Frost building on the Scottish connotations of his heroic name. The date of this letter – March 1936 – makes it clear that the book then going to press was *A Further Range*, published that May.[8] Frost had just been asked for manuscripts by his editor, and among the poems which he then released after a long period of secretion (it was near completion in 1911) was the famous 'Design' whose speaker encounters 'a dimpled spider, fat and white'. It makes that poem all the more powerfully disturbing when the reader knows just how well aware Frost was of the hope symbolized by the best known meeting of a man with a spider. It is further unsettling that, even if he was unaware of the implicit connection, Frost, at the very time of making that poem available for publication, could use a spider as a symbol of himself as artist. We are conscious here of the darker implications of his art.

Some of those darker implications may be related to his Scottish background, though it would be wrong to do this too crudely. 'Mr Frost

likes to sing old ballads', recorded Cox in 1915. (*Cox*, 84) In many of
those Border ballads which Frost's mother recited to her young son there
is not only a sense of ever-present doom, but also a concision and a dark
wit seen at its best in a piece such as 'The Twa Corbies'. The way that
ballad emphasizes bleak whiteness, leaving implicit the blackness of the
corbies (ravens), is not infinitely removed from Frost's whiteness gov-
erned by 'design of darkness'. Such pointed, dark wit is present in a Scots
poem which Frost taught to a class of girls at the New Hampshire State
Normal School in the academic year 1911–12.

> *Says Tweed to Till –*
> *'What gars ye rin sae still?'*
> *Says Till to Tweed –*
> *'Though ye rin with speed*
> *And I rin slaw,*
> *For ae man that ye droon*
> *I droon twa.'*
>
> (*EY*, 373)

It is easy to appreciate why Frost would relish such a piece, which
Thompson thinks must have been taught him by his mother. A similar
straight-faced humour with a grim conclusion characterizes many a Frost
poem; one that comes to mind is the ballad-like 'The Bearer of Evil
Tidings'. If some of Frost's most successful poems are narratives, it is
worth remembering that he was brought up on narrative poetry which
contained direct speech, and that much of it was recited or read to him by
his mother.

He was also brought up on 'voices'. His mother's voice read or re-
counted fairy stories, such as those of George MacDonald, the Scottish
fantasist, some of whose adventures took place *At the Back of the North
Wind*. This book, very popular in Frost's childhood, blends, as Thompson
pointed out, fantasy and realism. (*EY*, 35–6, 72) So, of course, would the
author of 'The Witch of Coös'. It may be significant that in 'Never Again
Would Birds' Song be the Same', one of the poems which comes closest
to enunciating Frost's cherished theory of 'speech sounds', it is the
mother of humanity, rather than Adam the namer, who brings birds to
add to their own voices, 'an oversound'. If childhood voices were associ-
ated with Frost's mother, they were present more mysteriously in the
work of George MacDonald, whose fascination with fairies and super-
natural fantasy fed into the later work of 'Fiona Macleod' and the Celtic
Twilight movement with which Yeats was associated. Little Diamond, boy
hero of *At the Back of the North Wind*, hears a frightening mysterious
voice which he traces to the wind blowing hard through a crack in the

wall. Eventually the North Wind (a female figure) is identified as the speaker behind the voice; as well as blowing Diamond into various adventures, she also enables him to move in the direction of the South Wind and so reach a celestial valley 'at the back of the north wind'. Elements from this story would reappear in Frost's 'The Aim Was Song'.

For the young Robert Frost, though, there were also the voices he heard in his own head.

> He was still a child in San Francisco when he first began to hear voices...he could not shut out the sounds of the voice, and the harder he pressed his hands over his ears the clearer and louder the voice came. Sometimes he could hear whole sentences. At other times the words were so indistinct that he understood only such meanings as were conveyed through the tones of the voice. At still other times he clearly heard the voice repeating something he himself had said a few minutes earlier, repeating and yet endowing his own words with tones so different from his that the effect seemed to be one of mockery. When he told his mother about these perplexing experiences, she seemed to understand them better than he did. Sympathetically, she hinted that he shared with her the mystical powers of second hearing and second sight. (*EY*, 36)

Some of Frost's ideas about poetry clearly derive from his childhood experiences. When he writes, for example, that 'Like a piece of ice on a hot stove the poem must ride on its own melting', he is recalling an incident when he borrowed his mother's thimble, froze water in it, then emptied the ice on to the lid of a stove where it skated with little friction.[9] Other seeds for his poetic ideas cannot be so precisely located, but when, in an important letter to John Bartlett (4 July 1913) Frost speaks of how he alone of English writers is determined to make music out of 'the sound of sense', the way in which he goes about describing this is surely reminiscent of those early fragments of heard voices. Frost in 1913 tells Bartlett that 'The best place to get the abstract sound of sense is from voices behind a door that cuts off the words'. He then goes on to offer a series of sherds of speech, asking Bartlett to imagine 'How these sentences would sound without the words in which they are embodied'. (*SL*, 80) Frost's apparent idea of disembodied sentence-sounds has more than a touch of the supernatural or spiritualist about it, a perception reinforced by his use of the word, 'summoned' (more commonly used of ghosts than of sounds) in his following sentence: 'Those sounds are summoned by the audile (audial) imagination.'[10] Small wonder that in a poem such as 'Snow' Frost delighted in the effects of sentence-fragmentation created by telephone conversation. When we remember his poem 'The Telephone' which deals with a voice mysteriously heard from a flower, we realize just how important to him was the hearing of voices in his childhood, encouraged by his mother and by his reading of MacDonald whose fantasy world was one of not always intelligible voices heard from fairies hidden in flowers and trees. These childhood voices which would be put to later lyrical and dramatic use were part of Frost's Scottish inheritance. Isabelle's Presbyterian upbringing led her eventually into Swedenborgianism, but just as importantly, she was aware of being part of a family possessing the gift of second sight which she inherited from her own father. When Frost used a quasi-oracular tone in a poem, or when as an old man he wrote to John F. Kennedy 'describing not so much what ought to be but what is and will be – reporting and prophesying', (*SL*, 590) that too was part of the tradition.

'Scott and Stevenson inspire me, by their prose, with the thought that we Scotchmen are bound to be romanticists – poets,' Frost wrote to Susan Hayes Ward, editor of the New York *Independent*, in 1894. (*SL*, 20) She was to publish his first poem. In his letters to her he began to develop his image as a poet. Here he could play Robert Burns, rather than Robert Bruce. Writing from Derry as a farmer-poet trying to get verse published, he cajoled with the postscript, 'A daimen icker in a thrave's a sma' request', alluding appropriately enough to Burns's 'To a Mouse', a poem not only involving a ploughman but also about the grave uncertainty of future prospects. (*SL*, 39) The supposed Scottish-American farmer-poet in New Hampshire was so successful in his cultivation of Miss Ward that by 1913 she was asking him to 'Give the bairns my love and blessing'. (*SL*, 107) By that time, though, Frost had crossed the Atlantic setting out for what, no doubt remembering his mother's words, he described to another correspondent as 'Glasgie mud and dirt'. (*SL*, 63)

Frost reached Glasgow in September; immediately he headed for London. For a man so affected by his Scottish mother and by Scottish stories, he took little interest in the country itself. Though he once retorted testily to Robert Lowell that 'Scotch is not a dialect. It's a language', partly, of course, Frost's Scottishness was a pose. (*Interviews*, 230) Today no Scotsman would describe himself as 'Scotch', which is neither a language nor a nationality but a drink. Frost's foreignness raised the hackles of the first native he met: 'I nearly got myself thrown overboard by a Scotchman for innocently calling the fleet I saw off the Mull of Cantire [*sc.* Kintyre] English instead of British'. (*SL*, 63) But probably just because his mother's view of Scotland and things Scottish had been so important, Frost did not wish to risk having any illusions blasted by the reality. A parallel instance might be his attitude towards a book of his student days: 'The book that influenced me most was *Piers the Plowman*, yet I never read it. When I realized how much the book had influenced me I felt I should read it. But after considering it I decided against reading it, fearing it might not be what I had thought when I started out to do what I have since done – what the book, unread, inspired me to do.' (*Interviews*, 68)

Often names and impressions, rather than accurate knowledge, were what mattered to Frost: 'I got as much out of seeing Dunfermline town from the train as from straggling around Edinburgh Castle for a day.... Places are more to me in thought than in reality'. (*SL*, 122) 'Dunfermline town' was of interest, surely because of 'Sir Patrick Spens', the ballad beginning, 'The king sits in Dunfermline town / Drinking the blude-red wine'. This ballad must have had a special significance for Frost whose father had drunk blood at the San Francisco slaughter-house, and whose Scottish grandfather, like Sir Patrick Spens, had died by drowning. (*EY*, 43) On a visit to Fife in 1913 Frost wrote to John Bartlett not so much about the real Scotland as of a land of the imagination: 'Pretty little village Kingsbarns – where the king used to store his grain when his capital was Dunfermline town and his Piraeus at Aberdour (read again the ballade of Sir Patrick Spens). Right foreninst us is the Bell Rock Lighthouse which was the Inchcape Bell of Southey's poem.' (*SL*, 91)

Not long afterwards, Frost told Sidney Cox that during his time at Kingsbarns he had had 'a narrow escape from drowning'. (*Cox*, 84) Partly this may be the imaginative Frost's mapping himself on to his reading and his grandfather's fate, but it furnishes a further reason for Frost's wariness about the land of his mother.

Frost had another, more obvious worry about coming to a landscape so soaked in poetry. Writing from Fife, he continues: 'I suppose it won't hurt my New Hampshire impressions as I have always been afraid learning a new language might hurt my English style.' (*SL*, 91) In fact, the effect was quite the opposite. It was through his engagement with the Old World that Frost constructed his New World literary self. He had never been able to see New England as clearly as from Old England. Similarly, when he visited Burns's homeland, he found that he was not swamped by its literary associations, but able to see it in terms of what, usefully, was most familiar to him as an American with Scottish blood. He told Cox that: 'The common people in the south of England I don't like to have around me. They don't know how to meet you man to man. The people in the north are more like Americans. I wonder whether they made Burns' poems or Burns' poems made them. And there are stone walls (dry stone dykes) in the north: I liked those. My mother was from Edinburgh....' (*Cox*, 31)

This man-to-man quality is a feature of Frost's New Englanders. They are not always distinguished for being pronouncedly articulate or emotionally honest, but they display a solid determination which does not

shirk confrontation and which presupposes the sort of direct egalitarian-
ism and scorn of affection exemplified in many of Burns's poems, and in
Frost's mother's attitudes: 'I remember well some of her sayings. She had
no patience with snobbery and pretence, and if anybody was boasting she
would say he was surely "the cousin of the Duke of Argyll's piper's son's
wee laddie".' (*Interviews*, 165)

In no poem is the concern with 'man to man' dealings and the scorn of
ostentation plainer than in the piece that Frost put at the head of *North of
Boston*. He later recalled that he had written 'Mending Wall' during a
period of homesickness in England. (*EY*, 432–3) Surely this longing 'for
my old wall in New England' relates to Frost's journey north to where the
people were 'more like Americans', and particularly to his liking for their
'stone walls (dry stone dykes)'. A dry stone or dry stane dyke is a Scots
term for a type of 'stone wall built without mortar' (*Concise Scots Diction-
ary*). Frequently these walls divide fields and are constructed from the
loose stones picked up there. This brings us very close to Frost's earlier
New England wall-mending with the French-Canadian farmer, Napoleon
Guay. (*EY*, 284) Unlike many of the other poems in *North of Boston*,
'Mending Wall' is not mentioned in Frost's earlier letters, a hint, perhaps,
that it was written not long before the book appeared. Other evidence
suggests that it dates from the period of Frost's Scottish visit. Various of
his 1913 letters take up the subject of belief in fairies. As well as delighting
in MacDonald's work, Frost had grown up with his mother's own fairy
stories, one of which was published as *The Land of Crystal*. This story
drew heavily on MacDonald for its picture of fairyland, even using such
phrases as 'the golden key' (title of a similarly toned MacDonald short
story published in his *Dealings with Fairies* of 1867).[11] Now as a man
Frost was encountering directly the Celtic twilight. He was clearly fasci-
nated by, yet sceptical about 'how perilously near Yates [*sic*] comes to
believing in fairies'. In this same letter, before passing on to recount his
Scottish experiences and his liking for dry stone dykes, Frost presents an
entertaining anecdote about the Scottish Celtic twilight writer, 'Fiona
Macleod': 'There's a good story I had pretty directly from Mrs. Sharp
about how she was out with her husband (Fiona Macleod) walking
somewhat ahead of him in an English lane one day when she saw
something childlike with a goat's legs scuttle into the woods. She stood
still with astonishment. Her husband came up. "William, what do you
think? – a faun! I saw him." "It's nothing," said William without coming
to a stand-still, "such creatures are all about this part of the country".'
(*SL*, 94)

There is little evidence that Frost thought his Derry New England farm
inhabited by little people or fauns (though he had toyed with the idea of

'Pan with Us'). It is surely his coming into contact with such stories at the time of writing 'Mending Wall' which prompted him to write of the agency which made the unmortared stones fall off his wall so easily:

> I could say 'Elves' to him,
> But it's not elves exactly, and I'd rather
> He said it for himself.

In Fife in August 1913 Frost had stayed for a few weeks with an archaeologist acquaintance, Professor E. A. Gardner, who tried the poet's patience and credulity by insisting on taking him to see what were, he claimed (Frost wrote to John Bartlett at the time), cave drawings done by 'paleolithic man'. (*SL*, 90) Frost was disbelieving, but when he sees the neighbour in 'Mending Wall' as an 'old-stone savage', that slightly odd locution 'old-stone' is Frost the Greek scholar's literal translation of 'paleolithic'.

Helping to tie down the poem's period of composition, these details also show Frost's ability to draw directly on his Scottish experience. All poets synthesize materials which come to them from different directions. What is striking here is how Frost translates the various specific elements (dry stone walls, talk of fairies, supposed paleolithic survivals) into a totally universal context, yet one which draws strength from an impression of particularity. The poem is written in England, sparked off by details seen in Scotland, drawing mainly on New England memories, but all these are so deeply embedded in the end-product that their foreignness is lost totally. To see this happening is to pay tribute to Frost's skill; it is also to see just how much his New England identity, however much grounded in actual experience, is a construct drawing on various, sometimes remote sources. Small wonder that while engaged in such construction Frost was pondering over the American-like northerners, 'I wonder whether they made Burns' poems or Burns' poems made them.'

The poem that opens *North of Boston* celebrates supposed northern values; stubborn persistence, traditionalism, refusal to waste words. Normally thought of as a very American poem, dealing with human independence, meeting, and confrontation, it is not simply a 'man to man' affair. It opens with that numinous 'Something' which is not a human agency but a mysterious force persistently present in nature (like the brook's power to generate 'thoughts' in 'A Brook in the City', or the river in Eliot's *Dry Salvages*):

> Something there is that doesn't love a wall,
> That sends the frozen-ground-swell under it,
> And spills the upper boulders in the sun,
> And makes gaps even two can pass abreast.
> The work of hunters is another thing...

The force is presented so as to seem as mysterious as possible. Of the gaps in walls which it makes we are told, 'No one has ever seen them made or heard them made'. To replace the stones on the wall is a magical activity: 'We have to use a spell to make them balance'. There may be accuracy in the figurative language of 'My apple trees will never get across / And eat the cones under his pines' since 'the acidity of pine duff would prevent apple seeds from taking root', (*Kemp*, 20) but the poem is dealing with a force apparently beyond science, one which comes closest to finding embodiment in the withheld word, 'Elves'. This magical idea leads appropriately to the primitive figure of the 'old-stone savage' who can repeat only the ancestral saying, left to him like a charm by his father, 'Good fences make good neighbours'.[12] Neither the narrator of the poem nor his neighbour really disputes the need for a wall, since both rebuild it annually. Doubt and interest centre, rather, round the nature of the force against which the 'saying' is used, this elfin 'Something' hostile to the walls of human order, perhaps, a milder version of the maleficent force of destructive 'design'. This sense of a sometimes menacingly animated landscape takes us back to George MacDonald in whose work was a thorough blending of reality and fantasy, as well as a strong sense of nature powered by quasi-human supernatural beings.

Such a sense is in much of Frost's poetry. In 'Birches' he writes, 'I like to think some boy's been swinging them', and goes on to interweave 'Matter of fact' and fantasy, until the imagined boy comes to seem far more real than any 'ice storm'. But it is important to remember that this boy is real and unreal. 'So was I once myself a swinger of birches' writes the poet, but the bulk of the poem is given over to a fantasy figure: 'I *like to think* some boy's been swinging them...I *should prefer* to have some boy bend them' (my emphases). In some ways even more striking, especially if we think of the boy climbing over them, are the birches seen

> Like girls on hands and knees that throw their hair
> Before them over their heads to dry in the sun.

In an abstract way this simile holds, and there may be similarities in attributes (birches and long-haired girls both look beautiful), but the more we think about the simile the more it approaches the absurd. These birches trigger imaginative excitement in the reader not so much because birch trees really are like girls, but because for a moment the poem seems to have the strange power to turn them into girls. This sudden animation of ordinary natural objects into often strangely sexual beings owes less to Ovid than to George MacDonald, of whose landscapes it is profoundly characteristic. Little Diamond climbs trees and sits in their branches to commune with the long-haired North Wind who so often hugs him to her bosom. Though Diamond's tree is not a birch but a beech, animated trees occur throughout MacDonald's work. Sometimes his woods, as they do in Frost's 'The Demiurge's Laugh', hold demonic terrors and, as in Frost's poem, there is the fairy-tale sense of something evil, an irrational force that is out to get you; on other occasions they are less dangerous though equally strange. 'Take care of the Birch, for though she is honest, she is too young not to be changeable', the narrator is warned among the fairy trees of *Phantastes*.[13] The hero falls in love with a beech-maiden. As often in MacDonald there is an erotic tone to the writing as the tree/girl confesses 'I fancy I feel like a woman sometimes. I do so tonight – and always when the rain drips from my hair...'. Frost's birches share this intimate sexuality.

MacDonald's prosaic natural environment soon metamorphoses into the marvellous, creating the sort of geo-sexuality that is found in the Frost of 'Paul's Wife' (a haunting poem, like an Indian legend), where a lumberjack marries a powerfully sexual star-like woman discovered (Ariel-like) encased in a pine log. She is the secret sexual life discovered in nature by the 'sensitive' woodsman. This sexual effect is at its most powerful in the sado-masochism of 'The Subverted Flower'. Though he once refers to 'daughters of Lilith', (*Cox*, 41) there is no proof that Frost read MacDonald's *Lilith*, but if he did that would make all the stronger the permeation of his imagination by a morbid sexuality seen in an animated landscape. Many of MacDonald's fantasies involve both flowers and overtones of sado-masochism. The strange feeling for nature as a sexual being permeates Frost's poetry. It may be most noticeable in a piece like 'Devotion', but it is also powerfully present in such passages as the conclusion of 'The Gum Gatherer' where the effect of the word 'breast' prepares the reader a little for the quasi-sexual satisfaction of what follows.

> I told him this is a pleasant life,
> To set your breast to the bark of trees
> That all your days are dim beneath,
> And reaching up with a little knife,
> To loosen the resin and take it down,
> And bring it to market when you please.

While Wordsworth also had something of the feeling for geo-sexuality, no English language poet other than Frost has presented so strongly the sexual qualities of trees. One of his strangest poems is 'Maple', which tells of a girl christened Maple by a mother who died in childbirth. Maple struggles to understand the significance of her own name, but is unable to do so. The poem is a flawed one. At its centre is a conversation between Maple and a man dictating notes to her.

> 'Do you know you remind me of a tree –
> A maple tree?'
>   'Because my name is Maple?'
> 'Isn't it Mabel? I thought it was Mabel.'
> 'No doubt you've heard the office call me Mabel.
> I have to let them call me what they like.'
> They were both stirred that he should have divined
> Without the name her personal mystery.
> It made it seem as if there must be something
> She must have missed herself. So they were married,
> And took the fancy home with them to live by.

The name mysteriously brings the marriage. Someone has managed to find her out without having 'to speak the literal'. Afterwards the couple discuss maples and the possible meaning of her name. Many of the maple images presented are distinctly sexual, such as that of the

>   maple in a glade,
> Standing alone with smooth arms lifted up,
> And every leaf of foliage she's worn
> Laid scarlet and pale pink about her feet.

In this poem the geo-sexual magic so effective elsewhere is used too crudely, but it makes plain what Frost is about. There is little doubt that maples in particular were associated by Frost with spring and with female sexuality. In a 1920 letter concerning a quarrel with his wife over the existence of a divine being, Frost interrupts with the protest that 'Spring, I say, returneth and the maple sap is heard dripping in the buckets', to which she responds 'Pshaw'. Soon we see Frost boring into a maple tree (actually boring right through it!), and his imagining that the tree is speaking to him scoldingly, just as his wife had been doing earlier. (*SL*, 244–5) The couple in 'Maple' eventually come to accept the meaning of the wife's name as necessarily secret, but only after thinking about a tiny maple sapling, small enough that a 'cow might have licked [it] up'.

> They hovered for a moment near discovery,
> Figurative enough to see the symbol,
> But lacking faith in anything to mean
> The same at different times to different people.
> Perhaps a filial diffidence partly kept them
> From thinking it could be a thing so bridal.

Not really successful, partly because it is unclear how much Frost is in control of all his material's implications, and partly because it oscillates too uneasily between the serious and the bathetic, 'Maple' nonetheless helps to make clear some of the stranger, and neglected workings of Frost's imagination. These are not aspects native to the New England farmer; they can be weird and fantastical, but George MacDonald would have understood such sexualizing of trees.

Among the phenomena leading to the greatest imaginative releases in MacDonald's work are stars. Little Diamond is nowhere closer to being a swinger of birches than when he is in his beech tree 'nest': 'I don't see anything more, except a few leaves, and the big sky over me. It goes swaying about. The earth is all behind my back. There comes another star! The wind is like kisses from a big lady. When I get up here I feel as if I were in North Wind's arms.'[14]

Diamond has a song which sums up some of his excitement.

> What would you get in the top of the tree
> For all your crying and grief?
> Not a star would you clutch of all you see –
> You could only gather a leaf.
>
> But when you had lost your greedy grief,
> Content to see from afar,
> You would find in your hand a withering leaf,
> In your heart a shining star.[15]

Some of the most lyrical effects in Frost involve not simply trees mystically bonded to the heightened human condition ('After Apple-Picking', 'Tree at My Window'), but also the conjunction of foliage and stars as if the two might be on the point of uniting, as they are brilliantly among the maples of 'Evening in a Sugar Orchard' when we catch

> Leo, Orion, and the Pleiades.
> And that was what the boughs were full of soon.

'Everywhere in Fairy Land, forests are the places where one may most certainly expect adventures', wrote MacDonald.[16] Frost must have been well versed in the location of the supernatural before he even saw his first New England wood, let alone wrote 'Into My Own', 'Stopping by Woods', or 'The Demiurge's Laugh', all of which are poems set very much in a MacDonald landscape. It is easy to see why Frost would hail Walter de la Mare's 'The Listeners' as soon as it appeared as 'the best poem since the century came in', (SL, 104) repeating that it was 'the greatest poem in English in recent years'. (Cox, 75) It is a poem to set beside 'Stopping by Woods', and both should be compared with the work of MacDonald.

As the fantasist did, so Frost continually sought and dreamed of seeking for the mysterious in the ordinary. He could make ironic capital out of this as in 'For Once, Then, Something', yet few actions seem more central to his imagination than speaking of going 'as though/ Commanded in a dream' and pursuing not the business of farming but a stranger activity,

> From following walls I never lift my eye,
> Except at night to places in the sky
> Where showers of charted meteors let fly.

Richard Poirier has drawn attention to 'A Star in a Stoneboat' as a magnificent Frost poem not among his best-known pieces, and one in which we see his imaginative activity at its height in making clear its own workings.[17] Fittingly, the central metaphor of the poem is very close to an activity found in *At the Back of the North Wind*. North Wind visits Diamond in the form of a shooting star which 'fell on the grass beside him'.[18] More interestingly, after descending a mysterious staircase in the earth, Diamond finds some boy angels engaged in an odd pursuit: 'Now let's go and dig for stars,' said one.... Each went by himself, walking slowly with bent shoulders and eyes fixed on the ground. Every now and then one would stop, kneel down, and look intently, feeling with his hands and parting the grass.'[19]

When they do excavate a star, the angels celebrate, then rebury it with a marker at the hole. The accurate portrayal of excited mundanity which MacDonald's prose here communicates is one of the devices which makes so successful Frost's account of searching for stars. MacDonald's sentimentality has gone, but there is a playful tone in which the supernatural aspects of the labourer's search are treated. The 'laborer' encounters the mysteriously alien, and mistakes it for the everyday. In this he is like some readers of Frost's poems. It takes the man with other knowledge or imagination, the poet or the sensitive reader, to appreciate what is discovered and translate it back into its proper sphere. If the narrator of 'Mending Wall' seems something of an outsider, then so in 'A Star in a Stoneboat' the searcher for the star is distanced from the labourer. We have to deal here with something other than the stereotypical New Englander as Frost's magic works 'to trip the reader head foremost into the boundless'. (*SL*, 344)

If his constructed New England self tended to make Frost seem all too comfortably 'homey', then this other supporting self which draws on his Scottish background can reveal him as sometimes darker, often more imaginatively exciting. It not only takes us to the 'man-to-man' dykes, but also illuminates some strange roads taken by his imagination into the sexualized 'lovely, dark, and deep' woods of a MacDonald-like world.

There is more than whimsical humour involved when Frost in 1917, worried about Amy Lowell's typecasting him as the simple New England farmer, writes to his confidant, Louis Untermeyer, 'I wish for a joke I could do myself, shifting the trees entirely from the Yankee realist to the Scotch symbolist'. (*SL*, 255) That is a remark worth pondering, and one which suggests both how flexible and how carefully constructed was the poetic identity of this 'identifying poet'.

III

Wildness certainly, but principally a sense of their being unfairly treated attracted Frost to Red Indians. Lawrance Thompson saw Frost's dream of fleeing to the Indian tribe in their secret valley as Frost's consolation against private wrongs. (*EY*, 38) Given his father's often irate temper, this seems plausible. It was not the first time Robert Frost would entertain ideas of escape when he felt he was being harshly treated. A much later remark reinforces the idea that the initial appeal of the Indians was their being ill-done-to: 'People say, "You were interested in Indians the way children are interested in cops and robbers." But it wasn't that way at all. I was interested in Indians because of the wrongs done to them. I was wishing the Indians would win all the battles.' (*Interviews*, 243)

A fierce sympathy with the inevitably defeated is a sentiment strongly present in some of the work of the author of 'The Lovely Shall be Choosers'. The first Indians to interest Frost were the northern tribes of Fenimore Cooper and the Aztecs of Montezuma in Prescott's *Conquest of Mexico*. Reading books such as *The Last of the Mohicans* must have impressed the boy with a sense of tribal cultural values handed down from generation to generation, and of how these could be destroyed. Prescott's Indians excited a love of freedom stirred also by the tales about Bruce and Wallace. As those leaders had fought for their people's independence, achieving a respite before eventual collapse, so Montezuma's victory staved off the threat of atrocities perpetrated by the Spaniards who would win terrible victory in the end. On such momentary stays against confusion Frost's imagination was nurtured. His first poem, 'La Noche Triste', celebrates the Aztec victory at Tenochtitlan, but over it hangs the knowledge of eventual defeat. The elegiac (*Last of the Mohicans*) and the freedom-loving strains are blended.

> The Montezumas are no more,
> Gone is their regal throne,
> And freemen live, and rule, and die,
> Where they have ruled alone.
>
> (*EY*, 94)

The Frost who in the year of this poem's composition (1890) argued vociferously on behalf of the Indian Bill, contending that 'some change should be made in the Indian's condition as it was very bad and growing worse', (*Newdick*, 25) was to continue to link himself with the Indians of North and Central America. In 1894 he defended to Susan Hayes Ward 'That Aztec consonant syllable of mine, 'l',' whose use she wished to temper. (*SL*, 21) Frost's references to Indians are often jokey in this period. 'Much of what I enjoyed at Dartmouth', he recalled, 'was acting like an Indian in a college founded for Indians'. (*SL*, 167) There Frost had taken part in what might be described as a scalping.[20] But he also enjoyed walking alone in the woods and liked to make himself out to be a wild man. When asked what he did on these walks he snapped back, 'gnaw bark'. (*EY*, 141)

If Frost's dream of safety with an Indian tribe was partly a consolation from his father's temper, then certainly his general interest in Indians went against his ancestral legacy. Frost wrote with grim irony about 'my bad ancestor the Indian Killer' (*SL*, 42) in a poem which he never published, entitled 'Genealogy' (printed in *SL*, 604–6). It is plain from reading it that Frost's feeling for the Indians is connected with his love of the woods. The seventeenth-century New Englander, Charles Frost, living in a time when 'they wasted the woods / With fire to clear the land for tillage', tried also to extirpate an Indian tribe. Both these acts would be terrible for the Frost who, encouraged by MacDonald and Fenimore Cooper, had made the woods a home for the imaginative life, and the Indians the people of his dream-life. Frost's mock-epic celebration of the Indians' revenge – they killed Charles Frost then dug him up after burial and hanged him – is not a great poem; he called it a 'Whitmanism'. But he writes that this ancestor 'explains my lifelong liking for Indians'. The poem is in part a celebration of human perversity, the evil designs of men. Yet it also acts as a rebellion against an oppressive genealogy and an assertion once more of Frost's own imaginative liberty. A combative individual, Frost liked to view the dealings of his father's family towards him in the worst possible light. The poem predates 1908 and comes from a time when the yet unknown poet was trying hard to prove his poetic integrity in the face of various demands imposed by family life. A poem which let him join the Indians was again a consolation.

Another clear instance of Frost's identifying his own cherished poetic ideas comes in the first interview he gave on his return to America in 1915. In it the core of his theory of poetry is linked with the Indians of his innermost dreams, though with Frost now a more successful public figure, these Indians are now more respectably academicized:

If we go back far enough we will discover that the sound of sense

existed before words, that something in the voice or vocal gesture
made primitive man convey a meaning to his fellow before the race
developed a more elaborate and concrete symbol of communication
in language. I have even read that our American Indians possessed,
besides a picture-language, a means of communication (though it
was not said how far it was developed) by the sound of sense. And
what is this but calling up with the imagination, and recognizing,
the images of sound?

When Wordsworth said, 'Write with your eye on the object', or
(in another sense) it was important to visualize, he really meant
something more. That something carries out what I mean by writ-
ing with your ear to the voice. (*Interviews*, 6–7)

This transition from primitivism to Wordsworth was not an unusual one,
and was encouraged by the opinions of anthropological writers such as
Max Müller. But Frost's use of the Indian image shows his imaginative
sympathy continuing from childhood, and his determination to present
his own poetic theory, largely developed in the England he had just left, as
aboriginally American.

Frost's best-known literary encounter with an Indian also dates from
this period. 'The Vanishing Red' begins on what seems a vaguely *Last of
the Mohicans* elegiac note, but a well-deployed enjambment means that
lines two and three immediately tie things down to a particular place, and
even to a particular sound.

> He is said to have been the last Red Man
> In Acton. And the Miller is said to have laughed –
> If you like to call such a sound a laugh.

This laconic poem about the murder of an Indian and, by clear implica-
tion, the destruction of the North American Indians, reminds the reader
that Frost came as an outsider to the New England mind, and is a useful
corrective to over-simple pictures of him. The tough practicality seen in
'Mending Wall' emerges here in a much less attractive light when the
Miller, on being told that the Indian is a last survivor sees that simply as
more reason for 'getting a thing done with'. Stubborn individualism here
reveals its dark side in the Miller's angrily asking 'Whose business' his
killing of the Indian is other than his own. The explanation of the
historical situation – 'It's too long a story to go into now' – seems
ironically bland and is in effect an easy elision of much of American
history. But, viewed ironically, the savagery of what is elided is made quite
evident; the 'guttural expression' of the Indian which 'Disgusted the
Miller physically' plays off against the morally disgusting laugh-like sound
emitted by the Miller when he remembers the Indian's fate. The forces of

the new, with their 'great big thumping, shuffling millstone' grind down what is left of the old, and the Red Man, led to his death under the trap door in the tortured waters of the wheel pit, yet giving rise to this uneasy anecdote, is like the brook in the city which robs away sleep. The details are particularly effective in their horrible mundanity, as the Miller, having rid himself of the Indian, 'said something to a man with a meal sack/ That the man with the meal sack didn't catch - then.' Casually, the life of Acton continues.

Yet for all that poem's irony, it is possible that it represents Frost's own suppression of the Indians. Certainly, like so many American dreamers, he was able to suppress or defuse awareness of them, most strikingly in his famous patriotic poem, concluding that 'we gave ourselves outright' to an 'unstoried' and 'artless' America which was 'vaguely realizing westward' and that 'The deed of gift was many deeds of war'. It takes some cool-headedness to reflect that these 'deeds of war' were not only wars of liberation from a colonial power, but also vicious wars of repression and suppression waged by colonizers such as Charles Frost; the land-deeds given to the Indians were well-nigh worthless. It is highly unlikely that Frost wishes these reflections to spring to mind in this poem but, particularly in view of earlier work such as 'The Vanishing Red', they are scarcely irrelevant. In 'The Gift Outright' Frost the artist is carried away with delight at the thought of the land as a virgin page; he conveniently forgets those whose stories and art enhanced an earlier America. Beautiful and moving, politically effective, the poem is also a piece of patriotic racism. By this time Frost has been unable to lead the vanishing red down to his own wheel pit. This is the unpleasant later Frost with his scorn of the politically or numerically minor:

> States strong enough to do good are but few.
> ...The most the small
> Can ever give us is a nuisance brawl.

So much for the Boston Tea-Party.

Frost's Indians could unsettle contemporary life, coming back most forcefully in 'The Vindictives' where, as in the earlier 'Genealogy', they wreak terrible revenge on those who have wronged them. The Incas have the angry power of the desperate:

> 'The best way to hate is the worst.
> 'Tis to find what the hated need,
> Never mind of what actual worth,
> And wipe that out of the earth.'

Yet this is the last time Frost's Indians will speak with a powerful voice.

Like their gold, they are put back underground, becoming there a force for desolation.

One way Frost seems to have suppressed his Indians was to archaeologize them. He had been interested in archaeology since at least his schooldays when he wrote not only on Aztecs but also on Petra. Here was a site already consecrated for poetry as 'A rose-red city – "half as old as time"!' but Frost's account seems to have relied on more accurate research. If later he was excited by Schliemann's discoveries, (*Newdick*, 36) read Flinders Petrie, (*Cox*, 145) and professed himself 'a frustrated archaeologist', (*SL*, 385) then there is no doubt where his particular interests would have lain: 'The first poem I ever wrote ['La Noche Triste'] was on the Maya-Toltec-Aztec civilization and there is where my heart still is while outwardly I profess an interest more or less perfunctory in New England.' (*SL*, 362) Typically, Frost is teasing here, but it is clear that his early interests persisted, just as it is clear that, having their origins in books, they become more bookish as he grew older. In 1929 he writes of 'a flood of Americana especially a great big portfolio of "Catherwoods Views in Central America Chiapas and Yucatan". – Did you ever see it? Now if I only owned Audubon's Birds, Audubon's Animals and Catlin's Indians wouldn't I be a gentleman? The Pueblo Potter is the thing. Thanks for it. The pictures are wonderful. The text is an amusing professorial attempt to be behavioristic in dealing with art.' (*SL*, 363)

There is self-mockery here, and mockery of academia, yet it is plain that Frost's interest in archaeology is essentially armchair in character. It was an interest which could produce poetry illuminating in relation to his major work, though itself lacking in sufficient electricity. When Frost returns to a 'raid / as Cortez on the Aztecs made' at the end of 'America is Hard to See' there may be present the private joke of self-reference, but the allusion does little to energize an undistinguished poem. By this time Frost the would-be Indian had been firmly overtaken by Frost the would-be archaeologist.

It is this archaeological self that is behind 'A Missive Missile', the poem concerning a pebble which apparently bears a hieroglyphic message left by 'Someone in ancient Mas d'Azil'. The pebble is now in the hands of the poet, who worries at what it might mean. When Professor Gardner had taken him to see that supposed paleolithic art near St Andrews, Fife, in 1913, Frost had reacted to the professor's fancies with amused disbelief, and had speculated that he, Frost, might be more of an archaeologist than was his guide. But in 'A Missive Missile' it is the poet who seems to be whimsically fantastical, pondering his pebble. Like the name Maple, this artefact is a simple sign handed down, yet one whose meaning is hard to discern. Frost learned from MacDonald to create a landscape of fantasy and reality. This archaeological piece is too much speculative fantasy. Yet, in a sense, its pebble is a paradigm for a Frost poem, simple, deeply ambiguous, apparently self-undercutting. Like many of his works, it also contains the theme of the difficulty and uncertainty of communication, and the theme of a barrier. Here the barrier is not just that of language itself, but also that of the ice-age, rendering the pebble's message unintelligible. It remains possible, too, that the pebble is not so much a sign as a natural accident. The poem is most successful in its conclusion, coming close to making something effectively moving out of the archaeological find, as it speaks (with an Arnoldian regret) of a sense of desolate futility.

> Far as we aim our signs to reach,
> Far as we often make them reach,
> Across the soul-from-soul abyss,
> There is an aeon-limit set
> Beyond which they are doomed to miss.
> Two souls may be too widely met.
> That sad-with-distance river beach
> With mortal longing may beseech;
> It cannot speak as far as this.

This poem ends *A Further Range*, and is followed only by blank paper, another white barrier between writer and reader. Its placing gives it a formal wit which makes it the more moving, but it is still uneven in its imaginative intensity. It does alert us, though, to just how much such a famous 'sign' in Frost's earlier poetry as that 'tuft of flowers' is also a message passed down, though again a message which seems unintended. As the pebble, so the tuft of flowers achieves a kind of communication, and prompts the thought 'Men work together'. That reassuring ending, however, does not eradicate, but tugs against, the earlier conviction that all are essentially alone. The mower has gone; he and the speaker who turns over the grass never meet. Maple has her mother's name but never meets her mother. The man holding the pebble thinks he deciphers it, but that does not lead him to the craftsman he thinks marked it, however embarrassingly the speaker may 'Suppose his ghost is standing by'. 'A Missive Missile' brings to the fore the anxiety present, though sometimes suppressed, in many other poems, such as 'Home Burial' where a couple seem cut off from each other by their own most intimate kinds of language or 'Snow' where the supposed medium of communication – the telephone – communicates through the blank snow, for a time at least, only a sense of desolation.

> 'A baby's crying!
> Frantic it sounds, though muffled and far off.

> Its mother wouldn't let it cry like that,
> Not if she's there.'

It could be said that the eye which 'reads' the tuft of flowers is an archaeologist's eye, fixed to the ground and constantly ready for small signs of a past human presence in the landscape; probably it is simply a countryman's eye or is like that of an Indian tracker. Indeed, Frost the archaeologist may have been most concerned with the awful empty spaces between fragments of the past which remain, the sites themselves functioning only to remind him of the Shelleyan 'lone and level sands'. In 1943 he writes to A. J. Armstrong, 'You can't help wondering what prompted me to write about Petra, sight unseen, when I was but sixteen and had never been outside of the United States. I can't help wondering myself. If I look into the matter I shall expect to find it was my love of desolation. I should have been an archaeologist. The evidence is written large in my books all down the years.' (*SL*, 513–14)

Many of Frost's strongest effects – 'the slow smokeless burning of decay' – rely on a sense of waste or of expansive emptiness,

> And miles to go before I sleep,
> And miles to go before I sleep.

The archaeologist of desolation, as well as the hopeful patriot, is behind that vast 'land vaguely realizing westward' with its Indians silenced. The archaeologist (like another of Frost's selves, the astronomer) deals with both empty tracts and small, eroding, barely perceptible objects. Particularly in romanticized versions of his activities he is a seeker in the soil for traces of the mysterious. The impulse which scrutinizes pebbles is also the impulse which searches with archaeological attention for a star in a wall, 'measuring stone walls, perch on perch'. MacDonald's angels dug for their stars. Frost recalled that 'In one poem I came near mentioning Petra in that part of Asia that "wedges Africa from Europe"'. (*SL*, 514) These last words occur in a bleak poem, 'The Census-Taker', set in a well-nigh desolate 'waste' permeated with 'decay'. The deeply ambiguous last line, 'It must be I want life to go on living' sums up Frost as poet-archaeologist. He is torn between archaeology as the discoverer of what survives and the revealer of the ruined or perished, the drive towards obliteration. Often it seems the latter that predominates. This archaeological Frost is linked to the self which seems to relish having to give up farming, in 'Bursting Rapture', and go instead to hear the statement of the physician about 'what a certain bomb was sent to be'. What began as a Californian's dream of life with miraculously preserved Indians, at the very time when the 'Reds' had almost been destroyed, becomes an archaeological fascination with waste lands. Perhaps this represents the eventual triumph of

Charles Frost. In any case, a bleak self is revealed, a self preoccupied with
the inane confusion not just beyond but also invading and undermining
the poet's momentary stays against it.

IV

Examination of Frost the 'Scotch symbolist' and Frost the Indian/archae-
ologist is valuable because it exposes other Robert Frosts predating and
helping to construct Frost the New England farmer, and closely associated
with the roots of his creative expression. Coming at the poet from these
different directions gives new insight into some of his major works,
revealing both richly attractive and unpleasant qualities; it also alerts us to
the importance of some of the minor works in the canon. It suggests the
possibility that there may be further aspects of this complicated writer still
requiring to be found out. Richard Poirier has pointed to some such
fruitful fields, such as Frost's interests in Bergson, astronomy, and evolu-
tionary theory. These are often alluded to, but seldom gone into with the
necessary attention. Perhaps the poet himself is partly responsible for this.
Even in 1917 he was pointing out to Amy Lowell that he was not for
simply pigeon-holing: 'Doesn't the wonder grow that I have never written
anything or as you say never published anything except about New Eng-
land farms when you consider the jumble I am? Mother, Scotch immi-
grant. Father oldest New England stock unmixed. Ten years in West.
Thirty years in East. Three years in England. Not less than six months in
any of these: San Francisco, New York, Boston, Cambridge, Lawrence,
London....' (*SL*, 226)

   Yet Frost's resistance against his public image was often only a token
one. He was to a large degree content with a portrait whose earthy tints
he had carefully ground himself. This could make him his own worst
enemy, particularly when he talked to reporters and loved playing with
them, extending the blanket of his persona until it covered his entire
personal landscape: 'I've always farmed ever since I was a boy in San
Francisco, in the backyard'. (*Interviews*, 119) As man and as poet (and as
'farmer') Frost loved to play tricks, to juggle selves, and to indulge in
'uncatchability'. (*Interviews*, 136) There can be no doubt that Frost is an
'identifying poet'. What we need to appreciate more fully is the way in
which his poetic self is, to adapt Bakhtin's terminology, multiply dialogic.
The Scottish self and the Californian self, the Indian self and the archaeo-
logical self are in dialogue with one another; the resulting conversation is
the 'identifying poet' with whose work we are familiar. Appreciating the
varied fusions and engagements out of which Frost constructed his literary
self should alert us all the more to his subtle resources. Frost may seem
homey; in his way he is as shy and subtle as the modernist writers beside

whose work his own is too often sidelined or patronized as 'regionalist'. Even such sharply insightful pieces as Tom Paulin's essay on Frost do not quite do justice to the complexity of Frost's selves.[21]

His tricks were not Old Possum's but they often achieved similar ends. It would be too easy to fit Frost into the modern theoretical model for Scottish poets, that 'Caledonian Antisyzygy' developed by MacDiarmid out of Gregory Smith. Yet it might do no more harm than thinking of him as a New Englander and little else. Frost is not merely a Jekyll and Hyde figure, though he is sometimes, just as he is other selves. Before we go on with the study of Robert Frost we should pay more attention to the examination of Robert Frosts.

2

MacDiarmid and his Makers

While the Caledonian Antisyzygy is an idea which might fruitfully be more discussed outside Scotland, and which might furnish a useful interpretative tool to apply to the work of Frost and a number of writers with significant Scottish connections, it is also, as I have suggested most fully in *Devolving English Literature*, an idea which is very much an outgrowth of late nineteenth-century Romanticism.[1] It is a concept valuable and typical as part of the emerging late Romantic and early modernist consciousness. It parallels and complements Yeats's self and anti-self, sits easily with Eliot's admiration of that Metaphysical poetry which yokes heterogeneous things together. Yet in Scotland it has also become something of a cliché. The standard thing to do with a Scottish writer is to show how he (or, very occasionally, she) corresponds to the well-established pattern of the Caledonian Antisyzygy. This model has been useful, but constricting. It is surely a measure of the theoretical poverty of much Scottish literary criticism that it has remained for most of the twentieth century the sole major interpretative model of the Scottish writer, and of Scottish culture as a whole.

It is time that we tried to supplement this undeniably useful model with others. There are a few signs, prominent among which is Alan Riach's recent work on MacDiarmid, that Scottish critics may now be prepared for a sometimes heady theoretical engagement with our literature. This may prove a confused and confusing time for Scottish criticism, but it is to be hoped that alongside literary history, an increased theoretical awareness may help end the at times extreme isolation of Scottish criticism from critical developments outside Scotland. As has been argued in the Introduction to this book, part of this increased theoretical awareness is likely to involve an examination or re-examination of the rich resources for Scottish criticism and theory which await exploitation in the work of Bakhtin.

Peter McCarey in his eminently readable study *Hugh MacDiarmid and the Russians* glanced at the relevance of Bakhtin's concept of Menippean satire to the interpretation of MacDiarmid and the modernist movement.[2] Kenneth Buthlay picked up this suggestion very briefly in the excellent introduction to his 1987 edition of *A Drunk Man Looks at the Thistle*, but argued that Bakhtin's theory of the 'carnivalesque' was more appropriate to MacDiarmid.[3] Both these Scottish commentators refer only to the Bakhtin of *Problems of Dostoevsky's Poetics* and the Rabelais study. It seems they point us in an important direction which remains to be explored. Yet potentially the richest theory for Scottish writing is found in *The Dialogic Imagination*.

As was indicated in the Introduction, when outlining the development of those dialogic elements which he sees as essential (not only to the development of the novel but also to the modern 'novelisation' of other genres) Bakhtin repeatedly explains how the emergence of dialogic strains in the novel is stimulated historically within societies used to either polyglossia (a presence of various distinct languages) or heteroglossia (a presence of several strains, dialects, or dialogic elements within the one language). Having used the example of Robert Frost to demonstrate how a poet may construct for himself out of a dialogue of various internal voices, and out of a dialogue between cultural traditions (in Frost's case American and Scottish), a poetic identity which allows him to identify with a particular region or territory, I wish in this present chapter to look at a similar process conducted in the work of MacDiarmid, focusing on *A Drunk Man Looks at the Thistle*. This chapter argues that we should view MacDiarmid's achievement not only in terms of antisyzygy. Rather, we should see it as multiply dialogic, rich in 'other tongues'. In particular, when reading *A Drunk Man Looks at the Thistle* we should bear in mind that the construction of that Scots poem takes place 'in the light of another language' – the potently dialogic, polyglot and heteroglot language of T. S. Eliot in *The Waste Land*. Both these great modernist poems are heteroglossic. Each may be seen in terms of Menippean satire. Here, however, they are viewed in terms of each other. In particular, *A Drunk Man* is seen in terms of *The Waste Land*, a poem constantly present in MacDiarmid's modernist consciousness. Loyal to the idea that good literary criticism can be a richly impure project, I have not hesitated to draw on our considerably increased knowledge of MacDiarmid's biography to supplement and illumine my reading of his work. Essentially what this chapter tries to demonstrate is that in creating for himself a cunningly structured, intensely 'Scottish' identity and a great poem obsessed with the identity of Scotland, MacDiarmid relied fundamentally on supplementing elements available to him in native Scottish tradition with other, clearly alien elements. His Scottishness might seem a cultural 'given'; in fact it is a clever cultural construct whose effect has been to develop and valuably alter many of our ideas about Scottishness.

Before 1922 Hugh MacDiarmid did not exist. And only Christopher Murray Grieve would have dared to invent him. Alan Bold's valuable biography points out that when the thirty-year-old Grieve began to write in the *Scottish Chapbook* under the pseudonym 'M'Diarmid', he was already editing the magazine under his own name, reviewing for it as 'Martin Gillespie', and employing himself as its Advertising Manager (and occasional contributor), 'A. K. Laidlaw'.[4] We tend to think of the subject of Bold's biography as the greatest voice of modern Scottish literature; more accurately, he is the greatest chorus. MacDiarmid is a chorus of voices which often sing against one another, producing sometimes brilliant, sometimes bathetic results. The achievement of his poetry as a whole is to unite his exploitation of Scotland's heteroglossic linguistic identity with his own personal love of splitting into a variety of constructed selves only slightly less stunningly multiple than those of Fernando Pessoa.

Born in 1892 in the Scottish Border mill-town of Langholm, Grieve, even before adopting the name Hugh MacDiarmid, was eager to give the impression that he was not just a writer but an enormous literary mill. Writing from World War One Macedonia (where he served in the Royal Army Medical Corps), Grieve tells his old schoolteacher, George Ogilvie, about his detailed plans for a hundred essays on Scottish Art and the Scottish Church. He is planning a Scottish Vortex, and is already fizzing with that energy which would make him a power-surge at the end of the Celtic Twilight: 'I can think out novels and plays in odd half-hours, visualize every detail, see them published and played, anticipate their criticisms in *The Times*, *The British Weekly* and *The New Age* simultaneously, write prefaces to new editions, sum up carefully on the business side, grant interviews and talk at great length and with indescribable sense and spirit ...'[5] This letter with its literary mill, crammed with dialogic voices, anticipates the technique of MacDiarmid's mature poetry.

The letters which the fledgling poet wrote to Ogilvie show how many of MacDiarmid's attitudes and determinations were present in Quarter-master-Sergeant Grieve of Salonika. The young Grieve describes himself as being in 'mental "spate"'; his intellectual life is 'a debating society', and he tells Ogilvie: 'I feel like a buried city'. (*L*, 11, 10, 20) These letters sizzle with energy; they also show an anxious desire to impress and, at moments whose scarcity only emphasizes their significance, they reveal an insecurity. The Grieve who initiates the correspondence with Ogilvie craves companionship and support. In 1920 he skids into the doubt that 'sometimes I think that I only think that I can think', and worries about struggles in his most private self that no one else will understand. (*L*, 50)

This may seem at odds with the man who writes of his hunger for any sort of publicity, but throughout MacDiarmid's career private anxieties and public pugnacity appear to have fuelled one another. The talented but vulnerable private individual could comfortably inhabit the noisy and polemical chorus.

From his earliest years MacDiarmid craved, deserved, but did not always receive, attention. Alan Bold's biography presents Grieve's childhood as rather lonely and biblioholic. The boy's talent for verse was encouraged by his local Free Church minister, T. S. Cairncross, before Grieve went on to Broughton School in Edinburgh where he met the remarkable and supportive George Ogilvie. Bold has done important work in assembling details of Grieve's early life, so that we see, not only Grieve the public friend of Red Clydesiders John MacLean and James Maxton, but also the private Grieve whose Scottish nationalism was encouraged by his rejection by English girls. Heady on his home-brew of Nietzsche, John Davidson and almost any other literary material he could devour, this proto-MacDiarmid emerges as something of a sexual predator. The year 1918, for instance, sees a passionate affair with a Spanish girl in Salonika followed by a marriage to Peggy, his Scottish sweetheart, that rapidly gives way to 'erotic abandon' with a French girlfriend. A dozen years later, MacDiarmid would be deeply wounded when Peggy left him for another man. For all his deploring of Harry Lauder, MacDiarmid himself in some ways conformed at various times to the easiest Scottish stereotypes: the boasting predatory male, the political motor-mouth, the pickled poet.

Yet his closeness to some of those crude stereotypes may have enabled him all the better to analyse the predicament of the Scot and of contemporary Scotland once he managed also to put a distance between the stereotypical 'Scottish' self in which he clearly often rejoiced and the other, more sophisticated and internationally conscious 'Scottish' self which he began to construct. Particularly acute is Alan Bold's demonstration of the importance of Lewis Spence to MacDiarmid. Bold argues convincingly that it was Spence's attitude to nationalism and to the Scots language that encouraged Grieve to reverse his earlier condemnation of the attempt to write in that medium, and so stimulated his first Scots lyrics. But Grieve was a late developer. Only after his cunning editing of *Northern Numbers*, a sort of Scottish Georgian anthology which brought him publicity and the attention of the literary establishment (several of whose members he included in the book) – only after this conventional debut by Grieve the douce editor, did another less amenable but poetically more exciting voice begin to emerge. Not until 1922 in Montrose did Grieve begin, falteringly, to find himself, or rather to locate Hugh MacDiarmid.

The 'Hugh MacDiarmid' who becomes the source of Grieve's texts is not so much a voice as a clashing chorus of voices or, in Bakhtin's terms, of heteroglossic elements. This is apparent from the start in the synthetic nature of the lyrics' Scots vocabulary where there is a constant and enlivening engagement between the familiar elements of couthy Scots verse – 'cauld', 'fegs', 'stane' – and the more obviously exotic and dictionaried elements such as 'how-dumb-deid' or 'yowdendrift'. It is possible that MacDiarmid's sensitivity to the 'exotic' qualities of Scots may have been heightened by the pointed isolation and exhibiting of Scots phrases in Kailyard texts, a phenomenon noted by Emma Letley.[6] Whether or not this is the case, alongside the heteroglossic strains in his diction, MacDiarmid presents in these lyrics of *Sangschaw* (1925) and *Penny Wheep* (1926) a rich, sometimes clashing dialogue between the familiar, pastoral elements of Scots verse – sheep, dykes, lullabies – and the aggressively modern ideas of Nietzsche, modern physics and a conscious twentieth-century cosmopolitanism which produces not only epigraphs from Yeats, Housman and Professor J. Y. Simpson, but also dedications to Herbert Grierson, and Denis Saurat, as well as signals of the Scots poet's international and contemporary awareness – 'After the German of Stefan George', 'Suggested by the Russian of Dmitry Merezhkovsky', 'Suggested by the French of Gustave Kahn.' Sometimes showy and ambitious, these various *seuils* and paratexts, like the notes and attributions in *A Drunk Man,* signal the modernity of works produced by dialogues between various elements – colloquial and arcane, folk and highbrow, native and foreign. Each of these binary oppositions might be seen as an antisyzygy, yet taken altogether they constitute a more complex pattern – the inter-penetrating strands of an evolving heteroglossic and dialogic imagination. We have reached the era when in *Penny Wheep* a Scots poem can be titled 'Bombinations of a Chimaera'. MacDiarmid's Scots is fruitfully aware not only of new developments in English literature, such as Imagism, but also of movements in literatures on the continent and beyond. In his lyrics, the Scots of Burns and the Scots of the earlier Makars not only sing together; they join a wider European heteroglot community.

The heteroglossic and dialogic quality of MacDiarmid's lyrics, as well as their Imagist techniques, bring them in line with modernism. It is coming to be more widely accepted that MacDiarmid should be seen as one of the major modernists, but the text which will most readily succeed in serving as his passport to the modernist pantheon is not a lyric but the long poem which he published in 1926. Buthlay's edition prints the text of *A Drunk Man* on the left-hand page and many of its source materials on right-hand pages. This arrangement allows us to see clearly how MacDiarmid in the poem achieves choral, typically Modernist effects. A good example is when Buthlay places a verse of MacDiarmid's host-text (an English version of Blok) beside the splendidly parasitic Scots revoicing of it in *A Drunk Man*. The English verse reads:

> I try, held in this strange captivity,
> To pierce the veil that darkling falls –
> I see enchanted shores; declivity,
> And an enchanted distance calls.[7]

MacDiarmid revoices this as

> I seek, in this captivity
> To pierce the veils that darklin' fa'
> – See white clints slidin' to the sea,
> And hear the horns o' Elfland blaw.

What we have now is a fully dialogic verse produced by Blok, his English translators, MacDiarmid and the Tennyson of *The Princess* with its 'horns of Elfland faintly blowing'.[8] MacDiarmid's Scots language is generally synthetic because it brings different dialects together with living words and long-obsolete ones. The way in which he likewise pools texts to achieve (like Eliot, Pound and Joyce) choral effects in a language that is and is not his own produces also a synthetic voice, a manufactured chorus. This technique is being developed in the early Scots lyrics, where he is not just using the dictionary but collaborating with it, and at times letting it use him as its wealth of definitions and citations affords him not just words but also whole lines and phrases. In a sense, MacDiarmid's work parallels the question asked by his Scottish contemporary, W. S. Graham: 'What is the language using us for?'[9]

MacDiarmid was well aware of the way a language structures and controls our view of reality. That is why he found the language of a good deal of nineteenth-century poetry in Scots insufficient for the expression of a modern consciousness. His entire output, the poetry in Scots and the later 'poetry of fact', can be seen as an attempt to push at the boundaries set up around language and what is defined as 'poetic'. His writings are very much an expanding universe, and his achievement in *A Drunk Man* of a classic examination of the Scottish psyche is made possible precisely because he was not content to remain within the confines of the existing Scottish literary consciousness. His triumph was to go beyond that by going outside it, then returning with foreign elements in order to rebuild and expand that Scottish literary consciousness using the most recent and most ambitious imported materials. His first major long poem is very much a product of modernist heteroglossia and polyglossia, and owes much to a specific engagement with the poetry of T. S. Eliot.

MacDiarmid's celebrated omnivorous reading at the well-stocked library in Langholm was followed by the painful kaleidoscope of his experiences in First World War Salonika, and in the Sections Lahore Indian General Hospital near Marseilles. The sometimes near-solipsistic speaker of the *Annals of the Five Senses* feels at times the strain of the vivid cultural metamorphoses which he undergoes, a rigorous multicultural jolting which surely contributes to the dialogic properties of MacDiarmid's mature work. – 'Thus, occasionally, he might have a shadowy sense of the incongruity of convening the Russian Duma under the woolly scalp of an undistinguished Scottish free-lance of two-and-twenty, or a hollow feeling (forthwith exorcised as a mean commercial instinct) that little profit to a fellow in his shoes lay in spending an hour or two as a Chinese Reference Library.'[10]

The compulsion 'To think o' China in Milngavie' would be with MacDiarmid all his life.[11] In Salonika, when not engaged in such speculations, he has his virtually autobiographical protagonist digest various fashionable contemporary intellectual topics: Bergson, Max Nordau, Gilbert Murray, the allure of the East, primitivism, psycho-analysis, and mysticism. These concerns are strikingly similar to those pursued just a few years before by a young Sanskrit and Pali scholar named T. S. Eliot. Entirely unknown to each other, both men also shared a strong attachment to the work of the poets James 'B. V.' Thomson and John Davidson, to whose influence and importance both Eliot and MacDiarmid later paid tribute.[12] These two Scottish Victorian poets had an important impact on *The Waste Land*, but one of the crucial differences between Eliot and MacDiarmid emerges in the attitude of each towards Scotland.

Eliot's attitudes towards Scottish literature and the importance of his reaction to the work of G. Gregory Smith have been discussed elsewhere.[13] His position on the chances of a Scottish literary revival appears to have been pessimistic. He was interested, polite, often supportive, yet ultimately unconvinced. MacDiarmid could be more bitterly vituperative about the impotence of his nation:

> God gied man speech and speech created thocht,
> He gied man speech but to the Scots gied nocht
> Barrin this clytach that they've never brocht
> To onything but sic a Blottie O
> As some bairn's copybook micht show
>
> (*MCP*, 115)

But MacDiarmid's asperity was the flipside of his passionate belief in the necessity and possibility of a Scottish Renaissance. His harangues are offset by such well-known pieces as 'Scotland Small?' and part of the key to MacDiarmid's renovation of Scottish writing was his sometimes suspicious, yet nevertheless deeply committed, internationalism. Such a policy made him ready to respond to the cosmopolitan, multicultural dialogic aspects of *The Waste Land*, though it was a policy which could be comic at the same time as serious. Readers of Eliot's poem would find it hard to resist the idea that a snook was being cocked by MacDiarmid in the conclusion of 'In the Slums of Glasgow'.

> And the fading sound of the work-a-day world,
> Dadadoduddadaddadi dadadodudadidadoh,
> Duddadam dadade dudde dadadadadadodadah.
>
> (*MCP*, 565)

There are innumerable references and allusions to Eliot's work in MacDiarmid's poetry, particularly but by no means exclusively in the early period. It is clear that MacDiarmid kept very much up to date with Eliot's output. So, for instance, in *To Circumjack Cencrastus* (1930) occur the lines,

> Even as youth's blindness hauds the body dear
> And only slowly, slowly, year by year,
> The dark thins and the een o' love grow clear,
> My hert'll stiffen and rejoice nae mair
> In the lost lilac and the lost sea-voices,
> Whaup's cry or goose's gansel o' mankind
> Nor set toom forms atween the ivory yetts
> Nor curtain them wi' siantan dubha, tears,
> Or Iolaire's, or angels', wings; but haud
> The warld a photo o' me as a loon
> I canna mind o' haen been at a'
> A state I put awa' wi' spung-taed pranks
> Wi' nae precociousness.
>
> (*MCP*, 259–60)

It is abundantly obvious here that MacDiarmid has not only read, but has assimilated and rechannelled a passage of *Ash-Wednesday* (also 1930):

> And the lost heart stiffens and rejoices
> In the lost lilac and the lost sea voices
> And the weak spirit quickens to rebel
> For the bent golden-rod and the lost sea smell
> Quickens to recover
> The cry of quail and the whirling plover

And the blind eye creates
The empty forms between the ivory gates
And smell renews the salt savour of the sandy earth[14]

Three years after he had printed Muir's enthusiastic review of *To Circumjack Cencrastus* in *The Criterion*, Eliot himself recalled episodes from his seaside experiences at Gloucester, Massachusetts, along with scenes from his youth as an 'arbitrarily chosen set of snapshots'.[15] Among a multitude of interests which MacDiarmid and Eliot shared, the sea and water life must rank highly. It would be possible to catalogue a variety of uses of Eliot in MacDiarmid's work after and including *To Circumjack Cencrastus* where direct mention is made of both *The Waste Land* and *Ash-Wednesday*. The most interesting aspect of the literary relations between the two men, however, lies in the germination of MacDiarmid's reaction to Eliot, and in the way *A Drunk Man* looks at *The Waste Land*, responding not least to what Bakhtin would have called its strong element of 'novelization', its continual play of dialogic strains. There is nothing new in simply noting the fact that there are links between *A Drunk Man Looks at the Thistle* and Eliot's poem. But no one, to my knowledge, has examined the connections in detail. Rather than back-tracking from MacDiarmid's poem, I want to try and work forwards, considering not only the imaginative encouragement that *A Drunk Man* received from *The Waste Land*, but looking too at the way in which reading MacDiarmid's work and Eliot's together is mutually illuminating.

First, though, it is necessary to stress further just how aggressively international MacDiarmid's poetics had become around 1922, the very moment when he was about to plunge from his early C. M. Grieve poetry in English into his 'Hugh MacDiarmid' work then mainly in Scots. The conscious encouragement of cosmopolitanism, often drawing on facets of his wartime experience in Salonika and Marseilles was continued during the early 1920s in a clutch of sonnets addressed to various international writers including Unamuno, Huysmans, and Amiel. MacDiarmid's use of Scots came about not at all as a gesture of parochialism, but as a move into a new, and renewed territory.

Like Eliot, he responded immediately and urgently to *Ulysses*. The importance of Joyce to MacDiarmid is self-evident. The whole concept of a 'poetry of fact' may be related to the Joycean love of facts, a love seen in torrent, for example, through Joyce's hymn to 'Roundwood reservoir in county Wicklow',[16] and in so many of MacDiarmid's water poems when, for instance, he urges,

Wheesht, wheesht, Joyce, and let me hear
Nae Anna Livvy's lilt,

> But Wauchope, Esk, and Ewes again,
> Each wi' its ain rhythms till't.
>
> (*MCP*, 333)

MacDiarmid first read *Ulysses* in 1922, and at once incorporated the Irish book from Paris into his plans for Scottish literature. Joyce's novel offers both the carnivalesque and the dialogic in profusion, and much has rightly ·been made of MacDiarmid's reaction to *Ulysses* in 1923, when he wrote of 'a resemblance ... between Jamieson's Etymological Dictionary of the Scottish language and James Joyce's *Ulysses*', and saw in this resemblance a possible release for 'puir auld Scotland'.[17]

It is simultaneously MacDiarmid's acute sense of that cliché-concept 'puir auld Scotland', and his determined refusal to accept it as final that energizes his work in its heroic attempt to convince his countrymen that Scotland's hope lies in looking out as well as inwards. The need for a change in Scottish literary values is put forcibly in MacDiarmid's 'Causerie' in the January 1923 issue of his magazine, *Scottish Chapbook*, where (with a play on Eliot's magazine title) he suggests that if Burns's poems were submitted to periodical editors as poems of today, then they: 'would be rejected in almost every case as hopelessly below the level by "The Glasgow Herald", not to mention "The London Mercury", "The English Review", and, say "The Criterion" (allowing for their difference in kind as well as degree from the now prevailing fashion which this comment in no way implies to be an infallible criterion) – it would appear that the prospects of Scottish literature would be greatly enhanced if an effective proportion of our literary aspirants turned their attention to James Joyce, Marcel Proust, Georges Duhamel, and others of their kidney. It is a significant fact in literary history that wherever there is a renaissance of a nation's literature nowhere else are the contemporary literatures of other countries more keenly studied.' (*TR*, 150)

Though we might recall his phrase 'other heroes of that kidney', (*ECP*, 44) there is no mention here of T. S. Eliot. What it is essential to realize, though, is that before January 1923, the date of MacDiarmid's piece, the only issue of *The Criterion* which had appeared was the first one, containing *The Waste Land*. Even more interesting is the fact that the Scottish poet responded to Eliot's poem almost as soon as it appeared. This response took the form of a sonnet, undistinguished in quality, but fascinating for what it represents, which MacDiarmid published in the third volume of the annual, *Northern Numbers*, a book printed in December 1922.[18] *The Waste Land* appeared that October, but MacDiarmid, living in Montrose at the time, was not only a journalist by training, but also a writer with many London contacts, gathered partly through his

work for the *New Age* and his friendship with Muir, then in London. To
print *Northern Numbers 3*, MacDiarmid used the Review Press, a local
printing firm which also produced the newspaper MacDiarmid then
worked for. He was used to writing poetry and prose at short notice, and
used to speedy liaison with the Review Press. Nonetheless, very little time
could have elapsed between *The Waste Land*, and the composition of
MacDiarmid's 'Spring, a Violin in the Void' whose title pinpoints three
crucial *Waste Land* elements. The specific spur is found in Eliot's lines

> A woman drew her long black hair out tight
> And fiddled whisper music on those strings
> And bats with baby faces in the violet light
> Whistled, and beat their wings
> And crawled head downward down a blackened wall
> And upside down in air were towers
> Tolling reminiscent bells, that kept the hours
> And voices singing out of empty cisterns and exhausted wells.
>
> (*ECP*, 73)

The MacDiarmid poem, written in a language which he was about to turn
against, reads

Spring, a Violin in the Void

> SPIDERS, far from their webs, with trembling feet
> Assemble on the ceiling, a charmed group,
> While the grey bow with many a swing and swoop,
> Draws from dim strings a music crying-sweet.
> Hard by the doorstep shelving to the street
> A fascinated lizard swells the troop
> Of mean hearts taken in the magic loop
> From terror freed, and given a cosmic beat.
>
> Even in the loft's profound behold a bat,
> But half-awakened from its winter sleep
> And hanging there head-downwards by a claw,
> In its small brain th' insidious tune has caught,
> And, swinging to the rhythm, has a deep
> Sense of at-one-ment with an unknown law.
>
> (*MCP*, 1215)

This odd little poem is a more complex response to *The Waste Land* than
it might at first seem. In its imagery it draws on Eliot's published work,
and even resembles some unpublished pieces. Where the Eliotic clairvoy-
ant, Madame Sosostris, saw 'crowds of people, walking round in a ring',

MacDiarmid presents 'mean hearts taken in a magic loop', but further extends this to the 'cosmic beat' which is later presented as 'a deep / Sense of at-one-ment with an unknown law'. This surely indicates a response to the laws sensed operating in *The Waste Land*, compelling, for instance, spring to prompt so many loveless couplings 'enacted on the same divan or bed'. Eliot presents a nearly surreal chorus of fiddling women, whistling bats, tolling bells, and inane singing voices. MacDiarmid's transforming this into his musical round emphasizes for us that *The Waste Land* is essentially a cyclic poem: even if the rain were to fall in 'What the Thunder Said', it would only reanimate those 'dried tubers' of the poem's start, 'stirring / Dull roots with spring rain'. In a cruder but analogous way, spring also brings out nasties for MacDiarmid – in the form of spiders, a lizard, and a bat. Yet there is an important difference. Eliot's bats, crickets, cicadas and other creatures seem only to reinforce the sensation of being trapped in a terrible cage of cyclic repetition where all are condemned to repeat ritual re-enactments without ever reaching that 'Shantih' which for the Buddhist is the peace which lies beyond the circles of creation. For MacDiarmid, though, the 'at-one-ment' seems to bring a kind of atonement, at least a sense of being 'from terror freed'. The poem brings together nightmarish elements, yet at its end seems to offer far more relief than Eliot's poem. There is a strange Orphic element, as music tames the bugs. This poem is MacDiarmid's first translation of *The Waste Land* into a kind of horror-facing optimism, an act of translation accomplished again when in 'On a Raised Beach':

> This is no heap of broken images
> (*MCP*, 427)

Such an act of translation is also accomplished in *A Drunk Man Looks at the Thistle*.

For the moment, though, the differences between MacDiarmid's poetry and Eliot's remain immense. MacDiarmid responds to *The Waste Land* initially with, of all things, a sonnet. He is fascinated by Eliot's poem, particularly by certain tones and images in it, but formally he remains far removed. In its form, his sonnet can take no account of the wild dialogic play of *The Waste Land* where in flights of heteroglossia and polyglossia, dialect confronts standard English, and quotations from a variety of languages are placed in 'intonational quotation marks' and allowed to engage with one another in the text. It will take MacDiarmid some time to come to terms with the formal possibilities offered by all these devices. It would be wrong to see 'Spring, a Violin in the Void' as any real response to the possibilities of novelization which *The Waste Land* made available, but it is a clear reaction to Eliot's poem which shows that the Scot's attitude is one of fascination, but also involves a refusal to succumb to the pessimism of *The Waste Land*. In 1923 such a difference in poetic attitude between the two writers comes not merely from temperamental differences, but from the simple fact that MacDiarmid, on the eve of his campaign for a Scottish Renaissance, had to see rebirth as hopeful. For Eliot in this period, 'Birth, and copulation, and death' seemed equally hopeless. For MacDiarmid, though he might present spring in a menacing and unorthodox way, it eventually had to be a season of promise. The path opened up by *The Waste Land* was there to be followed, but not to the same destination.

The need to see promise and to identify with the idea of re-birth leads MacDiarmid during this period to make the most amazingly provocative statements. So in March 1923 he writes that: 'It was anticipated that Spengler, in his second book – which has just been published – would reveal the East as the source of the civilisation destined to replace our own, that of the declining West, and in this connection it is well to remember in passing that we Scots are Oriental, the descendants of the lost tribes of Israel (sic) ....' (*TR*, 136) Daringly, before going on to draw his celebrated, eastward-looking 'Russo-Scottish parallelism', MacDiarmid attempts to place Scotland in the current of renaissance rather than decay. Both currents flow through *A Drunk Man*, and the prose of 1923 shows MacDiarmid using a tessellation of passages from H. G. Wells, Frederic Harrison, Graham Wallas and Spengler to build up a picture of contemporary civilization as a waste land in which 'Western Europe, with America, has exhausted her creative energies as Greece, Rome, Assyria, Babylon ...'. (*TR*, 135) Such a piling up of exhausted places draws on Eliot's technique:

> Falling towers
> Jerusalem Athens Alexandria
> Vienna London
> Unreal

We might sense now that MacDiarmid has continued to respond not just to *The Waste Land*'s tone but also to its technical devices. Confirmation that this is the case comes when we look at the organization of *A Drunk Man Looks at the Thistle*.

The Waste Land's hallucinatory technique did for Eliot's poem what the idea of being drunk did for MacDiarmid's, facilitating abrupt shifts and conjunctions. Though *The Waste Land* prompted various imitations, only MacDiarmid was both mature and independent enough to let Eliot help him on his way to a masterpiece. Eliot had shown how a work in related yet distinct units could function as a modern long poem, shifting from generalized comment to pub-scene to fleeting, intense vision, town to wilderness, confronting religious and sexual matters together, introducing unprefaced figures, mixing contemporary and traditional myths, blending dialogic elements. Eliot also incorporated (as would MacDiarmid) other literary material into his own poetic text, and continually juxtaposed the exploration of cultural roots with the evolution of physical and botanical roots studied by men like Mendel, de Vries, and Luther Burbank, with all of whose work Eliot was familiar. Learned commentators too often forget how frequently physical plant-life and its environment play a crucial part in *The Waste Land*, from those 'dried tubers' onwards.

> What are the roots that clutch, what branches grow
> Out of this stony rubbish?
>
> ...the dead tree gives no shelter
>
> 'That corpse you planted last year in your garden,
> Has it begun to sprout? Will it bloom this year?'
>
> And other withered stumps of time
> Were told upon the walls
>
>   ...the last fingers of leaf
> Clutch and sink into the wet bank.
>
> A rat crept softly through the vegetation
>
>   ...dry grass singing
>
>   ...the limp leaves
> Waited for rain ...
>
> The jungle crouched, humped in silence.

Such a list is not exhaustive, but it may help to suggest why the thistle, rather than, say, whisky, is the central symbol in *A Drunk Man* where again there is a preoccupation with physical at the same time as cultural roots, occasionally following Eliot's diction,

> The barren tree, dry leafs and cracklin' thorns
>   (*MCP*, 152)
>
> Here is the root that feeds
> The shank wi' the blindin' wings
>   (*MCP*, 99)

As in Eliot, plant life and human sexuality are intimately connected, whether in the lyric,

> O wha's the bride that cairries the bunch
> O' thistles blinterin white?
>
> (*MCP*, 102)

or in several visions of the thistle as a nightmarish phallus:

> Or new diversion o' the hormones
> Mair fond o' procreation than the Mormons,
> And fetchin' like a devastatin' storm on's
> A' the uncouth dilemmas o' oor natur'
> Objectified in the vegetable maitter.
>
> Yank oot your orra boughs, my hert!
>
> (*MCP*, 117)

When we see how many of the central concepts of *The Waste Land* would be triumphantly transmuted in *A Drunk Man*, it is hardly surprising that about a year before that work's appearance when MacDiarmid advertised his forthcoming long poem in the *Glasgow Herald* of 17 December 1925, the only other poet whom he mentioned was Eliot, whose name appeared twice. True, he mentions 'parodies of Mr T. S. Eliot and other poets', and 'a skit on Mr. Eliot's "Sweeney' poems"', but the spur of *The Waste Land* went beyond parody. Where Eliot had a London pub scene, MacDiarmid has a Scottish one; where Eliot had his hyacinth girl, MacDiarmid has his dreamlike 'silken leddy'. For MacDiarmid town confronts barren hillside and harsh thistlescape, for Eliot the confrontation is with scrubby desert. Cruivie and Gilsanquhar appear and go like *The Waste Land*'s shifting persons. If Eliot presents us with the pageant-like procession of deathly clerks over contemporary London Bridge, yet calls the scene 'unreal', so MacDiarmid has his drunk man wonder

> Or am I just a figure in a scene
> O' Scottish life A.D. one-nine-two-five?
> The haill thing kelters like a theatre claith
> Till I micht fancy that I was alive!
>
> ...
>
> The haill damned thing's a dream for ocht we ken,
> – The Warld and Life and Death, Heaven, Hell ana'.
>
> (*MCP*, 92)

As in *The Waste Land* the horror of London becomes that of all cities, a parallel theme marks *A Drunk Man*

> And in the toon that I belang tae
> – What tho'ts Montrose or Nazareth? –

> Helplessly the folk continue
> To lead their livin' death!
>   (*MCP*, 88)

For Eliot, Tiresias, 'throbbing between two lives', epitomizes the cage of sexuality, the links between opposing elements including dead and living. The thistle, true to MacDiarmid's version of the 'Caledonian Antisyzygy', has an analogous function as a 'creakin/ Hinge atween the deid and livin'...'. (*MCP*, 96) In Eliot's jazz age, being bang up-to-date is counterpointed by the presence of primitive and classical myth. MacDiarmid's poem too is aggressively contemporary, referring for instance to the General Strike of May 1926 as well as to modern cultural figures such as Eliot himself, Blok and Schönberg. But such references occur in the poem along with many details drawn from primitive and Christian ceremony, along with distinctively Scottish myths and practices such as those of the Langholm Common Riding, and the Burns cult. Pound was midwife to *The Waste Land*. When in difficulties about the assembling of the various pieces of his poem, MacDiarmid had the aid of composer F. G. Scott. MacDiarmid also followed Eliot in making lines of Dante part of his own poem, but took the process of textual embedding further by incorporating versions of whole poems translated from Russian, Belgian and German poets. MacDiarmid clearly signposts the borrowed nature of these passages which become at once elements of his own poem, native artefacts, at the same time as being clearly un-Scottish material, foreign bodies. This reinforces on the large-scale level what we have already observed at the level of detail: the poem's choral, deliberately heteroglossic quality. It emerges as crammed, like *The Waste Land*, with often competing dialogic voices. MacDiarmid's incorporation into his host text of whole foreign poems is companioned by a use of many shorter quotations from, for example, Mallarmé, and from Scottish writers including Burns (essential to the poem throughout, most of all as the poet of 'Tam o'Shanter'), and Robert Buchanan. *A Drunk Man* also discusses Eliotic themes such as impersonality, (*MCP*, 162) according to which the poet's personal voice is lost in the revoiced tradition. MacDiarmid's efforts in this poem seem geared to engaging his own poetic voice not only with other Scots voices, but also with those of an international chorus. *A Drunk Man* is at once obsessed with Scottish heritage and dilemmas while being at the same time aggressively modern and international. MacDiarmid uses what he has learned from Eliot's dialogic, heteroglossic poem to allow him to present a new model for the Scottish consciousness which is not the atrophied 'Blottie O' attacked in the poem so much as the multifaceted and multivocal sophisticated amalgam embodied by the poem. Where Eliot rings what sounds like the death-knell of a civilization, producing a

Menippean satire whose import may be ultimately nihilistic, MacDiarmid
produces a new constructed form of Scottishness which allows him both
to lash what he sees as wrong with Scottish culture and to provide a
sometimes carnivalesque blueprint for its rebirth.

Just as it would be perverse to deny that MacDiarmid used numerous
Waste Land elements to make a poem which is eventually very different,
so also it would be absurd to suggest that, among Eliot's works, it was
solely *The Waste Land* which was grist to MacDiarmid's mill. That early
line from *A Drunk Man*, 'Twixt Burbank's Baedeker and Bleistein's
cigar', (*MCP*, 85) alerts us to Eliot's poem where we find the lines,

> Chicago Semite Viennese.
>
> A lustreless protrusive eye
> Stares from the protozoic slime ...
>   (*ECP*, 40)

This seeing of humans as lower organisms haunts MacDiarmid's poem
where, a few lines before, he presents figures who are 'nocht but zoologi-
cally men'. (*MCP*, 85) Later he will say that 'Barbarians ha'e lizards' een',
(*MCP*, 153) and having mentioned Chicago in the eighth stanza of his
poem, he will go on to have his own worries about cultural incongruities,
not without a touch of uncharacteristic racism:

> You canna gang to a Burns supper even
> Wi'oot some wizened scrunt o' a knock-knee
> Chinee turns roon to say, 'Him Haggis – velly goot!'
> And ten to wan the piper is a Cockney.
>   (*MCP*, 84)

Eliot's quatrain poems may encourage the use of the word 'protoplasm',
(*MCP*, 125) or the imagery of the epileptic, (*MCP*, 140, 149) and there
are, of course, more direct connections, as when, antisyzygically,

> The circles of our hungry thought
> Swing savagely from pole to pole.
> Death and the Raven drift above
> The graves of Sweeney's body and soul.
>   (*MCP*, 150)

There are many other equally clear uses of Eliot's work. The 'broken
stone' of 'The Hollow Men' becomes MacDiarmid's 'broken stanes',
(*MCP*, 153) and he also weaves 'We canna tell oor voices frae the wund'
out of Eliot's 'Our dried voices, when / We whisper together / Are quiet
and meaningless / As wind in dry grass'. (*MCP*, 151; *ECP*, 83)

Yet MacDiarmid's poem no more 'derives from' Eliot's work than *The Waste Land* 'derives from' that of Dante. Realizing the closeness of *A Drunk Man* and *The Waste Land* lets us appreciate more finely the way in which their differences emerge. In doing this, and especially in comparing the two poems' conclusions, it becomes obvious that, as in his 1922 sonnet, so in the 1926 masterpiece, MacDiarmid has translated the darkness of *The Waste Land* into what becomes again his own brand of optimism won from horror. His alteration of the borrowed material is thorough-going. So, MacDiarmid several times alludes to Eliot's now famous water-dripping passage, (*MCP*, 88, 147, 150) joking that water is the last thing wanted for whisky. But the use of the passage moves far beyond the merely burlesque, taking MacDiarmid to levels of characteristically intense and macroscopic lyricism:

> I tae ha'e heard Eternity drip water
> (Aye water, water!), drap by drap
> On the a'e nerve, like lichtnin', I've become,
> And heard God passin' wi' a bobby's feet
> Ootby in the lang coffin o' the street
>
> (MCP, 147)

His poem may borrow its 'mony-branchin' candelabra' but it turns its material to ends other than those of Eliot. One of the central differences lies in MacDiarmid's attitude to sex, seen often as painful and frightening in *A Drunk Man*, but not as mechanical. So when the speaker cries ' – But sex reveals life, faith!', (*MCP*, 114) this is not a bitterly ironic cry, for though in many ways the setting of this poem is a tortured waste land, whatever his suffering, MacDiarmid's odd, but fundamental optimism pushes forward. At the very moment when he envisages that 'Scotland' may 'turn Eliot's waste – the Land o' Drouth', the Drunk Man continues,

> But even as the stane the builders rejec'
> Becomes the corner-stane, the time may be
> When Scotland sall find oot its destiny...
>
> (MCP, 134)

A saving humour is at work throughout much of *A Drunk Man*. *The Waste Land* is not totally humourless, but MacDiarmid's humour often in this poem at least involves a Joycean love of the carnivalesque and human which is not nearly so apparent in the agony of Eliot's masterwork. This difference, seen again in the attitude towards women in the two poems, emerges clearly in a comparison of the two conclusions.

The Waste Land ends precariously, toppling from nursery rhyme to high art, and stops with the Buddhist 'Shantih', that peace which passeth all understanding. The path to a transcendental Silence is also taken by MacDiarmid, here no doubt walking with Soloviev: 'Yet ha'e I Silence left, the croon o' a'.' Yet the conclusion comes brilliantly back to the everyday, warm world with the final finale deflation ' – "And weel ye micht," / Sae Jean'll say, "efter sic a nicht!".' (*MCP*, 167) In *The Waste Land* little real relief is offered. There seems more hope for the Drunk Man's 'aboulia'. (*MCP*, 93)

All this alerts us to the importance of MacDiarmid's most direct reference to Eliot in the poem:

> T. S. Eliot – it's a Scottish name –
> Afore he wrote 'The Waste Land' s'ud ha'e come
> To Scotland here. He wad ha'e written
> A better poem syne – like this, by gum!
> (*MCP*, 94)

The word 'this' may be taken to refer to what immediately follows – a parody of Eliot's 'learned' stylistic polyglossia:

> Type o' the Wissenschaftsfeindlichkeit,
> Begriffsmüdigkeit that has gar't
> Men try Morphologies der Weltgeschichte,
> And mad Expressionismus syne in Art.
> (*MCP*, 94)

But the word 'this' surely refers as well to *A Drunk Man* itself, and does not represent merely the author's confidence. It also invites the reader to look at *A Drunk Man* in the light of *The Waste Land*. To do this is not to suggest that Eliot's poem offers a 'key' to, or 'the source' of MacDiarmid's achievement. Looking at the two poems in tandem, though, does bring home just how receptive and active was MacDiarmid's reading of Eliot at this period. It also alerts us to some important, yet often insufficiently stressed aspects of both *A Drunk Man Looks at the Thistle* and *The Waste Land*. Those ubiquitous roots, so characteristic of both poems, are intertwined.

They are intertwined not only on the level of stylistic detail, but crucially, on the level of their formal music. Both are to an important degree 'novelized' poems, full of those clashing voices which Bakhtin sees as essentially characteristic of modern literature as manifested in what he calls the 'novel'. Both poems are produced chorally, by a chorus of voices which does not always sing in unison. The sometimes clashing dialogic voices of these poems prepare us for the music of Elliot Carter and the poetry of John Ashbery, but they both relate also to the attempt on the part of the poet to construct for himself a new cultural identity. I have discussed the complexities of Eliot's identity elsewhere, but wish to point out here that few contemporary observers of this complex identity were more astute than the C. M. Grieve who was himself so busily engaged in the assembly of a chorus of voices which would allow him to give voice to a new conception of Scotland and her culture.[19]

For a poet in many ways so different from him, MacDiarmid keenly understood much of Eliot's poetry and psyche, and, as so often, where he admired, MacDiarmid wished also to lay claim. This he did not only in *A Drunk Man* and elsewhere in verse, but also in prose, where he writes (wrongly), for example, that Eliot's 'first wife was a Scotswoman from Glasgow'.[20] In a 1928 letter to Neil Gunn this impulse is again apparent, and we realize too that it was just because MacDiarmid was not himself English that he understood some of Eliot's methods so well. 'Now as to Eliot, I believe (vide Drunk Man) he's a Scotsman by descent – but it's a damned long descent: and mentally he certainly fills the role you seem to have cast him for in your papers. He is pure Boston – ultra-English classicist in criticism: that's what makes him so unintelligible to mere English conventionalists – they can't follow their own ideas to their logical conclusions well enough to recognize their own supporters.' (*L*, 222)

For Eliot's part, he seems early to have recognized in MacDiarmid a poetic outlook very different from his own yet, perhaps for that very reason, one that was important. So, as well as having MacDiarmid's work reviewed in *The Criterion*, and publishing MacDiarmid's prose there, he also made space in the magazine for 'Second Hymn to Lenin' and 'Cornish Heroic Song for Valda Trevlyn'. As well as backing MacDiarmid's Scots work, and paying tribute to his writing in English, Eliot was one of the few people to appreciate the importance of *In Memoriam James Joyce*, pronouncing himself in 1945 astonished at such a magnificent tribute to language. (*L*, 455)

Eliot was not 'a Scotsman by descent' but he was like MacDiarmid an un-English writer aware of the culture power of the English metropolitan centre and its language, and particularly alert to heteroglossia. We may suspect that he reacted to *In Memoriam James Joyce* for reasons related to those behind MacDiarmid's reception of *The Waste Land*. Each poem depends fundamentally on a rich dialogic play of voices. Originally titled *He Do the Police in Different Voices*, Eliot's poem has its Cockney, Dantescan, nursery-rhyme, neurasthenic, prophetic, elegiac, and other 'voices'. MacDiarmid's later poetry has its scientific-informational, lyrical, humorous, polemical, native and variously other tongues. The voices of that late poetry, collaged together out of various discourses and interpreted best by poets who have learned from it (such as Edwin Morgan, Alan Riach, and W. N. Herbert), is a development of the heteroglossic and polyphonic technique which shapes *A Drunk Man Looks at the Thistle*. Though gradually his critics are coming to realize that the eclectic compositional strategies, the kleptomania of the late work in 'synthetic English', are in some important ways similar to the methods of assembly used in the early Scots poetry. This process of realization has still some way to go. MacDiarmid has come to be seen as the foremost representative of twentieth-century Scottish culture, and *A Drunk Man* as one of the most important artworks emerging from and dealing with the Scottish tradition. Yet more and more we are becoming aware of how much MacDiarmid, his work, and the Scottishness of both are complexly manufactured.

The pugnaciously confident Ecclefechan-among-the-stars Scottishness of MacDiarmid's work is very different from the Scottishness taken as the norm by the Kailyard writers. Scottishness is not an immutable quality but an evolving construct that varies from age to age. MacDiarmid himself was such a construct. His maker, C. M. Grieve was, by all accounts, a kindly and generous individual. His creation, MacDiarmid however, was made of different stuff.

MacDiarmid was never a man to be confined to the page, and readers attracted to his biography because they want a picture of one of the oddest writers of the century – endlessly provocative, percipient and crazy – will not be disappointed. The public life of MacDiarmid, a professional journalist with an insatiable appetite for publicity, affords numerous occasions for delight, horror and amazement. In his career the heroic and mock-heroic frequently scald one another. MacDiarmid designates his garden shed the Scottish Poetry Bookshop, and tries to set up a Hugh MacDiarmid Book Club to dispose of unsold copies of his work. He asks for writing materials in a pub: only a piece of toilet paper can be found – he writes a great lyric on it. On one of the hottest days of the year he wears a fur coat to keep the sun out. In 1964, having polled 127 votes against Sir Alec Douglas-Home's 16,659, MacDiarmid takes Douglas-Home (then Prime Minister) to court, denouncing him as 'a zombie'. Thirty-six years earlier, flown to Dublin by the Irish Government, MacDiarmid finds himself in the early morning pissing in the street with W. B. Yeats: 'I crossed swords with him and we became very friendly after that.' Bold's *MacDiarmid* supplies many such enjoyable vignettes, but resists (as C. M. Grieve sometimes did not) turning his subject into The Hugh MacDiarmid Show.

Yet C. M. Grieve's Hugh MacDiarmid Show was very much a deliberate, heterogeneous creation which does have a definite relationship with the poetry. For the MacDiarmid Show which so fascinated Scotland was not just the Caledonian Antisyzygy solo on the public stage. It was a discordantly choric production, the work of C. M. Grieve, Hugh MacDiarmid, Martin Gillespie, A. K. Laidlaw, Anon. and a number of other shifting identities. Similarly, the peculiar and frequently hypnotic effect of the texts we call 'MacDiarmid' comes from their blending and juxtaposing of heterogeneous voices – the voices of Scots and non-Scots, polemical, lyrical, lexicographical, demotic, bizarre, and banal. Among the producers of such a dialogic voice is certainly T. S. Eliot, but Burns and Joyce, Charles Doughty and Shestov are there as well. So too is Robert Frost, Kenneth Buthlay suggests, and certainly this would be appropriate given Frost's careful synthetic construction of his own complicated territorial identity.[21] We might speak readily of MacDiarmid and his maker, C. M. Grieve. But we would do better to speak of MacDiarmid and his many makers whose voices sound together, sometimes in harmony but more usually in a clashing but exciting near-Babel of tongues, a product not merely of any Caledonian Antisyzygy but of a fully heteroglossic imagination. It is a similar if more awesomely scaled imagination that is at work in *In Memoriam James Joyce*, a poem which should be seen again as the product of a choric rather than of an individual voice. This late work is a poem to intellectual DNA, to the creative energies of the human intellect and imagination: kaleidoscopic, supremely eclectic, it draws on the wide variety of sources and discourses. When the words 'I' or 'we' are used in the poem they should be seen as referring less to particular historical individuals such as Hugh MacDiarmid than to the whole of the human creative and intellectual potential. The choric 'I' of the poem brings together all knowledge, as if the *Encyclopedia Britannica* or Murray's *New English Dictionary* were to be given a self. This data-base-like poem is perhaps easier to comprehend in an age when computing technology and techniques are more generally familar. Blending or juxtaposing the dialects of exploration, bibliography, philology, physics, and many other technical and scientific jargons, MacDiarmid produces again, as he had done in *A Drunk Man* a potentially heteroglossic paean which has less a maker than a community of makers. In his late poetic career as in his earlier, one of MacDiarmid's striking legacies is that through his achievement such a dialogic imagination, in which Bakhtin could surely have revelled, has come to be readily identified as Scottish.

3

Somhairle MacGill-Eain/ Sorley Maclean

The finest poetry written by British subjects during the years 1939–45 was produced by T. S. Eliot and by Sorley MacLean. Each was a British subject in a very different way. Eliot, more interested in assuming English-ness than Britishness, had already taken the un-English step of giving himself a written constitution (Royalist, Anglo-Catholic, Classicist), and gave over one of his three great war poems to the investigation and celebration of his American background. MacLean, a Gael born on the Hebridean island of Raasay in 1911, almost gave his life in the service of the British Crown when he was blown up by a land-mine at El Alamein in 1942; holding strong Communist and Scottish Nationalist views, he had decided he would fight because he was convinced Hitler would attack Russia, and because (as he wrote to MacDiarmid in 1941) his fear and hatred of the Nazis was greater than his hatred of 'the English Empire'.[1]

Eliot and MacLean may be seen as poles apart. What they shared was more important. Each was impelled by a duty to his language, by the necessity of modernizing its capacities and fighting its insularities; each was to become a cultural figurehead, the quintessential representative of poetry in his language. A desire to bond the traditional to the avant-garde, an apocalyptic turn of the imagination, a difficult fidelity to ancestors – these also connect Eliot with MacLean, and with MacDiarmid.

MacLean's attitude to Eliot is a complex one which has altered over the years. Tómás Mac Síomóin reminds us that MacLean wrote in his verse of rejecting 'the way, trifling, mean and arid / of Eliot, Pound and Auden, / MacNeice, and Herbert Read and their crew'. Yet the poem which Mac Síomóin quotes goes on to suggest that MacLean came close to following a Modernist path.[2] If in 1970 MacLean could write sceptically of 'the preciously consistent humility of Eliot', then such an attitude marks a considerable revision of the view of Eliot which MacLean held during his early years as a student.[3]

The 1989 parallel text of MacLean's *Collected Poems* which contains almost double the material included in the 1977 Canongate parallel text *Selected* (and significantly more than the *Poems 1932–82* published in English translation only by the Iona Foundation in Philadelphia in 1987) opens with a helpful, lucid preface in which, among other things, MacLean recalls his time as an undergraduate studying English at Edinburgh University around 1930 when the influence of Professor Herbert Grierson was so potent. MacLean has described Grierson as 'outstanding among the Professors of English Literature in the British Isles' and recalls he was 'an awfully good lecturer'.[4] Celebrated not least for his anthology of *Metaphysical Lyrics and Poems of the Seventeenth Century* which had occasioned T. S. Eliot's review article 'The Metaphysical Poets' (1921), Grierson delivered to MacLean's first year English Literature class in 1929–30 a course of lectures which took the form of a survey of English poetry from Chaucer to Swinburne. Though his first language was Gaelic, MacLean chose to concentrate on English at university because the job prospects for graduates in Celtic were so unpromising. His own background in Gaelic culture was strong, and grew in his student days; yet alongside that growth there developed his interest in English-language writing, an interest already potent in the schoolboy MacLean. If the poet most familiar to us is the 'Somhairle MacGill-Eain' whose Gaelic work began to be collected in print in the 1940s, then there was also the English language poet 'S. MacLean' who used this form of his name when he published a poem in English in a 1933 Edinburgh University anthology edited by David Daiches.[5] The young MacLean wrote poetry in both languages. The mature work is written in the language to which MacLean is so magnificently committed. Yet what is noteworthy in the range of reference, styles and positions is that it has evolved out of a dialogue between the Gaelic and non-Gaelic worlds, a dialogue between 'Somhairle MacGill-Eain' and 'Sorley MacLean'.

MacLean has written of how 'in my later teens a dichotomy took me psychologically: my "pure" aesthetic idols of old Gaelic songs, and my humano-aesthetic idols of Blake and Shelley.'[6] This dichotomy involves not only aesthetics, but also a split between languages. Sometimes in his career MacLean has had to defend one language against the encroachments of another, but his bilingualism has also been a source of strength, allowing him to learn from another literature and to pursue in Gaelic a dialogue with the modern world, albeit a dialogue often conducted through an interpreter's parallel text. If 'Somhairle MacGill-Eain' has achieved poetic dominance, many of his readers continue to rely on the facing English-language translations of 'S. MacLean'. The dichotomy and the dialogue which were known to the student MacLean have continued, in modified forms, in his mature work.

When MacLean was a new student at Edinburgh, he recalls, the undergraduates were very keen on the work of Eliot, Pound and Hopkins, none of whose poetry was taught as part of the university syllabus. One lecturer in particular, Arthur Melville Clark, was especially hostile to Eliot, though this may only have encouraged the students' enthusiasm. MacLean began to read Eliot, Pound and Hopkins in his first year at university, ignoring Yeats who was then unpopular amongst the students who knew only Yeats's early Celtic Twilight work. Among the student poets J. D. K. Rafferty (who later wrote as Shaun Rafferty) was considered most promising and produced a pastiche of 'Hugh Selwyn Mauberley', a poem then very popular with the undergraduate writers. MacLean thought Rafferty 'brilliant in the Poundian manner', though he preferred Robert Garioch's early poems to those of Rafferty. (*CPGE*, xiv)

The young MacLean wrote English poems (now lost) in the style of Eliot and Pound, particularly the Pound of 'Hugh Selwyn Mauberley'. One can see how 'Mauberley' with its bitterness at Europe's 'botched civilisation' and the slaughter of her young men may have helped fuel the MacLean who was increasingly enraged at the oppression of his own Gaelic people, and prepared him to become a modern poet of war and of the strains between action and aesthetics. Some of his short early lyrics such as 'Edinburgh' and 'Aros Burn' surely draw on Pound's Imagism, while linking of the frustrated love of the eighteenth-century Gaelic poet William Ross to 'the Audiart who plagued De Born' (*CPGE*, 13) glances to the Pound of 'Na Audiart' and *The Spirit of Romance*.

More illuminating, however, is MacLean's early orientation towards Eliot. As a young student, MacLean preferred Eliot's work to that of Pound, admiring in particular his control of and insight into language. *The Waste Land* remained a very strange, though intriguing poem, and MacLean recalls a strong liking for the quatrain poems, particularly 'Sweeney Among the Nightingales'. Like the other quatrain poems, this poem brings together violence and the erotic, using the actual to question the ideal. A division between the physical and the ideal runs throughout Eliot's other quatrain poems such as 'Mr Eliot's Sunday Morning Service'. The spell of Eliot and Grierson, along with the enthusiasm of his student friends, drew MacLean to Donne, whom both critics saw as the great exemplar of the poet's synthesis of conflicting elements, of reason and emotion. Eliot's own imagination (into whose service Donne was easily recruited) was obsessed with division – whether the split between thought and action in the early verse, between human life and potential salvation in *The Waste Land* and *Ash-Wednesday*, between the halves of a 'dissociation of sensibility', or 'Between the emotion / And the response' in 'The Hollow Men'. Division, warring division, was to be MacLean's terrible muse.

Choisich mi cuide ri mo thuisge
a-muigh ri taobh a' chuain;
bha sinn còmhla ach bha ise
a' fuireach tiotan bhuam.

I walked with my reason
out beside the sea
We were together but it was
keeping a little distance from me.
(*CPGE*, 22–3)

MacLean throughout struggles 'with the divisive passion of my spirit' ('Glen Eyre', *CPGE*, 43), while holding to traditional forms. Division is bound up with his concept of poetic greatness, with 'acute Shakespeare struggling in the strife of his nature'. The stunning (occasionally, in English, awkward) long poem of 1939, 'An Cuilithionn' ('The Cuillin'), published in the 1989 *Collected Poems* for the first time as a whole work, has its speaker standing with 'a foot in the morass/ and a foot on the Cuillin'. (*CPGE*, 95) Thirty-three pages long, this is a clear-sighted, frequently beautiful work written in anguish over the fate of Gaelic and European culture on the raw edge of war. It looks fearfully and worshipfully towards the bare, saw-toothed mountains of Skye, seeing them in a focus both of appeal and suffering. Its range is world-wide as it surveys history, its subject-matter is hypnotically obsessive. It ends with the Cuillin seen 'rising on the other side of sorrow', but the pain of impending catastrophe is all-pervasive.

Considering 'Realism in Gaelic Poetry' in 1938, MacLean writes that 'As far as I can see the 18th Century Gaelic poet did not dissociate his sensibility from any aspects of life'. MacLean is here contrasting Gaelic poetry with English poetry, but his phrasing also shows how deeply his thought had been affected by Eliot whose questionable notion of 'a dissociation of sensibility' had first surfaced in his 1921 review of Grierson's anthology.[7] MacLean's 1938 essay, his most substantial critical work, focuses on Gaelic texts, yet it is also produced out of a dialogue with the world of non-Gaelic critical theory, poetry, and aesthetics. MacLean draws on T. E. Hulme, the darling of the Imagists; to aid his demolition of the Celtic Twilight, he makes use of the terminology of Eliot as well as Gaelic scholarship. He quotes C. M. Grieve as well as Mary MacLeod, and refers to Burns and Donne (now accused of 'nonsensical indecency') as well as to Gaelic writers.[8] MacLean is formulating his own cultural and poetic identity through engaging simultaneously in a study of Gaelic poetry and a dialogue with the non-Gaelic world. His greatest poetic subject may be division, but the poetry in which that is expressed is also nurtured by the dialogue. When this Gaelic poet sees the distinguishing feature of great poetry as its 'auditory effect', it is hard not to think that he has not engaged rewardingly with Eliot's concept of the 'auditory imagination'.[9]

Half of the poems in the 1989 *Collected Poems* were produced between 1939 and 1945. The poetry written throughout the Second World War intensifies and develops MacLean's early divided lyric voice which had been honed against that of Eliot before the student poet was converted by James Caird to the idea that Yeats was as great a poet as Eliot, and before he read for himself Yeats's later poetry. MacLean's poem 'The Knife' opens:

> Rinn sgian m'eanchainn gearradh
> air cloich mo ghaoil, a luaidh …
>
> The knife of my brain made incision,
> my dear, on the stone of my love…
> (*CPGE*, 144–5)

In the famous poem 'An Tathaich' ('The Haunting') 'the triumphant face of a girl / that is always speaking' obsesses the poet, urging him in terms like a reworking of lines from section V of 'The Hollow Men':

> Tha e labhairt ri mo chridhe
> nach fhaidar sgaradh a shireadh
> eader miann agus susbaint
> a'chuspair dho-ruighinn;…
>
> It is saying to my heart
> that a division may not be sought
> between desire and the substance
> of its unattainable object;…
> (*CPGE*, 158–9)

The poem concludes with an admission common to many of MacLean's sharpest lyrics: that in the fight between his reason and his fruitless love it is the latter which wins a costly victory.

Continuous awareness of painful division in MacLean's verse gives him a constant sense of *luasgan* ('unrest'). That word recurs in his long 1940 meditation in time of war, 'The Woods of Raasay'. Unrest and division also permeate the love lyrics, where, for all their tenderness, attachment to a beloved wars with the call to defend values threatened by imperialism and Fascism, whether in the early Thirties, in Spain, or in World War Two. The love affairs are internal wars, and the decision to go to 'the proper war' is only the exchanging of one conflict for another. Much of the verse which MacLean wrote during the war years, some of his finest work, was love poetry addressed to a figure who is a mixture of an individual woman and the poet's home and culture. Linking older Gaelic themes of heroism, lament, love and land-love, these poems are themselves strife-torn and haunted by political anxieties, with the result that they shade with scarcely a break into the poems which are literally and principally about the military hostilities of the Second World War.

It is precisely MacLean's rasping awareness that even love may be a destructive engagement which makes him such a tight-lipped, generous poet of war. His love poems are almost war poems; his war poems, written far from 'every loved image of Scotland' in a place where 'a foreign sand in History' is 'spoiling the machines of the mind', achieve a remarkable sympathy, very close to love, for those enemies whom he elsewhere derides. (*CPGE*, 205) The corpses of Nazis in the desert are seen as *neoichiontach* ('innocent') in the poem 'Going Westwards' with its loaded, Donne-like title. Now

> Chan eil gamhlas 'na mo chridhe
> ri saighdearan calma 'n Nàmhaid
> ach an càirdeas a tha eadar
> fir am priosan air sgeir-thràghad ...

> There is no rancour in my heart
> against the hardy soldiers of the Enemy,
> but the kinship that there is among
> men in prison on a tidal rock ...
> (*CPGE*, 204–5)

One thinks of Owen's 'I am the enemy you killed, my friend', but also of the Eliot who could see in 'Little Gidding' a German warplane as the Dove of Pentecost. MacLean writes neither as an Anglican nor as an Englishman, but develops as a war poet his ability to utilize the potent peculiarities of his Calvinist Gaelic tradition and his intense awareness of division to write strikingly angled poems that both take cognizance of the fissures of history and gesture across them. The poem 'Heroes' moves from Culloden to celebrating the heroism of a nameless small Englishman, 'knees grinding each other', (*CPGE*, 209) killed in a tank attack in the desert. 'Death Valley', started by the sight of the 'slate-grey' face of a dead German boy-soldier, passes beyond reflection on the evils of the Nazis and those who were led often unwittingly by them; that poem concludes forcefully, quietly that

> Ge b'e a dheòin-san no a chàs,
> a neoichiontas no mhìorun

cha do nochd e toileachadh 'na bhàs
fo Dhruim Ruidhìseit.

Whatever his desire or mishap,
his innocence or malignity,
he showed no pleasure in his death
below the Ruweisat Ridge.
(*CPGE*, 212–13)

These are some of the unforgettable poems of the Second World War, and
stand at the head of the distinguished treatment of the desert war in the
work of such Scottish poets as George Campbell Hay, Hamish Henderson
and Edwin Morgan. MacLean's work, like that of these other Scottish
poets is all the stronger because it is produced out of a painful dialogue
between the native identity and the identity of several 'significant others',
the desert, the enemy, and English culture.

There is a pained, grim quality to some of MacLean's verse – seen in
the impulse which leads him to translate the first twenty-six lines of
Paradise Lost into Gaelic, appending after the last line ('And justify the
ways of God to men') the date '1945'. (*CPGE*, 219) But there is also that
generosity of spirit, seen particularly in the poems about the desert war. I
am emphasizing these poems for two reasons. First, whether because of a
naive cultural imperialism or for other reasons, they are normally left out
of anthologies and considerations of the poetry of the period. My second,
greater reason is that these works seem to reveal how the rest of
MacLean's poetry is born out of war, out of the clash of warring elements
of the self, and out of divided loyalties, as well as out of the heroic fight for
the survival of his people's language and culture. It is no accident that the
last poem in this book, the recent 'Scrapadal' is a meditation both on the
clearance of Raasay in 1846 and on the possibility of a newer, greater
clearance. The last line of the poem reads 'Bom idrigin is neodroin',
which is the Gaelic for 'hydrogen and neutron bomb'. (*CPGE*, 312–13)

Post-1945 poems, including the beautiful 'Hallaig' with its 'vehement
bullet … from the gun of Love' and 'A Church Militant' with its fighting
talk, continue to exhibit MacLean's acute sense of war and division,
linking him not only with Eliot but also with other great modern poets
whose work is relevant to his own: MacDiarmid with his Caledonian
Antisyzygy, and the Yeats of self and anti-self, intersecting gyres, and a
poetic imagination so preoccupied with the inner war of his frustrated love
for Maud Gonne, the choice between poetry and action and the civil war
of his own country. It is in such an international company that MacLean's
oeuvre demands to be judged, as well as against the background of his
native Scottish Gaelic tradition.

This contention brings us inescapably to the question of language. It may seem absurd or scandalous to some readers that I am writing as a person without Gaelic, who is unable to read the original poems and who has to rely on the translations which Sorley MacLean has provided. Much of MacLean's work is about the nature of this scandal – what has been done to his people and their language. The dialogues in which he is engaged are angry as well as creative. My point has to be that his *Collected Poems* offers to readers of Gaelic and to those who have no Gaelic a chance to read the work of a great poet. This chance should be seized. There can be few who will resist the wish to steal something from the honed grace of MacLean's lyrics and who will not feel about them as one may feel about Zbigniew Herbert's poems: that even in English their sense of struggle, irony and determination convinces the reader that 'if the City falls but a single man escapes ... he will be the City'.[10] MacLean, like Eliot, is such a figure: his language and much of his technique seem to us remote from the polylingual pyrotechnics of much of Modernism, but in a unique manner this great bard of division, this war poet, managed to articulate his culture so as to speak for embattled small cultures around the globe. His work also matters to those of us who come from strong languages outside the Gaelic zone and who are ready to appreciate how the passionate clarity of a major poet writing in a 'minor language' can be seen as belonging to and enriching the world of 'Hugh Selwyn Mauberley' and *The Waste Land*, as well as the worlds of present-day cultures as different as those of Portree, Glasgow, London and New York.

MacLean's achievement, like MacDiarmid's, and like that of most major poets who have identified with a particular nation or territory, has been made possible through a dialogue between his sense of his native culture and his sense of other cultures with their non-native writings against which he can define his own work, and with which he can braid his own work in order to strengthen the native tradition. Though Norman MacCaig is not a Gaelic speaker, there are ways in which his work has done for Scottish poetry in English something similar to what MacLean has done for Scottish poetry in Gaelic. In MacCaig's poetry, the Gaelic world often functions as a strange 'other' which is both beautiful, having its own laws, and only partly accessible. MacCaig's dialogic poetry of multiple selves also grew out of an engagement with the Metaphysicals, but when he writes in the early poem 'Drifter' about sailing through 'the Gaelic sea', one senses that the adjective Gaelic emphasizes the otherness of a foreign element.[11] That foreignness is still there in MacCaig's later poem 'Aunt Julia' where it is also seen as important, intimate and be-loved.[12] Aunt Julia comes from a culture with which the poet wishes to identify, in which he sees value, yet which is also foreign to him. Many

Scottish poets feel this about at least one of Scotland's language-cultures. Yet just as we are coming to realize that MacCaig's English-language poetry has grown out of a dialogue with the intimate foreign-ness of his ancestral Gaelic culture, so we may also see ways in which MacLean's Gaelic poetry has been strengthened because the poet's poetic identity has been constructed out of and nurtured by elements which are not purely Gaelic.[13] MacLean's is a poetry which has reached across language differences to take what it needs, at the same time as resisting any suggestion that these language differences should be abolished. MacLean's ambitions reaching out from his strong Gaelic base have allowed him to enter into a creative dialogue with the major writers of our century, just as MacDiarmid too was able to braid native and non-native materials, forms and techniques in his own work. It is fitting that MacDiarmid should have sought out MacLean to translate Gaelic poetry for him, and that he should have produced his own verse 'translations' from MacLean's prose glosses. Here is one of the most visible signs of a creative dialogue within modern Scottish writing. MacDiarmid may have sinned by failing to let MacLean look over the versions before they were published, but then as MacLean the dialogic poet remarks, 'I could have forgiven him anything'. It is MacLean's willingness to interact with material from outwith his own culture, to be both 'Somhairle MacGill-Eain' and 'Sorley MacLean', which has eventually resulted in the strengthening of that culture, and in MacLean's being seen as a vital part of a heritage present to writers not only in Gaelic, but also in other tongues as far away as Canada and Australia.

4

Les Murray
Shaping an Australian Voice

'Australia' is the title of a poem by A. D. Hope; and of a poem by Bernard O'Dowd; and of a poem by Gary Catelano. Judith Wright has a poem called 'Australia 1970' and James McAuley has one called 'Terra Australis', as does Douglas Stewart. I once heard an Australian poet remark on the obligation Australian poets seemed to feel to write poems called 'Australia', yet I suspect this plays down the subtlety of much Australian poetry. You won't find any poems called 'Australia' in either Les Murray's capacious, expanded 1991 *New Oxford Book of Australian Verse*, or in John Tranter and Philip Mead's very different 1991 *Penguin Book of Modern Australian Poetry*, though you will find poem after poem which, obliquely or otherwise, seeks to articulate an Australian identity. This may be the urban, streetwise postmodern identity of John Forbes or John Tranter, or, looking in different directions, it may be the more rural-oriented identity of Judith Wright or Les Murray.[1]

The fullest, most vulnerable Australian literary identities are not really 'literary' at all, but oral, sung. Aboriginal poetries in their original languages have a cultural centrality and sacredness which make them all the more remote from English-language verse, though Les Murray and other English-language writers have been fascinated with both the sacredness and the powerful identification with the land which such poetries possess and which can only be hinted at in translations like those included in the *New Oxford Book* or in R. M. W. Dixon and Martin Duwell's *The Honey-Ant Men's Love Song and Other Aboriginal Song Poems* (University of Queensland Press, 1990). Almost all of Kevin Gilbert's 1988 Penguin anthology *Inside Black Australia* sounds a cry of pain felt by Aboriginal writers in English, but fails to articulate the more remote strengths of Aboriginal culture in the threatened original languages. It is those strengths, however remotely sensed, which may convince the reader that English-language Australian poetry still lags behind Aboriginal culture in its attempts to articulate and construct a poetic identity which will make for full identification with the territory of Australia – a territory which now includes mirror-glass skyscrapers as well as the bush, a territory where the great majority of inhabitants comprise one of the world's most highly urbanized societies. Many of Australia's cultural emblems, however – from kangaroos to lager advertisements – rely on the non-urban world of the minority.

To some who have never visited my own country, Scotsmen may be represented in terms of kilts and bagpipes, while Scotswomen as such do not exist. Stereotypes and vague, distant impressions can be misleading, though a foreign perspective may also, at times, promise illumination. Bakhtin is far from the only writer to suggest that. I can pretend to no insider-knowledge of Australian poetry, though I recognize its variety and liveliness, and feel that there is much to be learned from it. Perspectives have become all the more complex and shifting with the launch of a growing number of competing anthologies in the last few years. In 1991 in addition to the two major anthologies mentioned above there also appeared John Leonard's *Contemporary Australian Poetry* (Houghton Mifflin) and Vincent Buckley's posthumously published *Faber Book of Modern Australian Verse*, a provocative but dated anthology which, because its cut-off point is 1980, excludes a substantial amount of very fine recent Australian poetry, among it some of Les Murray's best work. For British readers, the messy state of Australian (and British) poetic imports and exports complicates the position further. Because he found a major British publisher, Chris Wallace-Crabbe was, until comparatively recently, better known in England and even in Scotland than either Judith Wright or Les Murray, although Murray's selected poems, *The Vernacular Republic*, was published in Edinburgh by Canongate in 1982. Again, because of the vagaries of publishing, work by A. D. Hope, Gwen Harwood, Dorothy Hewett, and Alan Wearne is more readily available in Britain than the fine, very different poetries of Bruce Dawe, John Forbes, Peter Goldsworthy, Robert Gray, Kevin Hart, Jan Owen, John Tranter, Amy Witting and others, both younger and older. This is a curious and regrettable state of affairs which will be remedied only if British publishers follow the lead of OUP, Carcanet and Bloodaxe in allowing Australian verse to jump the Hadrian's Wall of current publishing practices. It is ironic that though some of the major Australian poetry publishers, including Angus and Robertson and Penguin, are owned by multinational publishers which import non-Australian books to Australia, those same publishers are often unwilling to attempt to export Australian books to other parts of the globe.

All this means that, writing on the other side of the world and on the wrong side of certain publishing practices, my sense of Australian voices is bound to be a distorted one. Still, having written elsewhere of Murray only in terms of his non-Australian contemporaries, I have felt obliged to hint at least at the way he belongs to a complicated Australian poetic geography and history, too much of which has been reduced for non-Australian readers to a kind of white-noise. Having dropped that hint, however, in this present chapter I wish to focus on Murray himself, making one possibly provocative juxtaposition of his work with that of another major Australian poet. I then concentrate on the subtle way he uses his sense of an inherited Scottish culture to construct a poetic identity which allows him both to identify with a particular territory and to articulate what has been widely recognized as a commanding Australian voice. Beyond those parameters I cannot venture with confidence or competence, though I am aware, for instance, of the complex debts Murray owes to the earlier Jindyworobak grouping of Australian poets. I suspect that this and other matters of Australian literary ancestry and allegiance will be covered by Paul Kane and others in their forthcoming books on Murray, so let these excuses stand for the more concentrated focus of the present chapter.[2]

First, then, the provocative juxtaposition. From what I can gather, the state of Australian literary criticism and of literary culture generally, is so fissured and fractious that this juxtaposition may have a heretical edge there which it cannot have outside Australia. What I am proposing is that, from this distance at least, it is worthwhile setting the achievement of Murray beside that of Judith Wright. Wright is a consciously female poet well known for her espousal of radical environmental politics and Murray is a consciously male poet execrated by some in Australia for his suspicion of radical feminism and for his orthodox Catholic views on such subjects as abortion. Neither poet might be happy at being set beside the other; nor might either poet's supporters relish the alignment. Nonetheless, in the long view which I am proposing, the juxtaposition makes at least limited sense and suggests connections in an Australian literary scene which is becoming too readily, crudely and bitterly polarized.

Both Wright and Murray possess acutely a sense of the New World as old. One could say that the New World is founded on irony: it isn't a world, and it isn't new. The doubleness of the New World comes from its European 'discovery'. It was split-new to us and older than us. Both Wright and Murray have tried to take account of this doubleness, invoking not irony but a vision of the sacred. They have tried to negotiate between the more recent white native culture and that of the older native other. Both are poets of pluralism and of cultural twinning.

Such a twinning may be an illusion, and may be possible only after the native culture has been smashed. We can feel generous towards the

Highlanders, or the Native Americans, or the Aborigines, only after our foreign and dominant culture has got the upper hand. Yet we can feel generous towards the other culture also because we have lived in its country long enough to appreciate something of the way in which that culture has adapted to and has grown out of the land it inhabits. In the work of Judith Wright, which is almost wholly non-urban, as in the poetry of Les Murray, there is a sense of sometimes uneasy admiration for the Aboriginal, an admiration that grows from the poet's sense that the poet's ancestors, though incomers, have also suffered and delighted in this land. There is in Wright's work (and later in Murray's) a desire to twin with the Aboriginal culture, to twin with the amazing (yet by now familiar) nature of Australia. This sense of twinning with a dangerous, loved environment lies under Wright's work, a good deal of which has little explicitly to do with the Aboriginal. Wright like Murray is a broadly religious poet whose individual volume titles often look to the sense of an otherworld (of the non-self, of mirrors, of another sex, or another form of life). Here is the concluding, second stanza of her poem, 'The Twins', from her early collection, *Woman to Man* (1949):

> How sweet is the double gesture, the mirror-answer;
> same hand woven in same, like arm in arm.
> Salt blood like tears freshens the crowd's dry veins,
> and moving in its web of time and harm
> the unloved heart asks, 'Where is my reply,
> my kin, my answer? I am driven and alone.'
> Their serene eyes seek nothing. They walk by.
> They move into the future and are gone.[3]

The ending of that superb poem prefigures Murray's 'They have vanished into the Future' at the end of his poem 'The Future'. (*SP*, 65) Vincent Buckley has pointed out how a poem like Wright's 'South of My Days' prefigures Murray's enterprise.[4] Wright's 'Legend' and 'The Forest' are other such poems, but I suspect there are further connections – both particular and general – which have yet to be made. For the moment, though, it is worth lingering over and relishing those lines of Wright's 'The Twins' which have just been quoted.

These lines have a good music, as phrase answers to and links up with phrase. The music is utterly simple; the last two lines gain their power from a clipped closure which leaves speculation in its wake. The language is clear, as in much Australian poetry, and an accumulation of contextual details rather than vocabulary gives the poem its interest. 'The Twins' images a cut-off, longed-for twinning; coming near the start of *A Human Pattern*, a retrospective life's work selection published in 1990 when

Wright was seventy-five, it heralds the work of a poet with a purposeful religious gaze. It is that gaze which is one of the strongest links between Wright and Murray.

One of the images which Wright likes is that of Spenser's odd couple, Una and the lion – an image of vulnerable virtue twinned with hard nature, an image of another kind of 'interplay', to use a term Wright repeats in her work. The twinning of white and Aboriginal is clear in 'Jacky Jacky', a poem about a white colonial and an Aborigine. The poet longs for a vision of difficult pairing,

> that the smouldering flame in your heart might meet his eyes
> and be quenched in their comforting blue; that you both might ride
> through a nightmare country, mutually forgiven,
> black logical as white, and side by side.

This poem comes from Wright's collection *Shadow*, which followed *The Other Half* (1966) – again the titles speak of doubleness. Sometimes for Wright the interplay is that of marriage, sometimes other pairings, most frequently that of people and the land, of which she has a sharp, lyrical sense, which one might indicate by quoting the opening two lines of 'The Cicadas': 'On yellow days in summer when the early heat / presses like hands hardening the sown earth'. The song of the land is tough here, as it is in 'The Blind Man' where: 'The smoke sang upward, the trees vanished like dreams / and the long hills lie naked as a whipped back'. Yet that lyrical toughness, that willingness to confront the ironies of this life-threatening beauty, gives Wright's visions a rare conviction. At her finest she is a visionary poet in whose best work people and places pass into each other with a blaze of native fluency. Surely Murray is the poet who has most stunningly inherited this fluency and this gift of twinning.

Wright's finest poetry will become universally loved; in Australia she is well known for her support of Aboriginal land rights and environmental causes. As she is aware, her gift has often flickered of late. 'By the waterfalls of Cedar Creek / where there aren't any cedars / I try to remember the formula for poetry'. Here the untwinning of place and word turns Wright into a preacher. As Chris Wallace-Crabbe puts it in one of his fine essays, 'Moral Bludgeoning is the Higher Boredom'.[5] At their best, Wright's poems are lit with vision, at their worst they are rather crude television. Vision takes a long time to be disseminated, but Wright's finest poems will ring the globe. When, however, Wright's twinnings become too consciously formulaic, the vision is lost and replaced by a sermon, as in 'Two Dreamtimes', addressed to the Aboriginal poet 'Kath Walker, now Oodgeroo Noonuccal': 'We the robbers, robbed in turn, / selling this land on hire-purchase; / what's stolen once is stolen again /

even before we know it'. Here Wright is speaking *about* what matters to her, rather than presenting it and allowing the reader both visionary access and the space to think things out.

No doubt Wright's later and more propagandist work would encourage Murray to distance himself from his senior contemporary. Yet it is probable that in the long view they will be seen to have a good deal in common. Dissimilarities in style, orientation and background are easy to spot, yet each is clearly an important and importantly Australian poet driven by a sense of the sacred and a wish for some sort of 'sacred twinning' – a wish which, in Murray's case, seems fuelled by his Scots-Australian heritage, which has given him a reverence for ancestors and for the land. It is clear that Wright is one of Australia's major 'identifying poets', and is a poet who is religious, determined, sometimes visionary. It is equally undeniable that Murray is an Australian Catholic poet with two great themes: his religion and his country, and neither of these themes is simple.

Murray was born in 1938, in Bunyah, New South Wales, where he now lives. Though a native Australian, he is very aware of his Scottish ancestry, and often writes about it. He contended in the 1970s that 'This is not England; we don't need to snub and suppress and deny our Celtic inheritance – though we mustn't be colonized by it, either.' (*PM*, 155) Such assertions and Murray's own investigations have surely helped fuel a growing interest in links between Australian and Scottish cultures which has produced in Australia Malcolm D. Prentis's *The Scottish in Australia* (Melbourne: AE Press, 1987) and in Scotland *That Land of Exiles: Scots in Australia* (Edinburgh: HMSO, 1988). Though it might be easy to exaggerate Murray's Scottish connections, they are clearly important to him. As he told Peter Porter in a 1990 interview, his family background 'was tribal because they were from the Scottish borders, the Murrays, and came out in 1848 and stayed around the Manning River and not very many of them moved anywhere else for a long time. There was an intensely complicated world of cousins and relationships and inter-marryings, and this was the common talk of the place when I was growing up. A certain amount of poetry was mixed in as well: mostly Robert Burns, mostly recited by men who were drunk. Lots of fiddle music and dancing and that sort of thing before the radio came. And I caught the tail end of that and the family part of it is as strong as ever.' (*Porter*, 77)

Since the 1960s, Murray has visited Scotland many times. In the winter of 1967–8 (as recorded in his essay, 'Spirit Farming' (*PM*, 214–19)) he lived with his family in a cottage on the edge of Culloden Moor, conscious that 'Culloden had a special resonance for me because of the tragic battle there in 1746, in which some of my forebears were involved'.

Murray regards time he has spent in Scotland as 'research ... recovery ...
retrieval ... confirmation'. (*Verse*, 27) Yet all these are also words which
describe his relationship towards aspects of earlier Australian culture, both
in his work as writer and anthologist. Coming from a 'tribal' culture and
feeling closely bonded to his own Scottish and Australian extended ances-
tral family, Murray is white, but he sees his background as connecting him
closely with the Aborigines whom he links with his own family back-
ground, viewing all as part of the oppressed rural poor. 'At least some
country people' he writes in 'The Completed Australian' 'have a depth of
love for their region, their holding or district, which approaches that of a
tribal Aboriginal for his spirit country'. (*PM*, 97) Murray describes as
'what may well have been the natal day of my vocation as a poet' the day
when, aged twelve, he saw an old black man 'who stood by the roadside in
Purfleet with his hat in his hands and his eyes lowered the day my
mother's funeral passed by on its way out to Krambach cemetery'. (*PF*, 7)
These Scottish and Aboriginal concerns complicate and enrich Murray's
concern with and about nationalism. He has written of being 'stunned'
when he 'first read R. M. Berndt's translation of the great Wonguri-
Mandjikai Song Cycle of the Moon Bone', which Murray considers 'may
well be the greatest poem ever composed in Australia'. (*PF*, 22) Foiled in
an attempt to make an anthology of Aboriginal verse in the 1970s,
Murray has written poems in imitation of Aboriginal work, the most
notable of which is 'The Buladelah-Taree Holiday Song Cycle'. His *New
Oxford Book of Australian Verse* (first published in 1986) contains a
substantial amount of Aboriginal work, along with a range of poetry that
extends from 'The Bastard from the Bush' with its .

> 'Are you game to break a window?' said the Captain of the Push.
> 'I'd knock a fucking house down!' said the Bastard from the Bush.
> (*NOB*, 83)

to religious metaphysic. At the same time, however, Murray is alert to the
sensitive issues involved in making connections between his own work and
background and that of the Aborigines, yet he has wished to assert
strongly connections between the two: '... in Australia you had an old
culture with fantastically ramified family connections and structures. I
come from a white version of that'. (*Oles*, 28) Though he has acknowledged
that recent Aboriginal priorities have differed from his own, (*PT*, 9) he
maintains that he has aligned himself in many cultural struggles 'now along-
side, now in distant parallel with mainly black and Celtic allies'. (*PT*, 7)

In examining the variety of Australian poetry, Murray has also identi-
fied what he calls 'The Bonnie Disproportion', that is the unexpected
preponderance of Australian poets with Scottish connections. Murray has

written brilliantly on Scottish culture. He sees it connected with Austral-
ian culture by various lines, one of which is a common celebration of
nationality and a complementary antagonism to English cultural imperial-
ism. Another bond is clear in a passage which Murray quotes from
Stevenson's *Weir of Hermiston* about a Scots woman who '... at least
knows the legend of her own family, and may count kinship with some
illustrious dead. For that is the mark of the Scot of all classes: that he
stands in an attitude to the past unthinkable to Englishmen, and remem-
bers and cherishes the memory of his forbears, good or bad; and there
turns alive in him a sense of identity with the dead even to the twentieth
generation .... The power of ancestry on the character is not limited to the
inheritance of cells.' (*PF*, 68)

Here the strong bond is between the Scots and the Aborigines. Murray
often writes of Scots, particularly Gaels, in terms of Aborigines, and *vice
versa*. When he lived in Scotland and in Wales, Murray responded with
particular keenness to the poetry written in Welsh and in Gaelic, those
languages which we might describe as Aboriginal. In the mid-Seventies,
while insisting that 'from the beginning white Australians have been an
Anglo-Celtic rather than an Anglo-Saxon people', Murray wrote excitedly
about Gaelic tradition, complaining that 'to date, no Australian university
has a chair of Celtic studies, any more than it has, say, a chair of Aboriginal
studies'. (*PM*, 78–9). He responded enthusiastically to Derick Thomson's
Introduction to Gaelic Poetry, emphasizing the importance of Gaelic as a
sophisticated 'tribal' and popular poetic tradition which was at one time,
'From the time of collapse of the old tribal order right down to the
terrible dispersions of the Gael all over the world, a period of nearly two
centuries... perhaps the highest 'folk' civilization in Europe'. (*PM*, 81)
Murray's linking of Celtic and Aboriginal traditions would appear to lie
behind his advocacy, in 1975 (the year after his review of Thomson's
book), of a complex but genuinely 'public and "bardic" function for
poets' (*PM*, 183) when he took part in a debate at Macquarie University.

Such a gesture may be related also to Murray's childhood exposure to
Frost's early model, Robert Burns. Murray's Scotland is both Highland
and Lowland. He may be connected not only to the Gaelic bardic tradi-
tion and to the Aboriginal world, but also to that of the 'bardic', Burns,
another farmer poet whose sophisticated barbarian stance towards
academia and metropolitan culture was very close to that of the Australian
poet who calls himself a 'peasant mandarin'. Though the Burns of
Murray's childhood may have been a drunken, sentimentally distorted
figure, Murray, like Burns, appears interested in the collection and pro-
duction of verse which articulates a communal and national identity which
outsmarts the metropolitan in its vernacular drive for democratic values.

Murray's explorations of Scottish and of Aboriginal culture appear to have been carried out in the spirit recommended by the Bakhtin of the *Novy Mir* reply. Certainly a twining of the Scottish, Gaelic, and Aboriginal heritages is at the heart of Murray's pluralist vision of a multicultural or creole Australia which in his poem 'For a Jacobite Lady' he has called 'the Plain of Sports of the vision-poems' – that is, the Gaelic paradise. (*PO*, 1) But such a place is also the sacred site of Aboriginal vision. So Murray writes in 'Louvres' of

> the four-wheel drive
>
> vehicle in which to make an expedition
> to the bush, or as we now say the Land,
> the three quarters of our continent
> set aside for mystic poetry.
>
> (*SP*, 134)

That poetry is primarily Aboriginal, but Murray's hymning of his land shows, without denying the Aboriginal presence, that other Australians can partake in such a mystical sense of the Land. 'We have come to the sense, which the Aborigines had before us, that after all human frenzies and efforts there remains the great land'. (*PF*, 115) In adopting such a stance and in stressing the nourishing strength of Aboriginal models, Murray, who sees Australia like America as part of the New World, is refusing to subscribe to imperialist and racist aspects of the New World myth. (*PM*, 156) The potent version of this myth which sees the 'new' land as a virgin page for incoming writers is seen in one of the most famous poems by an early influence on Murray – Robert Frost – when (as pointed out in the 'Robert Frosts' chapter of the present book) in 'The Gift Outright' he speaks of giving oneself

> To the land vaguely realizing westward
> But still unstoried, artless, unenhanced.

The same urge is present in A. D. Hope's celebrated poem, 'Australia', when Hope speaks of Australia as being 'Without songs'.[6] Murray too is deeply concerned with his land, but part of that concern is a desire to join in weaving an Australian vernacular tradition, a people's poetry, rather than to adopt a position of destructive imperialism. Murray knows that Australia, like Scotland, is already rich in song, and it is significant that he should speak of his excitement on reading the following sentence in T. G. H. Strehlow's *Songs of Central Australia*: 'It is my belief that when the strong web of future Australian verse comes to be woven, some of its strands will be found to be poetic threads spun on the Stone Age hair-spindles of Central Australia.' (*PF*, 30)

If Murray's nationalism (articulated more aggressively in his earlier than in his most recent writings) is closely bound up with his deep and sophisticated sense of the Australian land, then so is his particular sense of religion. 'God' he writes, 'in Australia, is a vast blue and pale-gold and red-brown landscape, and his votaries wear ragged shorts and share his sense of humour'. (*PF*, 116) Murray puts this with deft, brilliant wit in the poem 'The Dream of Wearing Shorts Forever'. That poem is about going to a spiritual and physical 'home'. Its confident Australian-ness and the effortless eclecticism of Murray's language mirror his sense of his religion as being at once universal and precisely localizable in an Australia where shorts bring the speaker close to the world of classic Aboriginal nakedness, though not into it.

> Satisfied ambition, defeat, true unconcern,
> the wish and the knack for self-forgetfulness
> all fall within the scunge ambit
> wearing shorts or similar;
> it is a kind of weightlessness

> Unlike public nakedness, which in Westerners
> is deeply circumstantial, relaxed as exam time,
> artless and equal as the corsetry of a hussar regiment,
> shorts and their plain like
> are an angelic nudity,
> spirituality with pockets!

>   (*SP*, 129–30)

Murray's wit, his humour and irony, it becomes clear, are not alternatives to seriousness or powerfully emotional writing. Though it may not be one of his most sophisticated poems, 'An Absolutely Ordinary Rainbow', one of his best known pieces, shows just this; it also demonstrates his ability to localize the universal in particularly Australian places and terms, to do the equivalent of MacDiarmid's making Ecclefechan part of the eternal mood. (Murray has written of *A Drunk Man* as a 'great poem' – (*PM*, 163)). In 'An Absolutely Ordinary Rainbow' Murray describes a man who has burst out weeping in a Sydney street, and who strangely sets the onlookers 'longing for tears as children for a rainbow'.

> Ridiculous, says a man near me, and stops
> his mouth with his hands, as if it uttered vomit –
> and I see a woman, shining, stretch her hand
> and shake as she receives the gift of weeping;
> as many as follow her also receive it

and many weep for sheer acceptance, and more
refuse to weep for fear of all acceptance,
but the weeping man, like the earth, requires nothing,
the man who weeps ignores us, and cries out
of his writhen face and ordinary body

not words, but grief, not messages, but sorrow
hard as the earth, sheer, present as the sea –
and when he stops, he simply walks between us
mopping his face with the dignity of one
man who has wept, and now has finished weeping.

Evading believers, he hurries off down Pitt Street.

(*SP*, 13)

The sense of community in this poem, as much as the sense of suffering, is essential to Murray's work, to his religion, and to his view of Australian poetry of which he has written 'the memory and aspiration of community, it seems to me, have kept the best Australian poetry humane in a time when it has often seemed more natural to accept the apparent drift of things and become wholly elitist'. (*PM*, 196) Murray's nightmare vision is of a society divided by snobberies of class, sex, race, religion. His utopia (though it is not free from suffering) is an eclectic one. 'We are insensitive', he complains to his fellow Australians, 'to the mosaic of cultural heritages which have formed us'. (*PM*, 96) Murray's own religious sensibility, at the same time as being Roman Catholic is also catholic. Brought up in the Scots Presbyterian tradition, he has at once reacted against Calvinism with a convert's fervour and brought from it a desire for vernacular preaching which is manifest far beyond the title of a poem such as 'The Broad Bean Sermon'. (*SP*, 42) Some people may feel that one of Murray's weaknesses is a tendency towards epigrammatic preachiness. But his respect for and even qualified love of Aboriginal tradition also feeds into his religious outlook. He has written that, though the un-European nature of the Australian seasons has subtly undermined 'the ancient sense of consonance ... between nature and the supernatural', nonetheless such consonances do exist in Australia, both as recast by incomers and as known by Aborigines. Murray writes that 'Our culture has *places* for abandon, not seasons', and he sees this in Aboriginal terms, though we might note that his phrasing has a hint of 'Ecclesiastes' about it. 'And for every time there is a sacred place, somewhere along the paths of the Dreamings'. (*AY*, 5, 6, 12). Murray has catalogued his own list of blessed places. He has made major poetry out of this concept in one of his most impressive achievements, the verse novel, *The Boys Who Stole the Funeral*, in which several of his core concerns come together.

The Boys, published in Sydney by Angus and Robertson in 1980, is an Australian religious epic, with epic machinery. That machinery is provocatively unsettling, since it comes complete with an 'epic fight with women', a funeral scene featuring the removal of an old warrior's body in a Morris Nomad, and even small epic details like the modern augury when

> Reeby follows the flight of his question with sharp eyes
> but it falls through the ghost of a wink into wide fenced paddocks
>
> (*Boys*, 27)

In the epic tradition the opening lines hint at the plot to come, though it is not quite of arms and the man.

> It is the story of the boy
> with his gift of laughing at deadly things
> who stole a Digger's funeral
> and took it on the country roads.
>
> (*Boys*, 1)

Clarrie Dunn, a World War One veteran, has died in Sydney. His pseudo-sophisticated urban relatives are unwilling to spend the money necessary to transport him back to the rural place where he wished to be buried. But a distant relative, Kevin Forbutt (a young unemployed man), and his student dropout friend, Cameron Reeby, steal the corpse and transport it into the country for burial according to the old man's wishes. After the funeral the two young men are arrested. Hot-blooded Reeby attacks the policeman with a spanner and is shot dead. Kevin meanwhile escapes to the Bush where in a dream sequence he undergoes at the hands of Celtic-Aboriginals an initiation into religion and Australian-ness, sharing in the 'common dish', a meal that as a form of communion is reminiscent of the crying in 'An Absolutely Ordinary Rainbow' except that now both dead and living join together in their communal act.

> *Can I speak now?* When you've chosen. *I have chosen.*
> *Who made the dish?* It is human manufacture, boy.
> *Who carved the sides?* Nameless people. And name people.
> *Did my parents eat?* That'd be no guidance, Clancy.
>
> He takes the spoon that has always been in his pocket,
> digs in, and tastes. And tastes again, and savours.
> *It's – ordinary. It's – subtle. It is – serious.*
>
> The taste suggests the holiest thing in the universe
> is a poor family at their dinner. It is that dinner.
> Afternoon. The house raised on blocks, exposed to telegrams –

You've tasted the food that sobers intoxications.
Yes, your father did taste, and fled, and traded on it.
Your mother broke her spoon to be saved from tasting,
and Noeline Kampff denied the dish, and yearned for it.

(Boys, 131)

This eating from the common dish is the climax of the poem, but it is preceded by a dazzling spirit view of the Australian continent. Murray has said that 'all of my work is fundamentally religious, subsumed by a Christian consciousness, though. I would say that's where the geniality comes from, and a lot of the humour. And it's my sheet-anchor against nationalism'. (*Verse*, 24). He *is* a fundamentally religious poet, though his religion, like T. S. Eliot's, is a complex one. At the same time, while he has contended that nationalism is 'as a religion-substitute ... a monster that demands human sacrifice', (*Verse*, 24) Murray has been an outspoken republican nationalist and one to whom doodling Australian republican flags 'on odd sheets of paper was an aid to meditation while writing poems'. (*PM*, 239) Murray's ideal Australian flag includes stars and boomerangs. Another version includes a view of the earth's surface from space. These themes find poetry (rather than heraldry) in the vision of Australia that precedes the religious communion in *The Boys Who Stole the Funeral*.

They go up above the great land, holding on to their cords,

they go up higher   above the Divide's embraced erosions
till they can see the boomerang-and-shield   the continent
the drawn bow from ocean to ocean   the fistmele of delicate
austere ochre and flowering   that spiritualized the fencers
potch and opaline cities   molecular townships are under them
hard to tell from diggings   ruled lines attendance upon snake-lines

During all the new time, we've denied her our culminations:
natural that the Rabbit and Blue Heeler totems should rule her;
her human life isn't in government, it is in holdings
of literal and spiritual farming (government properly stands cow to them)
or else it's in platoons, reminiscent, cheerful, deadly dangerous;
denied singular work, we're drawn to them. That's our human Matter. –

The Njimbin stops speaking and they contemplate the great land.

(Boys, 127)

Murray is both a literal and a spiritual farmer. He is from a farming community, and he regards his own poetry as a medium of religious exploration. He writes particularly well about fertility, whether farmed or

untamed. The great twisting sentence that runs for thirty-five lines to
open 'Bent Water in the Tasmanian Highlands' is not only a tour de force;
it is also a delight of passionate accuracy. It celebrates, to steal a term from
Douglas Dunn, 'land-love'. In its eclecticism of vocabulary, especially its
use of geological terms it reminds the reader that Les Murray is tempera-
mentally as well as genetically related to Sir James Murray of the *Oxford
English Dictionary* (the relation of whom he is proudest) but also to
Christopher Murray Grieve (*Verse*, 23, 27). The poem is a flood of life and
precisely graphed energy.

> Flashy wrists out of buttoned grass cuffs, feral whisky burning gravels,
> jazzy knuckles ajitter on soakages, peaty cupfulls, soft pots overflowing,
> setting out along the great curve, migrating mouse-quivering water,
> mountain-driven winter water, in the high tweed, stripping off its
>   mountains
> to run faster in its skin, it swallows the above, it feeds where it is fed on,
> it forms at many points and creases outwards, pleated water
> shaking out its bedding soil, increasing its scale, beginning the
>   headlong
> – Bent Water, you could call this level
> between droplet and planetary, not as steered by twisting beds laterally
> but as upped and swayed on its swelling and outstanding own
>   curvatures,
> its floating top that sweeps impacts sidelong, its event-horizon,
> a harelip round a pebble, mouthless cheeks globed over a boulder, a
> finger's far-stretched holograph, skinned flow athwart a snag
>
>   (*SP*, 83)

Murray celebrates fertility. He celebrates the bare beauty of the bush –
'it'll kill you, but it's – decent'. (*Boys*, 136) His celebration of his land and
its detailed virtues is bound up with his religion; as is his attack on articifial
infertility in the form of abortion. This subject, one which has helped
make Murray so controversial, is also important in *The Boys Who Stole the
Funeral*, where the Aboriginal killing of 'surplus children' is paralleled by
the sophisticated urban feminists' desire for abortion.

> Then consumers of landscapes said Let us kill our children
> and be young forever; let us kill them and be famous;
> let us kill them by delegation; let's deny death and escape it
> We desire spacious life. Space costs the lives of children.
>
>   (*Boys*, 128)

Sometimes Murray becomes strident in this cause, and, occasionally it
seems to me, what we are intended to react against can seem attractive.

Not the rather forced lines about abortion, but the lines about buying beer make me warm a little to the villainess Noeline Kampff.

> *Swoop reckons you can't trust an activist who hasn't*
> *had her abortion? And don't you*
> *dare try to buy out of turn, you patronizing*
> *chauvinist shit? I'll get the fucking beer!*
>
> (*Boys*, 101)

Murray's concern with the sort of feminism which he sees as preaching abortion as a virtue is a serious one. As he puts it in an interview, 'Oh yes! Some people hated the book. It raised the uncomfortable question of how do you stay spacious. The old Aboriginal answer was infanticide. It has a terrible line in it which says: 'Space costs the lives of children'. The poem has some hard things to say against abortion, but it does make that point. Abortion has rather tragically been taken by some as a touchstone of liberation, of the modern idea of individuality, which I think a lot of the time is based on a notion that if you reproduce yourself you concede that there is a future – that you're not the final perfected people on earth. Reproduction relativizes you in a series of generations, which I think comes as very bad news to an extreme form of modern individualism. Hence the war against babies.'[7]

The controversial nature of such remarks is part of Murray's poem. But we should not allow the controversy of that aspect to blind us to the fact that this is *one* aspect of the poem, and the whole matter of abortion in the poem is not only part of what Murray calls in *The Boys* 'the blood-history of the continent' but also part of the theme of blood sacrifice which runs through the history of civilization as Murray sees it. (*Boys*, 128)

Murray is haunted by Chesterton's saying, 'Those who lose belief in God will not only believe in anything; they will bring blood offerings to it', (*PF*, 112) and the theme of blood offerings is particularly prominent in *The Boys Who Stole the Funeral* where from the First World War to the killing of Cameron Reeby, blood seems to be demanded in an Australian version of Geoffrey Hill's 'There is no bloodless myth will hold'.[8] The sacrifice of the unborn is part of this blood sacrifice. It is less messy but for Murray it is still murder. In a similar position is the relegation of the old in a culture which stresses style, fashion and metropolitan 'progress'. Always Murray opposes his own 'Boeotian' stance to the 'Athenian' metropolitan.[9] Cultural relegation is another form of maiming.

> Obsolete and therefore deaf
> both old men from the Battalion
> hang their heads and smile at boards,
> the sunlight under the veranda.

Obsolete and therefore blind
women nervously hand their toddlers
back and forth, small pastel bells
and little one-toothed woollen shouters.

Obsolete and thus irrelevant
farmers nod and shake their heads,
sharing with dated wives and cousins
subtleties of passé restraint.

Oblongs of the shed roof opposite
capture the sun's free-floating anger.

(*Boys*, 63)

Murray is angrily suspicious of what is 'interesting' as opposed to obses-
sively important, because he sees this fashion-following as making obso-
lete fundamentally decent people. 'Before you're dead you'll be out of
date. So will everything you love'. (*Verse*, 31) Again, the comparison
which springs to mind is with T. S. Eliot who emphasized in 'Burnt
Norton' the dangers especially present in the modern rat-race of city life
of being only 'Distracted from distraction by distraction'. Eliot's 'distrac-
tion' is close to Murray's fashionable 'interest'. Murray delights in various
aspects of the modern world which he has seized on – from earth-moving
equipment to vector geometry; but he is also sceptical of the slickly
displayed values of liberal consumerism. This is clear, for instance, when
the unemployed rebel Kevin Forbutt confronts his father (who has refused
to pay for the country funeral of the veteran Clarrie), and challenges the
casually assumed superiority of that father's life-style.

Father, Clarrie Dunn
was partly ruined by a war, but he had dignity.
You fought in an antiwar and you've got – white Levis?

(*Boys*, 95)

Though it was published in Britain by Carcanet in 1989, *The Boys Who
Stole the Funeral* is not included in Murray's British or American *Collected
Poems* and remains the least known of his major works. This is unfortunate
not least because many of the arguments and techniques deployed in the
poem have been developed in his more recent writing. Though selective
quotation can recast Murray in any one of several over-simplified moulds,
it would be wrong to present him as a simple neo-conservative. In many
aspects his stance has been and remains profoundly radical. He inveighs
against both the Australian 'cultural cringe' and against artistic snobbery
and elitism. The results of these emphases are his attack on the political
situation which leaves his country as an 'absentee monarchy' rather than a

republic. (*PM*, 264) Again, Murray's own cultural background is important in the precise nature of his alignments. 'If, in the wake of the Vietnam war, the intelligentsia here would adopt the sort of nationalist orientation taken up by their coevals in, for example, Scotland and Wales, the colonial hangovers which subtly cripple much of our life might be swept away'. (*PM*, 144) During time spent in Edinburgh, Murray was friendly with some of the staff of the nationalist cultural magazine *Cencrastus*, and he has had similar links with Welsh political and cultural nationalists. Murray's essay on 'The Australian Republic' is one of the finest pieces written on the theme of cultural imperialism, and it is significant that its matter would apply equally well to his ancestral Scotland as to his native Australia.

> Formal education and high culture in Australia, as in any other colonial territory, are systems of foreign ideas imposed from above whose usual effect is to estrange people from their own culture and injure their rapport with their own people. They are ways in which the ruling elites recruit people to their purposes. Some few think their way through the imposed ideas and overcome their alienating effect, but most are caught for good in their estrangement, and convert it into privilege or virtue. It has never been possible to get a distinctively Australian education through institutional channels. You must either give yourself one, or be taught by your elders in a more or less informal way outside the institutional system. This is the way all the vernacular cultures of Australia – Aboriginal, immigrant and mainstream – *are* in fact transmitted, though the mainstream one does also get disseminated to a limited extent through books and other media. The most comfortable way to educate oneself is to do it at a university; the library there tends to be better stocked than that famous and perhaps mythical one in the cells of Borroloola lock-up, which is said to have educated a generation of Queensland and Territory wanderers. I used and resisted my university in this way, though I don't claim much credit for it: it was an instinctive and precarious balancing act which I didn't really understand at the time and which must have looked merely perverse to many of my contemporaries. All I knew was that if ever I snubbed or denied my fellow country people, those who hadn't had the education I was getting, I would be lost. (*PM*, 150)

These fellow country people are those to whom Murray (like Seamus Heaney in Ireland) most wants to give voice.

> Where cattletracks climb
> Rice-terrace-wise to the hills
> I want to speak the names of all the humble.
>   (*SP*, 22)

More comfortably than Tony Harrison, Murray manages both to remain 'vernacular' and to produce both deep and complex utterance. He is neither a peasant nor a mandarin, but both, as that title of his first prose collection, *The Peasant Mandarin* (1978), proclaims. Murray is also an internationalist, a cultural eclectic, as well as a nationalist, a 'provincial', a cultural patriot. It is here he owes the greatest debt to modernism. He attacks Pound and Eliot for making 'more than anyone else ... a certain slangy-mandarin tone dominant in poetry'. (*PM*, 75) Yet the modernist combination of the demotic and the highbrow is just the combination to be found often in the writings of Murray the peasant mandarin – as in that off-Joycean title, 'Portrait of the Autist as a New World Driver'. (*SP*, 36) Significantly, when pressed on whether he was not 'attracted to any sort of synthetic impulse in modernism'. Murray responded, 'Yes. Very much. That's *the* great thing about modernism. That, and also its admission of a wide range of vernacular speech'. (*Verse*, 22) Murray's syntheses of cultural mosaic can be viewed as a development of modernism. It is hard to imagine a poem like '1980 in a Street of Federation Houses' or 'Aqualung Shinto' if modernism had not happened. (*SP*, 28, 146)

On the other hand, in his reaction against the thin air of the mandarin, Gaelic verse is a particularly attractive model and touchstone for Murray. He prizes it as an ideal towards which his own poetry aspires. So Murray connects with Australian life a passage describing the 'intensive cultivation' of unchangingly spiritual Gaelic poetry, and celebrates the way in which it 'can engage modern themes and complexities while retaining much of its characteristic flavour' since it comes from that Gaelic culture which 'was perhaps the highest "folk" civilization in Europe'. (*PM*, 126, 82, 81) It is Murray's attachment to a folk civilization beyond Europe which has led him to write of the Gaels in Australia how

> They had lost the Gaelic in them. It had become
> like a tendon a man has no knowledge of in his body
> but which puzzles his bending, at whiles, with a flexing impulse.
>
> (*VR*, 134)

But Murray has also stated in 'four Gaelic Poems' (*CP*, 151) that though he writes 'in the conqueror's language' his English is not European, and that it contains a Gaelic seed. Here again the Gaelic and the Aboriginal dovetail, as they do in the title of the collection *The People's Otherworld* which celebrates an Australia not only of the Aboriginal Dreamtime but also of the (partly Gaelic) poor who got away. A poem in Murray's earlier selected poems, significantly titled *The Vernacular Republic*, celebrates something brought over from Gaelic.

This, then, for the good you put on us,
round-tower of Gaelic, grand wrongheaded one,
now you have gone to the dark crofts:
the oldest tree in Europe's shed
a seed to us – and the Otherworld
becomes ancestral, a code of history,
a style of fingering, an echo of vowels,
honey that comes to us from the lost world.

(VR, 175)

Here again it is obvious that it is this Gaelic, as well as the Aboriginal heritage, which makes Murray long for a bardic poetry, a poetry of community that will unite his own community. Murray, who has a deep sense of how 'resurgent minority nations are themselves poems, slowly, cumulatively composed and refined and stubbornly memorized down the generations to keep them alive' can sense at times his own Australia as one of his 'Big Loose Poems that Rule Us'. (PM, 246; PF, 49)

In 'Sydney and the Bush' Murray wrote that 'Where Sydney and the Bush meet now / there is no common ground'. (VR, 143) Yet his poetry is directed towards providing just such a common ground. I am emphasizing here Murray's sense of the land because it seems to me remarkably deep and worth exploring. The point should also be made (and could be developed) that he can write of urban life with elegance and accuracy as in 'The Sydney High-Rise Variations' (SP, 75) or 'Mirror-glass Skyscrapers'. (DFF, 48) In linking the modern world to the land, the new world of high technology to the ancient world of the earth, a crucial connecting link in Murray's work as in Australian culture is the motor vehicle. The car is most important in Murray's verse. His epic The Boys Who Stole the Funeral moves mainly on wheels, whether of the Morris Nomad or the truck or the Holden. As Murray writes in 'Portrait of the Autist',

Indeed, if you asked
where the New World is, I'd have to answer
he is in his car

(SP, 37)

The car is what takes the dweller in the urban anthill out into the Bush, back to the land, and the car (the shell) is also part of the familiar Murray mythology.

Of course we love our shells: they make the anthill
bearable. Of course the price is blood.

(SP, 37)

In one of Murray's best known early poems the careering vehicle is a symbol of the evil inherent in civilization; it is 'The Burning Truck'. (*SP*, 11) Elsewhere, though, cars are more benign. Richard Tipping's fine film of Murray perceptively includes shots of the poet driving home through the landscape with a voice-over of his reading 'Driving Through Sawmill Towns':

> In the high cool country
> having come from the clouds,
> down a tilting road
> into a distant valley,
> you drive without haste. Your windscreen parts the forest,
> swaying and glancing, and jammed midday brilliance
> crouches in clearings ...
>
> (*SP*, 9)[10]

Blake Morrison has rightly praised Murray as a poet of cattle. Yet few poets have written so well of cars whether as seen by other drivers or (in one instance) by an eagle which, far above them, notes how 'dying, they open little wings, releasing humans'. (*Boys*, 67)

To his wife Murray dedicates the series of 'Machine Portraits with Pendant Spaceman', which largely celebrates vehicles, from bulldozers to a river ferry, which can bring contact with the simple business of the earth. (*SP*, 97) 'I don't think Nature speaks English', Murray has written, but he knows that out there are 'bush-encyclopedists'. (*SP*, 25, 37) Murray is a sophisticated and international bush-encyclopedist who managed to react enough against *Literature* (which stereotyped the bush as 'alien') and realized that 'the bush wasn't alien to me at all'. (*PF*, 153) He learned to read in Bunyah from a copy of Cassells 1924 *Children's Encyclopedia*. (*PM*, 90) Significantly, his 'Absolute favourite' childhood book was *Huckleberry Finn* (*Oles*, 36) and Murray has always been sceptical about being too blandly '"sivilized", as Huckleberry Finn would have spelled the word'. (*BT*, 93) Equally significantly, Murray's enthusiasm for poetry was sparked by encountering the work of Hopkins; (*Oles*, 32) in their expanded English language and their search for 'inscape' or 'presence' Murray and Hopkins are alike. His education he describes as 'picking up lots of *disjecta membra* of learning around the university', and he jokes that 'a poet should know everything.' (*Verse*, 28) He is aware of a drive in his own writing to stress 'the simultaneous interconnectedness of all things'. (*PF*, 1; cp., e.g., *PM*, 133) There is a modernist aspect to this that looks to Pound, Joyce and MacDiarmid. There is also a distinctly Australian Bush aspect, though. Writing in praise of 'Eric Rolls's regional-ecological history *A Million Wild Acres*, in 1982, Murray praised the way

the book's logic was 'really accretive, made up of strings of vivid, minute
fact which often curl around in intricate knottings of digression':

> ...everything is in motion yet held in a sort of dynamic tableau,
> measuring some thousands of square miles by about 160 years. In
> contradistinction to most European art since the Middle Ages, there
> is little sense of foreground and background, that perspective of
> heroic agents acting out their drama before a series of sketched-in
> theatre flats, the Renaissance schema by which the aristocratic prin-
> ciple was able to triumph over an older Christian 'field' (the sense of
> Everyman, or Piers Plowman's Field Full of Folk) in which promi-
> nence was reserved for supernatural figures. In Rolls's presentation,
> things human and non-human are all happening interrelatedly, and
> the humans barely stand out. Through a fusion of vernacular ele-
> ments with fine-grained natural observation, and a constant move-
> ment of back-reference, he breaks through sequential time not to
> timelessness but to a sort of enlarged spiritual present in which no
> life is suppressed. (*PF*, 161)

This linking of the Bush with Catholic artworks and vernacular egalitari-
anism looks directly towards *The Boys Who Stole the Funeral* and other
Murray poems, particularly 'Equanimity' which seems to be one of the
poet's personal favourites, and which comes from his 1983 collection, *The
People's Otherworld*. In this poem come together Murray's sense of his
nation and his religion as themselves poems of grace and delicate balance,
as he goes back to that forest near which as a child he had carefully
balanced towers of drinking glasses.[11] Now he balances words and ob-
serves both Australian and divine equipoise.

> From the otherworld of action and media, this
> interleaved continuing plane is hard to focus:
> we are looking into the light –
> it makes some smile, some grimace.
> More natural to look at the birds about the street, their life
> that is greedy, pinched, courageous and prudential
> as any on these bricked tree-mingled miles of settlement,
> to watch the unceasing on-off
> grace that attends their nearly every movement,
> the crimson parrot has it, alighting, tips, and recovers it,
> the same grace moveless in the shapes of trees
> and complex in our selves and fellow walkers: we see it's indivisible
> and scarcely willed. That it lights us from the incommensurable
> that we sometimes glimpse, from being trapped in the point
> (bird minds and ours are so pointedly visual):

> a field all foreground, and equally all background,
> like a painting of equality. Of definite detailed extent
> like God's attention. Where nothing is diminished by perspective.
>
> (*SP*, 86)

This poem's conclusion in turn looks forward to the conclusion of 'The Assimilation of Background' where

> we saw
> that out on that bare, crusted country
> background and foreground had merged;
> nothing that existed there was background.
>
> (*DFF*, 62)

Murray's poetry of the late 1980s and early 1990s has taken the form of a deep homecoming, a profound re-emergence into and through the world of his own upbringing. This re-emergence has not involved the suppression of what he learned from his visits to the Celtic world or to Sydney University or to Canberra, but has resulted in the full combination of all this knowledge of other cultures into that of his own native culture. In this sense, *The Daylight Moon* (1988) is an Ithacan volume. Joyce said that his favourite section of *Ulysses* was the one called 'Ithaca'. Ithaca is home, but home seen by the returning traveller, who perceives the ancestral ground in a new, exciting, sometimes provocative way. After twenty-nine years spent largely in other parts of Australia, Murray (aged fifty) returned to his native Bunyah, that small back-of-beyond farming community – the sort of place some Americans might call 'flyoverland'. But Bunyah is as important to Murray as Dublin was to Joyce, and his love of it is much less equivocal than was Joyce's of his Ithaca in Ireland. Murray knows the cosmopolitan snobberies that exist around the idea of going home. 'Forty Acre Ethno' is a poem which confronts such snobberies head on. Though it is not the strongest poem in the book, it makes explicit a theme that runs throughout *The Daylight Moon*.

> Sight and life restored by an eye operation
> my father sits nightly before the glass screen
> of a wood-burning slow combustion stove. We see
> the same show, with words, on television.
> Dad speaks of memories, and calls his fire homely;
> when did you last hear that word without scorn
> for something unglossy, or some poor woman?
> Here, where thin is *poor*, and fat is *condition*,
> 'homely' is praise and warmth, spoken gratefully.
> Its opposite lurks outside in dark blowing rain.
>
> (*DM*, 61)

One of Murray's favourite words is surely 'verandah' – this term recurs throughout *The Daylight Moon*, a sign that it is on the verandah that home is truly located. A lot of the longer pieces in that book incorporate narrative fragments, pieces of tales told on the verandah at night, oral histories of Australian places and people. The concluding poem, the most ambitious, 'Aspects of Language and War on the Gloucester Road', celebrates not just Bunyah and environs but the achievement of Australian history. It celebrates Australian words and deeds, but also that a sense of history has been achieved, that the bush country, for instance, is now seen not as empty, but as peopled with memories, dreams, and changing names, Aboriginal and Gaelic, a true spirit country. This poem also states that

> Peace, and the proof of peace, is the verandah
> absent from some of the newer houses here.
>
> (*DM*, 85)

Sometimes Murray seems worried that his verandah-culture is being lost, that Ithaca is becoming only another location for 'ethnic' outside broadcasts. Yet what becomes clear when one reads the book is that *The Daylight Moon* is not just a celebration of nostalgia, any more than is his listing of 'A Generation of Changes' in his prose collection *Blocks and Tackles* (1990).

Murray makes it clear that he rebelled, that 'At eighteen, I made a great vow / I'd never milk another bloody cow.' (*DM*, 70) Another poem, 'Variations on a Measure of Burns' demonstrates again that Murray is not sorry to have left home. The man who returns is the Peasant Mandarin, who has worked as an international translator, who has squeezed what he needed from universities from Australia to Scotland. This poet who returns to the vast Ithaca of Australia, and the particular Ithaca of a Bunyah verandah, has an eye far less for bush *bons mots* and simplicities, than for the peculiar canniness of mentality and the technological complexity of modern rural life, particularly in Australia. The stanza which opens *The Daylight Moon* exemplifies this perfectly as it describes travelling on 'Flood Plains on the Coast Facing Asia'.

> Hitching blur to a caged propeller
> with its motor racket swelling
> barroom to barrage, our aluminium
> airboat has crossed the black coffee
> lagoon and swum out onto
> one enormous crinkling green.
> Now like a rocket loudening
> to liftoff, it erects the earsplitting

> wigwam we must travel in
> everywhere here, and starts skimming
> at speed on the never-never
> meadows of the monsoon wetland.
>
> (*DM*, 1)

Few poets write about technology better than Murray, and one of the great pleasures of his verse is the way his technology is so firmly earthed and tactile. Murray's snake-infested Eden isn't colour-supplement escapism; it is a place made real in sometimes hyperarticulate language, a place where

> farmers take spanners
> to the balers, gang ploughs
> and towering diesel tractors
> they prefer to their cows.

Murray's *Collins Dove Anthology of Australian Religious Verse* uses the word 'religious' in a wide sense, and includes much work which others might have excluded. Murray seems to see poetry as exhibiting a sharpness of vision and depth of attention which gives it a religious quality. In 'Poetry and Religion' he writes that

> A poem, compared with an arrayed religion,
> may be like a soldier's one short marriage night
> to die and live by. But that is a small religion.
>
> (*DM*, 51)

Such thoughts are clearly related to the essays on 'Embodiment and Incarnation', 'Poems and Poesies' and 'Poemes and the Mystery of Embodiment' in *Blocks and Tackles* – essays which themselves develop not only from Murray's earlier poetry and his editing of the *Anthology of Australian Religious Poetry*, but also, I suspect, emerge in part at least from his reaction to reading the work of Lévi-Strauss, expressed in the 1979 piece, 'The Big Loose Poems that Rule Us'. (*PF*, 49–51)

The religious poems of Murray's which work best are of the kind for which he shows such a good eye in his anthology – those that are implicitly religious. There are times in *The Daylight Moon* when a poem seems to have too much of a design on the reader, as in these stanzas (the most abstract ones) from 'At Min-Min Camp':

> From the Rift we also carried the two kinds of fear
> humans inherit: the rational kind, facing say weapons
> and the soul's kind, the creeps. Awe, which warns of law.

The two were long bound together, in the sacred
cultures of fright, that called shifting faces to the light's edge:
none worse than our own, when we came dreaming of houses.

Then the sacred turned fairytale, as always. And the new thing,
holiness, a true face, constant in all lights,
was still very scattered. It saved some. It is still scattered.

(*DM*, 42–3)

It might be argued that, in the context of a poem partly concerned
with incarnation, these rather bodiless stanzas play their part, but surely
Murray's skill is stronger when he is less preachy, as he is in the simple,
splendid bodilessness of the stanza which ends this poem:

We left that verandah next day, and its ruined garden
of wire and daylilies, its grassy fringe of ancient pee scalds
and travelled further west on a truck that had lost its body.

(*DM*, 43)

While only one poem in this same collection ('Joker as Told') buckles
under the pressure of explicit sermonizing, there are moments in others
where this becomes a threat. Far more immediately enjoyable are poems
like 'Louvres' where, seen through louvres' slats

visitors shimmer up in columnar gauges
to touch lives lived behind gauze
in a lantern of inventory,
slick vector geometries glossing the months of rain.

(*DM*, 20)

Here we see and hear again the Murray who is a poet of accurately
observed pleasure. A poem such as 'Variations on a Measure of Burns'
makes it clear both that Murray is glad to have followed the literary career
that took him away from home, and that he is glad to have confirmed his
rootedness in his home community by returning to it. Like Burns, Murray
is bicultural, and enjoys such a situation. That sense of pleasure has
continued in his recent writings, but in *Dog Fox Field* in particular it is
shadowed and sometimes overcome by pain and even despair.

With the publication of *Dog Fox Field* in 1990, Murray received the
surrender of the Poms. This new book, like his poet's previous collection,
was a 'Poetry Book Society Choice' in Britain where it became increas-
ingly common to hear him described as one of the finest living poets. The
book's diction extends from 'ickilier' and 'tae yer neb' to 'pheromones'
and 'Luciferian', as if to hint in its use of Scots and an almost
MacDiarmidean synthetic English that Murray's home lies outside the

polis of Received Pronunciation, and that he wishes to articulate confidently something of this cultural difference in his writing. Increasingly in *Dog Fox Field* and in *Translations from the Natural World* (1992) Murray has developed an Australian English tinged with Scots, neologisms and scientific diction, a language of Shakespearian impurity.

Murray knows that words are bonds, but also means of exclusion. It emerged at the Nuremberg trials that a Nazi test for feeblemindedness was 'to make up a sentence using the words *dog*, *fox* and *field*'. Those who failed, Murray reminds us, 'had to thump and cry in the vans / that ran while stopped in Dog Fox Field'. (*DFF*, 50) The 'Idyll Wheel' sequence and many of the poems in this book are as rich and arresting as anything he has written, but they often reveal what it is to 'cross into Dog Fox Field'. The poetry takes us to the urban beauty of mirror-glass skyscrapers ('their decoration's anything that happens'), and to the vast Australian otherworld beyond the cities, the place where in 'Feb' there are 'Two cultures: sun and shade'. (*DFF*, 3) Yet often we move into a darkness visible, a zone of extreme experience which may be 'where the poet Brennan wandered / the soaked steps of his mind' (*DFF*, 42) or else when we glimpse 'terror radiant up the night sky'. We are aware of the 'real pain' on which our civilization is conveniently grounded – the 'high Sugar' of slavery's plantations whose wealth underwrote 'the liberal mind', and the pioneer brutalities that shaped Australia. Sometimes as well as pain there is a bitterness, as Murray again turns preacher, the lashing, epigrammatic prophet of the Book of Les. Eager to explain what has gone wrong, and eager to castigate, he is also wise enough to write the three-line poem 'Politics and Art':

> Brutal policy,
> like inferior art, knows
> whose fault it all is.
> (*DFF*, 75)

In the finest poems of *Dog Fox Field* Murray's amplitude and far-sightedness rhyme. 'The Transportation of Clermont' takes the physical moving and relocation of a timber-built town as a metaphor for flux and continuity. We see 'Everything standing in its wrong accustomed place' as 'My generation's memories are intricately transposed'. (*DFF*, 2) The dangers of the relegation of the decent by the chic continue to haunt Murray's imagination. So does the wish to achieve a rich 'television' – provocatively in 'The Tube', Murray uses that word etymologically to emphasize the need for a long-range visionary quality in our lives. 'The Emerald Dove' and 'Cave Divers Near Mount Gambier' use verse like prayer to try and reach past the boundaries of our mind-sets and touch what might lie beyond. Poetry as religious exploration is illuminating and dangerous, offering us either, that increasingly familiar Murray – 'nothing that existed there was background' (*DFF*, 62) – or leaving us stranded in a dark deep cave 'at the apex of a steeple that does not reach the day'. (*DFF*, 18)

Dog Fox Field frolics, swoops, rhymes in mid-air, and has bouts of stinging darkness. A sense of faith and desperation is mixed in Murray's hauntingly beautiful poem 'The Gaelic Long Tunes' which again relates the Australian-centred emotions of much of the book to Murray's older ancestral root. That poem concludes with an image of perseverance, of being taken into the otherworld, and of potential vast emptiness with 'Earth-conquest mourned / as loss, all tragedy drowned, and that weird / music impelled them, singing, like solar wind'. (*DFF*, 91) A sense of perseverance, and of threat is present also, yet triumphed over, in the explicitly Scottish poem of Murray's next collection, *Translations from the Natural World* (1992). 'Equinoctial Gales at Hawthornden Castle' opens not with 'solar wind' but 'tidal wind'. Yet nature provides not only bleakness, but also offers the promise of a triumphant fresh flowering to the defeated or 'licked' Robert Bruce, who watches his famous spider. It is as if Murray, in his own time of trouble (he suffered from recurrent depression in the late 1980s and early 1990s), looked for sustenance to various ancestral myths, among them those of his Scottish heritage. Murray at one time considered calling this book *Bob Spider*,[12] drawing on a phrase from the Bruce poem, and that poem, offering us the man who translates and is sustained by the natural world, without naively anthropo-morphizing it, may act as a useful interpretative key to a volume by a poet who has suggested that his work might suggest at times less pantheism than 'panentheism, God in everything rather than everything being God'. (*Porter*, 84)

It is surely significant that Murray's use of a myth from his Scottish heritage may help readers find their way into this book. At the same time, it would be foolish to pretend that Murray's 'Scottishness' has become more than one of a considerable number of strands pleated in his work. The blending of inheritances and materials in his recent poetry is more inward and subtle than in some of his early writing. Explicitly at least, Murray is less interested now than he once was in national identity or in the Celtic tones to be heard in the Australian voice. His Scottish lore and study have helped him articulate an Australian identity. But if for Peter Porter (quoted in the blurb to the Carcanet edition of *Dog Fox Field*) Murray has become 'the true spokesman of the whole nation, the custo-dian of its soul', then unlike his kinsman MacDiarmid, that earlier Voice of Scotland, the Murray who has constructed his Australian poetic voice is

wary about becoming set in the concrete of any slick or chauvinistic
image-making. As he writes in 1988, 'Making images of Australia is
arguably something we do too much of'. (*BT*, 113) Though much of his
recent prose has been concerned with the rediscovery of earlier Australian
vernacular poetry, he has become increasingly wary of 'the Australian
Identity industry' (*BT*, 116) and has been writing more and more about
the relationship between poetry and religion, expanding the sense of both
these words. Having achieved poetic and imaginative liberation from the
distant metropolitan establishment of his youth, Murray has no intention
of putting himself in thrall to another, perhaps equally limiting establish-
ment – whether that of now fashionable republican politics or of the
universities. *Blocks and Tackles* contains Murray's superbly provocative
flyting with academia, 'The Suspect Captivity of the Fisher King', and his
Preface to that volume of essays makes it clear that

> I have stepped back noticeably from the republican aspirations of my
> earlier two books of essays, though without advocating any sort of
> return to an older colonial set-up .... Since in fact the republic has
> arrived in all but name and some insignia ... I have thought it
> opportune to examine the reverse sides of many thoughts and
> dreams I had entertained in the past. (*BT*, viii–ix)

Murray's wish to 'keep at a tangent', to use Seamus Heaney's phrase, is
the ultimate sign of his poetic liberty and strength. Again, the parallel that
comes to mind, for all its improbabilities, is the Burns who exalted the
man of independent mind.

Looking back over Murray's poetic career in the light of *Translations
from the Natural World*, which has just been published as I write, it is
clear that the long 'Presence' sequence in that book is in one sense
another version of the extended 'identifying poem' which Murray has
attempted repeatedly from 'The Buladelah-Taree Holiday Song Cycle'
through *The Boys Who Stole the Funeral* to 'Aspects of Language and War
on the Gloucester Road' and beyond. Other, less purely poetic attempts at
this 'identifying poem' have taken the form of the poetry, prose and
photographs book *The Australian Year* and such essays as 'In a Working
Forest' in *Blocks and Tackles*. The otherworld of nature, familiar yet
foreign, has always attracted Murray and he found a peculiar grammatical
expression for it in 'The Cows on Killing Day' in *Dog Fox Field*. Further
examples of this biological community voice occur in the 'Presence'
sequence in *Translations from the Natural World* which is part of a book
that constantly explores the tension between human assimilation into
nature and human distance from the natural world. Continuing Murray's
fascination with incarnation and embodiment, the poems in this sequence
continually hover on the edge of self and other which so fascinated

Mikhail Bakhtin. If Murray's earlier poetry reveals the confident and increasingly sophisticated shaping of a national voice, then these poems move beyond that to develop the concern with sacred sites and the sacred in nature which is one of the main bonds between the work of Murray and that of Judith Wright. Murray's interest in the limitations of language and in ways of sneaking up on the unsayable in these poems may mark him out as peculiarly contemporary, yet there are also strong signs in the verse of a remarkable affinity with nature which may parallel the communion with nature felt in Duncan Ban Macintyre's 'Ben Dorain', the great Gaelic poem best known in the English translation by the bilingual Gaelic / English poet Iain Crichton Smith, whose own 'Deer on the High Hills' may owe something to Macintyre's Gaelic.[13] Crichton Smith has written about Gaelic Australia, and shares with Murray the same British publisher, so I suspect that, consciously or not, in the 'Presence' sequence Murray's title 'Deer on the Wet Hills' pays homage to this tradition. If so, it seems fitting that in the work of this religious poet who has constructed for himself a poetic voice which identifies his work with his poetic territory so clearly that he has been able to move beyond many of the anxieties of cultural and political identification, there still persists a Gaelic seed.

5

John Ashbery
A Dialogue Across Time

Museums then became generous, they live in our breath.
'A Mood of Quiet Beauty' (*AG*, 8)[1]

From the work of Les Murray to that of John Ashbery may seem a vertiginous leap. Yet driving in the United States, among the neons of Las Vegas where whole buildings sparkle like transitory hoardings, through the dirty, gleaming juxtapositions of New York, or across vast, clean, and lyrically historic expanses of Arizona, it becomes more and more apparent that the contemporary poetry whose tone most unites the remarkably differing anthology of states is that of Ashbery. Where Whitman sang of the open road, Ashbery constructs a poetry for and of the age of the multi-lane highway. His verse, dialogic, heteroglossic and frequently deracinated, is constantly on the move. It is full of peculiar drifts and seeming urgencies, yet can give the impression of being endlessly directionless – a spy-satellite view of the freeway traffic as well as an account of the flux and unending spool of the self which delights in the continuous linguistic play of novelization. Such a view might be odd, even invidious, to Ashbery himself. Interviewed by John Murphy in *Poetry Review*, he said, 'It's rather strange to me, the people who get taken up as spokesmen for everybody living at a certain time', yet he also wished to present himself as a distinctly *American* writer.[2] Still a controversial poet in the United States, Ashbery is also increasingly a welcomed, accepted, even a historical presence, a major voice of America. In Britain to some people his work remains strange, even threatening. That condition is changing, but it is true to say that his work highlights major differences between British, particularly English, and American poetry. Ashbery, championed by Bloom of Yale as the heir of Stevens, is culturally other, disconcertingly American, as remote in his own way from the orthodox English tradition as is the later Hugh MacDiarmid. That may be a reason for reading him. His alertness to the languages of corporate advertising, cartoons, popular culture and art criticism, as well as to those of colloquial conversation and many varieties of literariness results in a poetry that is supremely heteroglossic. Not only many of its cultural references but also its modes of constant rapid transit from register to register, its intercuttings and sophisticated mélange, make it a poetry of later twentieth-century media-saturated America, particularly metropolitan New York. When the protagonist of Martin Amis's *Money* is in New York he stays at the Ashbery.

Ashbery's verse then has achieved a new poetic articulation of American-ness through a particular exploitation of the novelized, dialogic mélange which for Bakhtin characterizes modern writing. Postmodernism itself may be seen as the late twentieth century's ultimate development of novelization, a development which transcends older artistic boundaries so that we find not only demotic speech engaged in a dialogue with literary registers in poetry, we also find in the visual arts the dialogue, in architecture for instance, between neo-classical, rococo, and Bauhaus elements all carried on within the one building. Ashbery's poetic identity, articulating the identity of contemporary America, has a similar structure. It is a dialogic identity in which dialogues are certainly conducted not only across spatial cultural boundaries – Ashbery's identity has been constructed out of extra-American voices, including notably that of Raymond Roussel.[3] Yet Ashbery's identity is also constructed out of a crossing of temporal cultural boundaries. The dialogues of his identity constitute a striking example of what any poet must do. He crosses into the past and makes that past part of his own poetic self. The way in which Ashbery has done this, however, is peculiarly his own. This chapter is designed to show how Ashbery's dialogic identity involves important crossings into the area of nineteenth-century British literature in order to construct his own particularly American idiom.

Ashbery's poetic world is a varied one. At one end of the spectrum of his work might stand that *memento mori*, 'At North Farm' from *A Wave*, and at the other a poem such as 'A Life Drama,' one of the avant-garde experiments in verbal texturing from *The Tennis Court Oath*. In between is a piece such as 'The Instruction Manual' from *Some Trees*, which Marjorie Perloff reads as a fairly traditional romantic vision poem, though she does not point out that the reader might wonder at its quaint or faded diction.[4] There are also the few short pieces in *As We Know* such as

I HAD THOUGHT THINGS
WERE GOING ALONG WELL

But I was mistaken.

(*AWK*, 94)

which are simply constructed as a title playing off against a one line poem. These pieces might stand as simple models for that favourite Ashbery trick of having the title apparently fought by the poem which follows it. Again, there are poems with an ostensible subject and a pained lonely eloquence such as 'Self-Portrait in a Convex Mirror,' the poem which (though it is not his favourite) Ashbery has suggested might appear more approachable than other poems which he prefers. (*Murphy*, 24–25) Then, more often, maybe too often, there are poems which (unlike the cut-ups and arrange-ments of *The Tennis Court Oath*) look as if they can be read as 'normal' poems, but amuse and baffle the reader by the apparently 'crazy weather' of their sudden, surreal switches. An example of this type might be 'The Pursuit of Happiness', the opening poem of *Shadow Train*, beginning

> It came about that there was no way of passing
> Between the twin partitions that presented
> A unified façade, that of a suburban shopping mall
> In April. One turned, as one does, to other interests
> Such as the tides in the Bay of Fundy.

Lastly, in this probably not exhaustive catalogue of Ashbery poem-types, there come the recipe poems. Sometimes Ashbery will include sections in poems dealing with how the poem gets written or read – as in 'Revisionist Horn Concerto'. (*HL*, 146) Other times he will let a poem itself act as an instruction manual. In *Houseboat Days*, the piece 'And *Ut Pictura Poesis* Is Her Name' would be a clear example. This recipe poem itself contains particularity and abstraction rubbing against one another, a peculiarly dialogic continuum which involves strange collocations ('humdrum testa-ments'), surreal mixing, an apparently endless motion (like the music of Philip Glass), and, after the fun, a final alienating gloom.

> Now,
> About what to put in your poem-painting:
> Flowers are always nice, particularly delphinium.
> Names of boys you once knew and their sleds,
> Skyrockets are good – do they still exist?
> There are a lot of other things of the same quality
> As those I've mentioned. Now one must
> Find a few important words, and a lot of low-keyed,
> Dull-sounding ones. She approached me
> About buying her desk. Suddenly the street was
> Bananas and the clangor of Japanese instruments.
> Humdrum testaments were scattered around. His head
> Locked into mine. We were a seesaw. Something

Ought to be written about how this affects
You when you write poetry:
The extreme austerity of an almost empty mind
Colliding with the lush, Rousseau-like foliage of its desire to
    communicate
Something between breaths, if only for the sake
Of others and their desire to understand you and desert you
For other centers of communication, so that understanding
May begin, and in doing so be undone.

(HD, 45–6)

Ashbery is the best explainer of his own poems. This does not mean, though, that they are incomprehensible to other readers whom large tracts of Ashbery's poetic landscape may amuse, but also weary and appal. Having, I hope, indicated that this landscape is a varied one – not just the flat plain that Ashbery's attackers, and some of his defenders would make it – I wish to suggest one possible way of viewing Ashbery as maintaining a continuing dialogue with the British nineteenth century, a dialogue which helps to constitute Ashbery's own American poetic identity.

Ashbery has a great love of Victoriana, a powerful nostalgia. As a child he spent much time with his grandparents, 'both born in the 1860s. They were actually Victorian people'. The young Ashbery pored over Dickens and Thackeray. The 'I' of one poem 'would like to write a Victorian novel'. (HL, 104) The poet pronounces that he is attached to Victorian architecture, an architecture characterized surely by excrescences, elaborate façades and complex, cluttered ornamentation. Ashbery's grandfather 'was the first person in America to experiment with X-rays', and Ashbery too is preoccupied with lighting up the human interior.

To flash light,
Into the house within, its many chambers,
Its memories and associations, upon its inscribed
And pictured walls, argues enough that life is various.
Life is beautiful.

Most of these lines from Houseboat Days, Ashbery recalls, are taken from 'one of my favourite writers', Walter Pater.[5] An art critic communicating emotions through the supposed viewing of other artworks, a man preoccupied with a shimmering, cadenced style whose refinements of art are shot-through with occasional violent and erotic pangs, Pater is a figure whose work is worth setting beside Ashbery's. For Ashbery, as for Pater, there is a stress on the 'multiplied consciousness'. If for Pater 'Not the fruit of experience, but experience itself is the end', then for Ashbery experience seems constituted by a hypnotically varied language which 'comes to you', like Pater's definition of art, 'proposing frankly to give nothing but the highest quality to your moments as they pass, and simply for those moments' sake'.

'It is with this movement, with the passage and dissolution of impressions, images, sensations, that analysis leaves off – that continual vanishing away, that strange, perpetual weaving and unweaving of ourselves.'[6] Ashbery's dialogic imagination continues the Paterian 'dialogue of the mind with itself' to use a phrase from *Plato and Platonism*, a book Ashbery loves, and which is filled with material developed in Ashbery's work. As the passage from 'And *Ut Pictura Poesis* Is Her Name' suggested, Ashbery with Pater likes to consider 'a mind trying to feed itself on its own emptiness', remaining aware that 'From first to last our faculty of thinking is limited by our command of speech'. Pater and Ashbery are both preoccupied with the search for a language which shows 'the search for and the notation, if there be such, of an antiphonal rhythm, or logic, which, proceeding uniformly from movement to movement, as in some intricate musical theme, might link together in one those contending, infinitely diverse impulses.' Both these art critics share a Heraclitean interest in something which both 'is and is not'.[7] Since I first suggested Ashbery's involvement with Pater, the connection has also been pointed out by J. D. McClatchy.[8] But, while Pater tires us because the refined air he breathes is too thin, Ashbery is attracted as well to a more mundane flow of details, the humorous common-ness exemplified in what he describes as 'another of my favourite books', George and Weedon Grossmith's *Diary of a Nobody.*(*Ash*, 33) Because titles are particularly important to Ashbery, as he has admitted,[9] it is worth pondering the importance of that title to his work which so often has the appearance of diary-like chronicling and intimacy, yet gives the impression of being generated by virtually a blank, a nobody, a rather sad speaker whose very existence may be called into question as pronouns flicker and merge. Ashbery's own preferred setting has something about it of melancholy as well as closeness:

> I was always very attracted to the cosiness and the gloom of Victorian life, and always felt very much at home in that environment. Now I'm happily ensconced in my gloomy Victorian villa ....

> Would you say that in buying this house and preserving and restoring it you were trying to recapture your time with your grandparents?

Yes, that's exactly what I was doing. It may be rather a sick
enterprise really, but when I first stepped into this house which
had been on the market for a long time because nobody wanted
it, I thought, 'This is perfect for me'. There's a kind of morning
room where the sun comes in, where I like to sit and read the
morning papers – as you might expect. Then I go upstairs to the
other living-room which is more unapproachable, where you're
protected from people looking in the window. (*Ash*, 33)

The idea of existing in a protected place, a 'more unapproachable' region,
is not an uncommon one in the work of this poet who is attracted to 'safe
houses' (*HL*, 3) and to Pater's 'The Child in the House'.[10] Such a place is
an art-world, like the realm presented in the last lines of 'Hop 'o' My
Thumb'. (*SP*, 33)

There are still other made-up countries
Where we can hide forever,
Wasted with eternal desire and sadness,
Sucking the sherbets, crooning the tunes, naming the names.

The space presented here is a dreamscape in which the pressures of the
outside world are transformed, made purely verbal and enjoyable, though
it is a space not without the awareness of death. It is a dreamworld that
can only be created by the motion of words. Contingent upon time, it is
aware of mortality.

The dark is waiting like so many other things
Dumbness and voluptuousness among them.
It is good to be part of it
In the dream that is the kernel
Deep in it, the unpretentious, unblushing,
But also the steep side stretching far away:
For this we pay, for this
Tonight and every night.
But for the time being we are free
And meanwhile the songs
Protect us, in a way, and the special climate.
('Robin Hood's Barn', *SP*, 63)

The idea of a world apparently open but protected recurs in Ashbery's
poetry. The art-world provides a refuge, but it also exacts a
confinement.

...it is life englobed.
One would like to stick one's hand

> Out of the globe, but its dimension,
> What carries it, will not allow it.
> (*SP*, 69)

The hand of the figure in Ashbery's poem-painting, 'Self-Portrait in a Convex Mirror' is

> thrust at the viewer
> And swerving easily away, as though to protect
> What it advertises.
>
> (*SP*, 68)

Though sceptical about much of Ashbery's undertaking, James Fenton has written of his strong admiration for this poem which he describes as 'didactic', and it is surely the case that the peculiar emotional force of the piece comes from the at times anguished tension between life and art. Not for nothing does Fenton pick for quotation the following passage:

> The soul has to stay where it is,
> Even though restless, hearing raindrops at the pane,
> The sighing of autumn leaves thrashed by the wind,
> Longing to be free, outside, but it must stay
> Posing in this place. It must move
> As little as possible. This is what the portrait says.
> But there is in that gaze a combination
> Of tenderness, amusement and regret, so powerful
> In its restraint that one cannot look for long.
> The secret is too plain. The pity of it smarts,
> Makes hot tears spurt: that the soul is not a soul,
> Has no secret, is small, and it fits
> Its hollows perfectly: its room, our moment of attention.
> That is the tune but there are no words.
> The words are only speculation
> (From the Latin *speculum*, mirror):
> They seek and cannot find the meaning of the music.[11]

This powerful, painful conception of a soul, even a sham-soul, bound to inhabit only art and unable to move from the mirror, or rather art's representation of the mirror, leads us on to what is surely the most crucial of Ashbery's relations with the nineteenth century.

Ashbery is reported as saying that a favourite poem of his is 'The Lady of Shalott'.[12] Tennyson's long musical poem treats of loneliness and failed love, and particularly the sad, beautiful loneliness of art's mirror-world which is separated from life despite the Lady's fatally lyrical attempt to intersect with it when, wearing her text written round the prow, she floats down to the Camelot which appears to represent reality.

Real life here is death for art, which may be why Ashbery's most 'serious' pieces such as 'At North Farm' (*W*, 1) and 'Light Turnouts' (*HL*, 3) deal with death, and why frequently his poems gravitate towards a foreboding gloom, as does the end of 'The Ice-Cream Wars'.

> A heaviness in the trees, and no one can say
> Where it comes from, or how long it will stay –
> A randomness, a darkness of one's own.
>
> (*HD*, 61)

'The Lady of Shalott' offers material that is instructive to compare with Ashbery's work not only because both poets seem possessed by art and life, but also because the comparison throws up significant differences. Ashbery's revision of and dialogue with Tennyson does not leave us with 'many-towered Camelot' as a representative of the 'real world'. The place of such an entity in a poem is continually questioned. For the modern world Camelot is already half-way to Hollywood, a version of 'the city of painted scenery' (*HL*, 58), and Ashbery, literally in 'Daffy Duck in Holly-wood', gives us an entire landscape whose reality seems only a media-hype, fascinating in its comic juxtaposition, its carnivalesque dialogues of register, but remaining a business of 'naming the names' rather than articulating a world of actual contacts and responsibilities.

> Something strange is creeping across me.
> La Celestina has only to warble the first few bars
> Of 'I Thought about You' or something mellow from
> *Amadigi de Gaula* for everything – a mint-condition can
> Of Rumford's Baking Powder, a celluloid earring, Speedy
> Gonzales, the latest from Helen Topping Miller's fertile
> Escritoire, a sheaf of suggestive pix on greige, deckle-edged
> Stock – to come clattering through the rainbow trellis
> Where Pistachio Avenue rams the 2300 block of Highland
> Fling Terrace.
>
> (*HD*, 31)

Ashbery's words make all fantastic and artificial. As he put it in an interview – 'I wrote about what I didn't see. The experience that eluded me somehow intrigued me more than the one I was having, and this has happened to me down through the years.'[13] The sense here is of the Lady of Shalott in reverse, of life pining at being cut off from art. A word-world as lush as Ashbery's, as free to break rules, is an adventure-playground. Reality can be made safe by being converted into fiction.

In this film you saw a python swallow a live pig.
This wasn't scary. In fact, it seemed quite normal,
the sort of thing you would see in a movie – 'reality'.
                              ('The Lonesdale Operator', *W*, 48)

The landscape for Ashbery is so often just words, admitting of immediate metamorphosis.

An inexhaustible wardrobe has been placed at the disposal
Of each new occurrence. It can be itself now.
Day is almost reluctant to decline
And slowing down opens out new avenues
That don't infringe on space but are living here with us.
Other dreams came and left while the bank
Of colored verbs and adjectives was shrinking from the light
To nurse in shade their want of a method
                                   ('Scheherezade', *SP*, 9)

Elsewhere spring means that 'New sentences were starting up' (*SP*, 1) or a figure appears 'wearing a text. The lines/Droop to your shoelaces.' ('Crazy Weather' *HD*, 21) The constantly shifting kaleidoscope does away with judgements and beliefs, holding all in suspension,

But I don't set much stock in things
Beyond the weather and the certainties of living and dying:
The rest is optional. To praise this, blame that,
Leads one subtly away from the beginning, where
We must stay, in motion.
                                   ('Houseboat Days', *HD*, 39)

'The mind' in this poem, this world, is 'hospitable, taking in everything / Like boarders', so that the poem's dialogic play of elements seems endless, and often, most particularly in *The Tennis Court Oath*, we seem in a world that is purely literary, sheer Shalott where the tension is not between life and writing but between the kinds of writing which compose the poems' dialogic identity. Ashbery warms to talk of Spasmodic poets, nineteenth-century writers such as the Scottish poet Alexander Smith and 'Festus' Bailey who can be seen as part of the New York poet's 'Other Tradition' (see *TP*, 56). Smith also attracts him as someone who tried to write in a melodious way using urban material.[14] For many readers the self-conscious literariness of Smith's style must be offputting, but surely this is what attracts Ashbery, a poet often naming his own poems after works of art. When he takes Smith's title 'A Life Drama' for an early poem it alerts us to the posing, artificial nature of what is going on. Ashbery has spoken of his admiration for a line from Tennyson's 'Mariana,'

> The broken sheds looked sad and strange

This line is a dialogic juxtaposition of two registers, one pointing towards the hard, ordinary world of 'broken sheds', the other towards the languidly 'poetic' – 'sad and strange'. A delight in combining such materials (again what happens in 'The Lady of Shalott') can be seen in Ashbery's own work not just on the large scale but also on the level of individual lines, such as 'A fine rain anoints the canal machinery' from the first poem of *Some Trees*. Here the Audenesque canal machinery belongs with those broken sheds, but the word 'anoints' is taken from a religious vocabulary and used in such a way that its 'poetic' nature is highlighted. For Tennyson, the strangeness and sadness contribute to a clear overall pattern. For Ashbery, however, the word 'anoints' seems used with mischievous gratuitousness. He is delighting in the power of being literary, of engaging in a hedonistic dialogue between the mundane and the portentous, the vague and the precise within a structure which confers upon his material the unity of music that can unite the grandly rhetorical to the banal. Ashbery's reducing and enlarging all to the same level is a technique that, when prolonged, can give his verse an offputtingly bland flavour. It does, however, permit that humorous avoidance of value-judgements and programmes which has been examined by Thomas A. Fink. While Ashbery's technique does not preclude Marxist interpretation, the attraction to a language self-consciously cut off from reality might seem more likely to lead to a reinforcing of the status quo, letting us see Ashbery as ultimately a neo-conservative poet.[15]

Ashbery's delight in the power of a poetic music to contain and give apparent unity to strange combinations of materials is certainly present in early poems like 'Two Scenes'.

> A fine rain anoints the canal machinery.
> This is perhaps a day of general honesty
> Without example in the world's history
> Though the fumes are not of a singular authority
> And indeed are dry as poverty.

Is there anything which holds together the elements of this first piece in Ashbery's first book? The final laughing cadets of the poem

> say, 'In the evening
> Everything has a schedule, if you can find out what it is.'

and the first of the 'Two Scenes' tells the reader that

> Destiny guides the water-pilot, and it is destiny.

But isn't this also part of the game? The 'schedule' cannot be discovered unless it is the poem itself, ordering its own constituents in an unresolvable play of dialogues. The redundant statement that 'destiny ... is destiny' makes us aware that destiny may just be a word, albeit a rather grand one. On a larger scale this technique of enjoyment of verbal textures juxtaposed dominates *The Tennis Court Oath*, as exemplified in 'A Life Drama', and gives us the Ashbery which has appealed most to Charles Bernstein and the L=A=N=G=U=A=G=E poets, and it is Ashbery's determination to play the whole language circus which is one of the most immediately exciting things for the new reader.[16] This poet's vocabulary is open to all comers in a process of novelization which seems to exclude nothing. As Ashbery puts it, 'Everybody knows Mallarmé's dictum about purifying the language of the tribe. In my case I don't feel it needs purifying. I try to encourage it.' (*Murphy*, 20)

Simply encouraging language is an essential element in any poetry, but it is only an element. *The Tennis Court Oath* does mark one extreme of the Ashbery spectrum. His sense of language as a physical entity which obscures, distorts and sometimes oppressively governs, though it may also carnivalize, our efforts at communication is something which has been developed by the L=A=N=G=U=A=G=E poets much of whose work may be viewed in terms of a purer form of novelization in which all content is illusory and all that remains is an interplay of dictions and registers. This is a poetic 'novelization' that has gone far from the conventional novel, yet one wonders if within Bakhtin's extreme emphasis on dialogic properties there is not the potential for certain developments which, as in some contemporary avant-garde poetries, preserve an interplay of dialogic voices, registers and tones while dumping any narrative content. Whereas it seems that some of the L=A=N=G=U=A=G=E poets do this, it may well be true to contend that the more interesting members of that school do not, but, like the Michael Palmer of 'Sun', maintain a tension between history, self and more abstract pleasures of textuality.[17]

However painterly he may be with his words, it appears that Ashbery too has a wish to keep at least part of one foot on the ground. In some senses his own later work withdraws from the extremities of *The Tennis Court Oath*, though it is worth noting that even those extremities are beginning to be deciphered by John Shoptaw in terms of the poet's individual biography and aspirations.[18] Ashbery likes to maintain some sense of an albeit fluid relationship between the texts which he produces and their producer. It is this which allows consideration of his verse as love poetry, for example.[19] There is certainly in his work a perceptible delight in dialogues between registers for their own sake.

Still, just as the reader would lose interest in the Lady of Shalott if she remained for ever weaving her web, so the mere juxtaposition of verbal textures is not enough for prolonged enjoyment. Ashbery has a sharp sense of the literary. He is attracted to 'faded charm' (clear in 'The Instruction Manual'). (*Ash*, 32) He is attracted even to 'deathly pallor' in a work he recalls fondly, Alexander Smith's *Dreamthorp*. But his work is most interesting when the tension is felt between 'The Palace of Art' and something beyond, an absent something which may be transcendental or ordinary, but which rubs anxiously and often comically against the pressure to live only in words. So we find in 'Worsening Situation' (*SP*, 3) the exclamation 'The name you drop and never say is mine, mine!' Here, as often in Ashbery's work, an apparently portentous note is introduced only to be dismissed, yet bringing with it an awareness of ageing. Growing older Ashbery has described as 'something I've been writing about all the time'. (*Murphy*, 23) Such an awareness of time passing goes hand in hand with the comic unease of having to exist only in the world of words. Ashbery is fascinated by words, and clearly by names, not because they can fix the real but because they can precipitate the reader into the fantastic or ridiculous, as happens with a virtuoso sting in the tail here:

> One day a man called while I was out
> And left this message: 'You got the whole thing wrong
> From start to finish. Luckily, there's still time
> To correct the situation, but you must act fast.
> See me at your earliest convenience. And please
> Tell no one of this. Much besides your life depends on it.'
> I thought nothing of it at the time. Lately
> I've been looking at old-fashioned plaids, fingering
> Starched white collars, wondering whether there's a way
> To get them really white again. My wife
> Thinks I'm in Oslo – Oslo, France, that is.
>
> (*SP*, 3–4)

The tension between the real world and the poemscape is here at the pitch of laughter, though reflection shows again that the themes include not just time passing, but isolation. Such wriggling fluently but upsettingly in the word-world is a device which Ashbery has made his own, setting his poems time and time again

> in a novel that has somehow gotten stuck
> To our lives, battening on us. A sad condition ...
>
> ('A Wave', *W*, 76)

Yet there is a danger of staleness. It is important to realize that Ashbery's poems are not all uniform. It may be equally crucial to realize that, as in

'Litany', Ashbery's peculiar presentation of 'a dialogue of the mind with itself' is both imaginatively exciting and ultimately insufficient. Ashbery catches the jumble and juxtapositions of a world which is a version of the Paterian 'multiplied consciousness', and which is rich in dialogic pleas-ures. But along with that goes a sense of the aesthete's thin-ness of the air in so many poems. Little seems to govern the length of many of Ashbery's works. Many would scarcely suffer by having lines omitted; Ashbery has shortened the *Selected Poems* version of 'The Skaters'.[20] 'Litany' in *As We Know* gives us a piece that is impossible for an individual to read according to the author's directions. The Paterian dialogue of the mind with itself splits entirely in two (as happens in 'My Erotic Double', *AWK*, 82) Poetry itself becomes narcissistic. In 'Litany' language turns back on itself totally defeating the reader. It is as if the Lady of Shalott had come out fighting. Ashbery describes the effect of the poem's being read in New York by two voices: '... one thing that did happen was that whenever there was a break in the poem and the other person carried on reading, suddenly being able to hear what was being read for a few seconds was rewarding after hearing two things at once. There seemed to be a tremen-dous illumination at that point'. (*Murphy*, 25) But is it enough that in a poem of sixty-five pages of double columns around 5 per cent should be comprehensible? The poem is theoretically interesting; it is a logical devel-opment in Ashbery's oeuvre, but like Derrida's *Glas* is likely to be more discussed than read. Fenton grows splenetic: 'This vaunted depiction of consciousness, of experience, this excursus into the meaning of meaning-less, this way of nattering on the whole night, this derogation of sense...'.

The Ashbery of 'Litany' most invites the 'etc' contained in the title of Edwin Morgan's '"In a Convex Mirror", Etc.'[21] At the same time, though, the poem clearly is a product of a dialogic imagination, one which delights in letting varying currents of language intersect, mix, clash, and separate. These voices are not attributed to individual speakers, they are simply sources of articulation, products of language itself, as impersonal and stylized as the stereotypically-named Cuddie and Colin of Ashbery's early pastoral 'Eclogue' (*ST*, 12–13) 'Litany' like much of the rest of Ashbery's poetry alerts us to the way Bakhtin's concept of a dialogic imagination is particularly appropriate to much modern art because it does not depend on a dialogue between individuals, but between ele-ments, and it does not necessarily involve any resolution (like a Socratic dialogue or the dialectical materialist process of Marxism), but may simply result in potentially endless juxtaposition of dialogic constituents. This juxtaposition may result in a pure, rarefied or decadent aesthetic pleasure, as well as, or instead of a working-out of those energies which make for social change. The endless juxtaposition of registers may come to seem unduly repetitive in a poetry which, for all its engagement with the nineteenth century seems to have little interest in the element of narrative which was fundamental to so much extended Victorian verse.

Ashbery is a poet whose work will call for selective editing, as does Swinburne's. Like that poet Ashbery loves to weave a world of words ('reptiles in rep ties', *HL*, 69) which seems almost, but not quite independent of the real. Eliot wrote of Swinburne that in his work 'the meaning is merely the hallucination of meaning, because language, uprooted, has adapted itself to an independent life of atmospheric nourishment'. The same, surely, could be said of much of Ashbery's output. Eliot also paid tribute to Swinburne since 'Only a man of genius could dwell so exclusively and consistently among words'.[22] But Swinburne, like Ashbery, possessed a sense of humour and of parody. Swinburne's best work is effective (and mattered to Eliot) because through the flickering surface of the language comes a painful sense of fragments of memory and desire. The same is true of Ashbery. As Pater found his concerns clearly mirrored by word-painting Leonardo's *Mona Lisa*, so Ashbery finds his own deepest concerns mirrored when he word-paints Parmigianino's 'Self-Portrait in a Convex Mirror'. This is the Ashbery, too, who with Tennysonian concern ends 'A Wave' with talk of 'the amazingly quiet room in which all my life has been spent', and of how 'each of us has to remain alone'. (*W*, 89) It is also the Ashbery who is liable to some of the criticisms most often levelled at Swinburne. It makes good sense, and helps make sense of Ashbery's work, if we set it beside the work of some of the writers of that nineteenth century which the New York poet so much admires. Ashbery may be a hi-tech poet; he is also a late Victorian. His poetic identity which seems to us so very American, is the result of a continuing engagement with the British poetry and aesthetics of the preceding century whose language and tones are hybridized with those of Popeye and modern New York. Ashbery's poetic identity is constituted by an unexpected dialogue that crosses temporal as well as spatial borders.

That is clear when one reads *Flow Chart*, Ashbery's *magnum opus*, a poem of Victorian amplitude whose 214 pages of long-lined verse provide the fullest demonstration to date of this poet's fascination with what Pater described as 'that strange, perpetual weaving and unweaving of ourselves'. Exploring the shifting web of the self which is bound up with the dream-web of art, the poem exhibits a continuing delight in a richly dialogic mélange whose roots once again lie in the mid and late nineteenth-century. Ashbery, though, produces a flavour that is sharply contemporary in its verbal registers, its blend of literariness and the colloquial:

                                                                    – I
      just lay down in a boat and slept, Lady-of-Shalott style. Soon I
          was gliding among you,
      taking notes on your conversations and otherwise making a pest
          of myself.

                                                            (*FC*, 133)

Like many passages of Ashbery's verse, these lines with their reference to
one of his favourite poems both enact and explain the dynamic of the
work from which they come. They speak of an aesthete's isolation, a
loneliness, but also a pleasure in mischievous polyphony, and a delight in
'gliding'. They hint too, at a finitude and death, which will end that
motion. In 'The Lady of Shalott' it is the act of writing which marks the
voyage to death of the isolated artist who is the poem's protagonist – 'And
round about the prow she wrote / *The Lady of Shalott*'. Gliding down to
Camelot, carried on the stream, the individual Lady of Shalott eventually
comes to rest, dead, and becomes art-work with a title – 'And round the
prow they read her name, / *The Lady of Shalott*'. In Tennyson's poem
those who read these title words fail to understand the lady, the artist who
wrote them.

   Suggesting that such a fate is inevitable, Ashbery's poem enacts some-
thing similar. It produces a relationship between gliding or flowing, and
being fixed or completed, dead. Art freezes living motion, changing the
flow of 'weather' (a word and a fluid phenomenon which Ashbery loves
for its craziness) into 'clouds stacked up in a holding pattern / like
pictures in a nineteenth-century museum.' (*FC*, 167) These words might
make us think of the jacket picture on Ashbery's previous book, *April
Galleons*, which shows a few black specks of gulls riding the thermals in
one of a series of *Cloud Studies* by Constable. This is a painting of motion,
at once frozen and fluid. It is a 'flow chart'. Ashbery has always been
brilliantly attuned to management-speak and its whacky idioms – 'Busi-
ness Personals', for instance, or 'Everything is modular now, even the
trees'. (*HL*, 78) He has seized on the term 'flow chart' because it unites
fluidity with fixedness. A chart is fixed, a flow is not. With its sense of
ironic fraying resignation, its tragi-humour, its lyrical office-language, its
Baudrillardian media-produced America of B-movie 'reality', and its sense
of urgency and death hidden yet present under the gliding surface,
Ashbery's poem offers us a graph of the way we live now.

   His graph might be seen as focused on the pronoun 'I'. The act of
producing that simple downstroke on a page simplifies the enormously
complex, unresolved and shifting nature of its producer. It creates the
illusion of a clear, simple, unified self: 'I'. Yet if 'I' is the gateway to
identity, it is also the gateway to the playground of fiction, since, on paper

in a poem, that 'I' is no longer the historical John Ashbery but is a linguistic sign suitable as the subject of a myriad of sentences, tales, fictions. That sign is in one sense fixed, unchanging; yet it is also infinitely fluid, able to be the subject of any number of written sentences which readers will interpret for themselves. As Ashbery puts it in another poem of this period, 'I have had so many identity crises/ in the last fifty years you wouldn't believe it'. (HL, 6) Fixed and fluid, a crystallization of our inner weather, but also a gateway to fantasy through language, the personal pronoun is itself a tiny 'flow chart'. The 'I' of this poem recurs, graphically the same, yet endlessly flowing

> It was then I discovered the pavements were made of the same
>   flagstones found underseas
> except there they were arranged more brightly in schools; here, clusters
> are the thing. School is for kids. I think I'll go, Miss MacGregor, honest
> I will, this time or bust?

> (FC, 122)

Given the utterly protean nature of this 'I' within language, the charge of narcissism may be inaccurate. Language takes over, hinting from time to time that there may be something beyond words – a realm of politics, sex, death and humour, a master narrative – yet making us aware too that this can at best be glimpsed only, and that language will hold and carry us off into its endless labyrinths. Text and living are both fluid processes, which may or may not intersect, are both kinds of weather in a climate where 'weathers wash so many of what we are'. (HL, 140)

> It's like the wind has taken over,
> except that one can be aware of, keep an eye on oneself in that
>   medium:
> this one is more like a pock-marked wall, in which spalling occurs due
>   to stress
> and anxiety at regular, key points in one's career
> (if it can be called that – 'progress' is a better word, implying a
>   development
> but not necessarily a resolution at the end), and which enfolds you even
>   as you
> marvel at its irregular surface before you feel yourself beginning to sink
>   into it,
> toes first.

> (FC, 85)

What makes us read on in this huge poem is the constant liveliness of the language – 'toes first'. If referents often seem to be left far behind,

nonetheless words have a pert strangeness of their own. Sometimes the
text is knowingly camp. It delights in secrecy, in withholding as it seems
to offer hints. Yet the effects which it produces are unique to our time,
and pioneering. They are 'Ashbery effects', seen nowhere to better,
stranger advantage than in the work of *Flow Chart* and *Hotel
Lautréamont.*

Readers who dislike such effects will find *Flow Chart* far too protracted.
Yet it has to be said that the scope of this work undeniably contributes to
its power. It is a wrap-round poem, like a panoramic painting, or a wide-
screen cinematic experience which catches up its audience in its huge,
consuming rush, attempting to present 'the picture, so vast and ener-
getic/ It gets seen by nobody'. (*HL*, 135) In contemporary English-
language poetry on this side of the Atlantic we have few analogues. Our
modes are more conservative. We read Ashbery with fascination, but like
to keep at least one foot fully on the ground. At times, relishing the mock-
grandiosity which recurs in *Flow Chart*, I was reminded of reading some
passages in Frank Kuppner's *Ridiculous! Absurd! Disgusting!* As part of his
huge imaginative flights and self-metamorphoses, Kuppner attempts to
duck charges that may be levelled against his work. Ashbery too is con-
cerned to do this in *Flow Chart* where the 'I' acknowledges the way others
may view him. We are given an 'I' 'whose personal-pronoun lapses may
indeed have contributed to augmenting the hardship / silently resented
among the working classes', (*FC*, 150) and who may

> feel I have
> wandered too long in the halls of the nineteenth century: its exhibits,
> talismans, prejudices, erroneous procedures and doomed expeditions
>   are but too familiar
> to me; I must shade my eyes from the light with my hands, the light of
>   the explosion
> of the upcoming twentieth century.
>
> (*FC*, 151)

Ashbery's work does bear relation to the work of modern literary theory –
not least to the fascination with novelization, polyphony, dialogic iden-
tity, and life-as-change in Bakhtin. Yet Ashbery is simply far more enter-
taining to read than any literary theorist. His verbal rococo is so full of
invention, his climate so spectacular in its shifts, that he is likely to be seen
as the defining voice of his nation at this time. His post-Tennysonian
palace of art, his Shalotts, his Paterian and Wildean fascination with the
self, its construction, and with artifice, exemplify nowhere more clearly
than in *Flow Chart* the way in which he has created out of a dialogue with
the nineteenth century an immediately identifiable voice of 'Not quite late

twentieth-century panic' (*FC*, 173) that is full of 'respect for the junk we call living/ that keeps passing by'. (*FC*, 213) As in the work of many of the painters about whom Ashbery has written in *Reported Sightings*, system and flux are in strained but creative relationship. The poem ends by plunging into our century's man-made weather – the endlessly shifting movements of traffic. It avoids closure, leaves by a Bakhtinian loophole. Its last lines read

> By evening the traffic has begun
> again in earnest, color-coded. It's open: the bridge, that way.

In this 'end', having charted the sensation of the way we often live now (but seldom acknowledge doing so, preferring earlier models), Ashbery directs his poem back towards the eventually submerging flow, the constant making-new of America in which his identity is found and lost. That identity, even when (as he often does) Ashbery writes of rural America, is one moulded by and articulated through urban perceptions – rapidly shifting, juxtaposed, improvisatory as the New York traffic. His art is 'The Art of Speeding', (*HL*, 42) written out of and about a culture where identity is an identity crisis, though one that can often be relished. His work shows that postmodernism may have its own identifying poets.

6

Frank Kuppner's
Dynastic Songs

Frank Kuppner and John Ashbery share more than a British publisher for their poetry. They have in common a postmodern concern with the wry presentation of life as a confused flux of 'crazy weather'. Indeed two of Ashbery's favourite metaphors for this – clouds and traffic – are also prominent in Kuppner's prose book *A Concussed History of Scotland* (hereafter *CH*), published by Polygon in 1990. Kuppner's works tend less to progress than to drift, and the 'I' of *A Concussed History* wonders in Chapter 290 'why should a brain not come into existence much as it degenerates – much like clouds, in fact?' Behind Kuppner, as behind Ashbery, lies French avant-garde writing, though in the case of Kuppner's recent work the most prominent model is a nineteenth rather than twentieth-century one – the Comte de Lautréamont (1846–70) whose shape-changing and monstrous *Chants de Maldoror* are recognized as a potent precursor of surrealism and who as obscure, oft-flitting hotel resident is the presiding spirit of Ashbery's 1992 collection *Hotel Lautréamont*. But where the ground-bass of Lautréamont would seem to be horror, in Kuppner's work the enormity of the universe is met with a constantly bemused sense of humour. Kuppner, like Ashbery, is a writer preoccupied with the urban sensibility and with the instability of the self. Beside Ashbery's dissolving of the 'I' we might set Kuppner's 'I, or whoever this person is who so more than intermittently occupies the space where I am' as Chapter 285 of *A Concussed History* puts it. Where Ashbery admires *The Diary of a Nobody*, Kuppner writes 'The Autobiography of a Non-Existent Person'. Like W. S. Graham and Ashbery, Kuppner is fascinated by the teasing possibility of contact between writer and reader which occurs through the probably illusory 'textual self'. If Ashbery is a bookish poet who is nonetheless alert to the demotic, enjoying mixing up literary and slangy registers, street-talk and the finely exotic, then a delight in such sometimes gangling polyphonies is there in Kuppner's writing also. These writers are experimental, prepared to take risks, including the risk of monotony. Their experimentalism is not, however, po-faced; it is accompanied by a sense of humour which, particularly in Kuppner's case, is insistent.

In linking Kuppner to Ashbery I am not suggesting that Kuppner is imitating the latter's work. Differences between the oeuvres of the Glaswegian and the New York poet are as striking as similarities. Yet Ashbery and Kuppner are alike not simply because they are an older and a younger contemporary. For readers of the work of each there is the interest in how the postmodern writer, fascinated by flux, instability and the deconstruction of identity, may nonetheless function as an 'identifying poet' who articulates something of the identity of his own particular culture. Indeed, in Kuppner's writing this concern has come to the fore increasingly as he confronts the absurdity and fact that in a universe which has such vast temporal and spatial dimensions, and which has such amazing evolutionary mechanisms, it should matter that there is such an entity as Scotland.

It is one of the virtues of Kuppner's work that it does not conform to the ready stereotypes of 'Scottishness' or 'Glasgow literature'. This means that his writing may have something useful to offer to people who are uneasy about those stereotypes. It may also mean that his work receives less critical attention than that of other Scottish writers. Nevertheless, I wish to suggest that in approaching Kuppner's writings to date there are some Scottish connections which it is worth bearing in mind, and that Kuppner's work has shown some interest in the question of how one may be at once a writer who identifies at least part of his multiple self with a particular territory, at the same time as being a postmodern artist deeply sceptical of notions of fixed identity and over-simple affiliation. Shy, witty, cosmopolitan, Kuppner is also a constructor of a postmodern identity for a country which may be more concussed than most in an era when unstable identity is the norm.

It was in the second half of the 1980s Frank Kuppner became unignorable. The five books he published between 1984 and 1990 established him as the leading younger poet of the Eighties Scottish literary avant-garde. There was a time when the use of that last phrase might have raised eyebrows, but few would deny now that if there is a strong line of aesthetically conservative modern Scottish poets which includes Muir, Mackay Brown, MacCaig and Dunn, then there is also a Scottish line which links such radically experimental poets as John Davidson, MacDiarmid, W. S. Graham, Ian Hamilton Finlay, and Edwin Morgan. In considering modern Scottish poetry it is not necessary or even desirable to choose between various dynasties, but they do have their uses. If we reel in the experimental line a little further, we find Frank Kuppner on the end of it.

A Scottish poet who appears to have learned from the New York School and from Language writing, but who is in thrall to neither, Kuppner can be directly emotional as well as postmodern. He is independent rather than modish. He's quite prepared, for example, to give the thumbs down (in the pages of the May 1988 *Edinburgh Review*) to the work of the widely-admired Polish exile poet Adam Zagajewski. Though an experimental poet in English, Kuppner appears wary of experiment in Scots. At its weakest, his work risks the charge of being clever-clever, but as a critic he is suspicious of the pretentious. Kuppner's awkwardness makes him valuable. Writing about his work is complicated by the fact that much of it remains unpublished. His early plays are still in manuscript; he is a young, prolific writer. His published books, the subject of this chapter, are probably Early Mid-Kuppner. They establish him as a writer of singular achievement.

Kuppner is a native Glaswegian, born in 1951. His father came to Britain in 1945 with the Polish army; his mother is Scottish. He grew up in Glasgow's West End and continues to live there. Having studied English and German for a time at the University of Glasgow, he left without taking a degree. Later he qualified as an Electronics Engineer, 'although', as the blurb of his 1989 Carcanet collection *Ridiculous! Absurd! Disgusting!* (hereafter *RAD*) puts it, 'he has never practised'. In the early 1980s he described himself as 'semi-unemployed', typed theses, did theatre reviews, and was all too familiar with the DHSS. Glasgow boasts Europe's largest municipal library, the Mitchell Library, and Kuppner is surely, like a number of other distinguished writers, a product in part at least of the city's democratic book-culture. His writing reflects vast amounts of time spent in various Glasgow libraries reading material that ranges from Hume's letters to current literary periodicals, from guidebooks to Islamic theology.

Kuppner writes poems that deal ostensibly with regions he has visited only in the pages of books – China, Czechoslovakia and the whole of time and space – as well as with the more local concerns of Kelvinbridge and West Princes Street. Juxtaposition of the cosmic, the supposedly Immensely Significant, with the apparently trivial but essentially human details of mundanity is a hallmark of Kuppner's writing. He is fascinated by our mistaken notions of what really matters, and by our grand theories about matter itself. He is also obsessed with a form of bilocation, with being at once an outsider and an insider in whatever society he is dealing with. One suspects that this relates to his own background. He jokes about his name being Scottish, but also part-Polish, part-German. 'I suppose my family background is a sort of European stereo .... It's harder to delude yourself that you are at the absolute sole centre of the universe when you are actually in two places at once'.[1] Being in two places at once is a major theme of Kuppner's writing. His first book, *A Bad Day for the Sung Dynasty* (Carcanet, 1984), consists of 511 quatrains whose form, he tells us on the back cover, is taken 'from the common usage of translators of Chinese poetry'. Kuppner was drawn to writing the poems after looking intently at Oswald Siren's *Chinese Painting: Leading Masters and Principles*. Reading the sequence, we are both inside and outside the world of Chinese culture.

> 24.
> Enchanted by the artistry of the ch'in player,
> The sombreroed fisherman lets his craft drift nearer;
> One of the two listeners has raised his right hand;
> The man seated in the river may also be listening.

Here as often Kuppner catches an intriguing sense of stillness, and of mysterious small gestures that approach a stereotypical 'inscrutability'. The 'ch'in', the drifting boat, the attentive listeners – all these bring us close to the world of Chinese poetry. Yet at the same time we're distanced by the incongruous verb, 'sombreroed', and by the temptation to snigger at some odd alien action (why is the man 'seated in the river'?). In this book, written before Christopher Reid's *Katerina Brac*, along with the apparently 'authentic' Chinese features, seems to go a relishing of translatorese. One might wait for hundreds of years before hearing in ordinary English the words 'Enchanted by the artistry of the ch'in player', or that odd combination of the demotic 'a bad day' and the remotely exalted 'the Sung Dynasty' which makes up this book's title. Kuppner's manipulations of translatorese at once lead us up the petalled paths of classical Chinese culture, and remind us that we are far outside it. In this big sequence of poems Kuppner (as elsewhere) is interested in the apparently endless yet finite; the Sung Dynasty was strong, yet it is distant now in both space and time. Translatorese lets him be comic and delicately wistful simultaneously, robs us of the sense of a precise location of the writer's 'voice'. In diction and subject-matter, cultural juxtapositions run throughout the poems, along with the connecting of the little to the large and the questioning of which is which.

> 38.
> If Newton at this moment is dying in a distant bed,
> And a light is now shining through the entire world,
> What does he care, that planter of chrysanthemums,
> Uttering his own sighs, not final sighs.

China and the West, life and death, a revolutionary theory of optics and an act of gardening are here brought together, and the relative status of each is made teasingly uncertain. The status of the 'I' of these poems is also uncertain. Sometimes the 'I' seems clearly Frank Kuppner in the library, (11) at other times the 'I' appears to have moved into the pages of the books being examined, (44) and for considerable stretches the 'I' disappears entirely. Yet its appearances are sufficiently frequent and intrusive to keep us aware of the comically vast disjunctions between insider and outsider, between the native 'real' world and the alien art world. These disjunctions are made plain through the artfully honest daftness by which the two are linked.

10.

Looking stunningly like that mad geography teacher of mine of twenty
    years ago
One of the fishermen, with ease, resettles his creel;
The other, chatting volubly, reaches an arm deep into his basket;
Feeling a hand grip his own, he hesitates.

Here writer and reader are insider-outsiders caught between the world of Chinese fishermen and that of Kuppner's schoolteacher (and, perhaps, of James Kelman's Glasgwegian short story, 'The Hon').[2] Kuppner's idea of an artificial China is not new. One of his Glasgow mentors, Alasdair Gray, had developed an idea from Kafka to striking effect in the 'Five Letters from an Eastern Empire' in Gray's *Unlikely Stories, Mostly* (1983). There are similarities between a few of Kuppner's poems in *A Bad Day* and the Gray story. The notion of translatorese is scarcely alien to the multilingual Scottish imagination, the imagination of James Macpherson's Ossian, of Scott's 'Gaelic' speakers, Carlyle's *Sartor Resartus*, MacDiarmid's synthetic languages, and Edwin Morgan's linguistic crossovers. Kuppner's work makes sense in a Scottish context, while relating to contemporary French and American preoccupations with the materiality of language. Yet none of this takes away from the more than merely comic surprise of *A Bad Day for the Sung Dynasty*. If one were to ask the simple, valid question 'What is this book about?' the answer would have to be that in a sense it is identifiably about Chinese customs; but it is also about pseudo-customs, misinterpretations, jokes, the misunderstandings which will arise in any attempt at understanding another culture, another person, another text. Kuppner's subject matter and his style are bonded. The stylistic waywardness is a crucial part of the point: all acts of interpretation are acts of waywardness, of fantastic, sometimes absurd border-crossing. This interest in interpreting other texts, times, cultures is something Kuppner shares with Edwin Morgan, with many Scottish writers, and with his friend the Glasgow-based English novelist Charles Palliser, author of

The Quincunx (Edinburgh: Canongate, 1989). But, unlike Palliser and Morgan, Kuppner seems to have little interest in conventional narrative. This gives his writing a sometimes zany excitement, and an obsessive fluidity that over-rides storytelling. To some readers, this lack of interest in narrative will be rebarbative, to others liberating. Yet Kuppner does tell a multitude of short stories in his first and his later books; he loves anecdotes and speculations; narrative-interest may be kaleidoscopic in his work, rather than simply absent.

Kuppner's first book announces several of the obsessions of his later work. Both the real China and his constructed China fascinate him because, to put it simply, 'China is such a vast country'. (400) This sense of vastness, of lyrical desolation and tiny life-signs, vital choices made within it, often draws from Kuppner poems which seem almost (but not quite) entirely unironic, as in quatrain 398 where the hugeness of geography and history counterpoints a tiny decision.

> A flawless abandoned road snakes its way among the mountains,
> The legacy of some other forgotten campaign;
> Occasionally a panda wanders across it,
> Looks to the left, to the right, and strolls across it.

What introduces irony here is the slight suggestion that the panda is following the pedestrian highway code – it becomes for an instant like Frank Kuppner crossing a Glasgow street. Kuppner takes well-known Chinese motifs and does not make fun of them but has fun with them, as when (without mentioning it directly) he plays variations on the story of the Taoist sage Chuang Tsu who dreamed he was a butterfly, then wondered if he was a butterfly dreaming he was Chuang Tsu. (419–24) Kuppner delights in anachronisms, often with a Scottish flavour. One might set Iain Crichton Smith's 'Chinese Poem' to Seumas Macdonald beside Kuppner's poem 326:

> All over the river valley they have met in houses
> To discuss the latest reports from the capital:
> How can there possibly be a MacPherson Dynasty?
> No troubled times could be as troubled as that.

Throughout the whole sequence, with its typically Scottish cross-cultural humour and concern with literary and cultural continuity (the dynastic song), there is a sense of a powerful formal imagination at work. Kuppner's fun comes both from alien cultural conventions and from the conventions of verse.

The obsessive repetition of the four-line verse unit throughout the book, the thematic near-repetitions and slight variations signal that this work is the contemporary of Eighties minimalist music (in his *Intimate Voices* Kuppner's fellow Glasgow poet Tom Leonard has a jokey poem on minimalism in the arts). If some audiences find that Kuppner's music is monotonous, that there is an attention-problem in reading him, then this is a problem his work shares with the music of his minimalist contemporaries. Yet that music has found a large audience of its own; in its defence, and in Kuppner's, it might be pointed out that minimalism is far less interested in repetition than in variation; what seems at first sight monotony turns out to be pluralism. Edwin Morgan's book-title, *Themes on a Variation*, suggests the celebration of the ability to discover whole new areas of difference in the slightest change; such a gleeful interest in the possibilities of modulation is apparent in Kuppner's writing.

Though many of them seem unrelated observations, some series of the *Sung* poems, such as 145–9, share a common first two lines, each closing couplet developing the poem in a different direction. This sense of allowing the work to develop in a variety of alternative ways, of taking the road not taken, recurs. Kuppner alerts us to writing as a constant business of making choices, and he rejoices in a creative indecision which (like his name and heritage) allows him to be in two places at once. He loves a pluralism of alternatives, as we see not only in the formal patterns of his first book, but also in his work of the later Eighties. Identity becomes plural, but also a bit 'concussed'. A typical technique is to offer the reader an apparently impossible option such as 'Pterophryne, that peculiar fish which I do not guarantee that I have not just not invented, or the opposite ...'. (*RAD*, 183) Where the structuralists offered us binary oppositions as essential to literary composition, Kuppner the electronic engineer makes us aware in his 'Eclipsing Binaries' that the signal can always be rerouted in an alternative direction. In an age when it is fashionable for poems to resist closure, Kuppner's do this in the most marked of ways.

3.

<u>What is this net that holds us in place so insecurely?</u>
We are not fishes, are we? Were we ever?

<u>Might it not prove possible to slip through it entirely?</u>
I believe the fishes in general once did something like that.

Perhaps this <u>room</u> is still in <u>the water</u> anyway.
      arm   ·   this room

<u>Why is it we are not drowning</u> in this invisible sea?
What is it we have sighted
         (from *Verse*, Vol. 6, No. 2, June 1989, 52)

Making us preternaturally aware of what the writer does and chooses, of the materiality and plasticity of language, Kuppner likes to make fun of these with a poststructural or deconstructionist ludic bounce:

> This was a curiously reassuring feeling to have,
> Although I forget it now. (In fact, on reflection,

> 3 I think I would replace the word 'reassuring'
> With the word 'conditional', and the word 'curiously'
> With the sentence, 'I hope I may be allowed to say so
> Without being accused of bathos'. Although, for 'bathos',

> 4 I suspect the phrase: 'without wild accusations
> Of political opportunism being levelled at me'
> Would equally well fit the bill. And of course
> The word 'absence' has been left out as usual.)

>   (*RAD*, 121)

That last joke might appeal to readers of Derrida, but it might equally appeal to readers of the Alasdair Gray who inserted in the first edition of *Unlikely Stories, Mostly* a small 'slip' which read

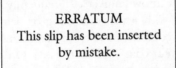

It was the formally impish Gray who designed the slant-eyed 'Sung Mona Lisa' which is the striking cover picture on *A Bad Day for the Sung Dynasty*. A sense of formal impishness certainly connects Kuppner with other late twentieth-century Scottish poets, from W. S. Graham and Ian Hamilton Finlay to the writers of his own city, such as Gray, Leonard, and Morgan.

In the very relevant context of Glasgow writing, Edwin Morgan is surely one of Kuppner's major poetic predecessors. Morgan's own interest in formal play and in the materiality of language manifests itself in such works as his sequence of 'Unfinished Poems' (dedicated to the Veronica Forrest-Thomson whose work Jerome McGann in 'Postmodern Poetries' (*Verse*, Spring 1990) has linked to that of the Language poets), in his concern with randomness and typographical slips ('A Jar Revisited'), and his own explorations of translation, a powerful motivating factor in his work. Such preoccupations surface in Kuppner's own interest in the incomplete (*A Bad Day*, quatrain 299), or hard-to-decipher, seen most clearly in his liking for faded inscriptions, for a text supposedly 'From a Moth-eaten Ethnographical Manuscript',[3] or for the half-scrutable:

244.
Stolidly he ponders the old text in front of him;
Delight something buttocks pliant something;
Sunburst something buttocks something balcony;
He frowns at the girl noisily pouring out wine.

Like Morgan, Kuppner loves jokes; like Morgan he has a playful formal
imagination; like Morgan again, his jokes lead somewhere, often into the
alien and strange. In Kuppner's case the jokes often move towards
thoughts on evolution, both verbal and universal. As Bakhtin suggests one
should, Kuppner voyages receptively into another culture without re-
nouncing his own. The resultant dialogue alerts us to all sorts of incon-
gruities and anachronisms. This is less a drunken voyage than a tipsy one
which covers huge distances. The other 'cultures' which Kuppner's 'I'
explores include not only human but biological and cosmic ones also. The
whole of the known universe confronts, dwarfs and comically defines the
human self or selves who remain (to themselves at least) important,
though they are also aware of the oddity and potential bathos of that self-
importance.

It is unsurprising that one of Kuppner's favourite childhood books was
about the nature of the known universe.[4] Frequently he is interested in the
apparent randomness with which one thing or being survives while an-
other does not: '"Of course we wanted a daughter," / I insisted to her.
"Of course we wanted you."' (*RAD*, 133) On the level of words,
Kuppner is interested in his own poems' linguistic evolution. Hence those
choices proferred in the draft-like yet complete 'Eclipsing Binaries' and
elsewhere. Language can suggest both a thing and its opposite almost
simultaneously, though one tends to think of a fine poem as the survival of
the fittest words. Author of 'The Opposite of Dreaming', Kuppner likes
to play with such ideas, teasing them out and teasing us with them. In
passing, it is worth indicating that this links him not just with other
Glasgow writers, but also with the avant-garde on a much wider scale.
Edwin Morgan's work has been related tentatively to that of the Lan-
guage writers, and he has shown a marked interest in them and their
forerunners, lecturing on Language writing at the universities of Liver-
pool and St Andrews in late 1989.[5] Beside a Kuppner text like 'Eclipsing
Binaries' one might place a quotation such as this from the Language
writer Michael Palmer's 'Notes for Echo Lake 1':

That is, snow

    a) is
    b) is not

        falling — check neither or both.[6]

or from 'Notes for Echo Lake 2' the sentence 'We have never been happy here have never been happier'. (12) This is not to say that Kuppner has read Palmer or is a mere slightly-belated Scottish imitator of the Language writers. He is not. But it is to suggest wider contexts in which his writing may be placed, with its concern with language and the way language constructs and distorts a world, and with its fascination with juxtaposed registers, its teasing.

That teasing, though, gives Kuppner's work a much more human face than is seen in most Language writing, and his second book also reminds us that his work isn't simply knowingly postmodern, but is also quite directly emotional. *The Intelligent Observation of Naked Women* (Carcanet, 1987) offers us five poems, again predominantly made up of four-line units. The expansiveness of China is replaced by the hugenesses of astrophysics, the subjects of the poems range from Glasgow tenements and the cityscape to love, to Prague. Yet the writer's obsessions are developed from his first book. The narrative voice is still frequently presented by various strategies as that of an insider-outsider, a 'semi-stranger' (14) often regarding his subject-matter through the medium of a book about it. In one way 'An Old Guide-Book to Prague' does for photographs of pre-war Prague what Kuppner's first book had done for Siren's Chinese paintings. We are again faced with the problem of inter-pretation, of the 'scarcely knowable', but the subject here is not Chinese inscrutability, but a society at once vividly present in its daily routines, and irreplaceably removed by history ('Surely the absence of the Second World War / Ought to be more apparent in the quality of the light' – 20). Again we're in a library ('The old man slumped asleep nearby at the library table, / With *One Hundred Years of Scottish Football* cradled against his lifting chest' – 20) and in a book within a book. The 'I' changes from distant reader to involved participant and back again, from insider to outsider. Odd locutions are employed to highlight the distanc-ing of observer from observed ('Three women exist variously' – 20) and the lovingly, fascinatedly-detailed part-imagined events of routine life ('Why, she wonders, should anybody want to take a picture of this?' – 20) are presented with a sense of the unseen menace of a history which will obliterate them – 'At this moment, in the neighbouring country, Hitler begins to play with his penis'. (33) Kuppner's imagination often gravitates towards the threat of engulfing catastrophe. He is distant in this Prague poem, yet involved: 'Some of my German relatives must be here or hereabouts'. (34) There is that interest also in calm, tranquillity. If the photographer in this work is described sometimes as a 'philosopher', then he recalls the still hermits of *A Bad Day for the Sung Dynasty*. But this is a markedly urban poem, intent on what buildings hide and reveal. Secrecy

and revelation, what's glimpsed, misinterpreted or obscured, fascinated
Kuppner in his China where each of the four-line poems was like a little
unfamiliar room into which, for a moment, we could glance. The photo-
graphs of Prague afford this pleasure also in a manner that is now explicitly
urban. Kuppner's postmodern consciousness involves a relishing aware-
ness that it is 'Somehow surprising that ordinary real lives should go on /
In what seem such extravagantly picturesque surroundings, / Like living
on a set for *Fidelio*'. (27) Yet this impression of ephemeral routine life as
oddly potent art is balanced with a cruder pull of minutely accurate
curiosity and imagination:

43.
There are only two open windows in the whole building.
Who opened that window second from the left on the middle floor?
Who opened that window at the far right on the top floor?
Why am I sure they are sitting beside each other?

Such a sense of trying to peer through the walls into the past, and into
other people's lives is linked to Kuppner's interest in jokey, off-porno-
graphic voyeurism. That can be bonded to horror as in 'A Real
Drumchapel Pastoral',[7] where the incongruous antique pastoral style dis-
tances us, like translatorese, from a hypnotically horrible murder; but a
closely-related voyeuristic impulse can be comically deployed as in the
many glimpses of strange sex in *A Bad Day*. It's as if Kuppner has his eye
at many keyholes in a large building; many of his works convey a sense of
living in close proximity to a lot of people into whose lives we only
occasionally glimpse. Kuppner's art manifests an awareness of being part
of a co-operative community where privacies can embarrassingly, hu-
manly, amusingly lapse. A tenement dweller, he shows in what he writes a
tenemental imagination.

This tenemental imagination is present in the structuring of Kuppner's
texts. He has a fondness for large structures built out of fairly small
repeated units. Like the rooms in a tenement, some of these units
(whether the quatrains of *A Bad Day* or the chapters of *A Concussed
History*) lead into one another, while others seem at first sight discrete,
though they may have some structural relationship to the other parts.
Constantly in Kuppner's writing we are made aware of activity in a room
above or below the one in which the writer is located, or else we are made
aware of a gaze from one room into another. These small, even petty local
interactions may be dwarfed by the size of the overall structure (whether
of the poem or the universe), yet they are seen as important within it. It is
their smallness which makes them treasured and significant. Kuppner likes
to drop a placename – Kilmarnock or Vienna – into his free-ranging text.

The result is sometimes bathetic, the place seems insignificant in the face of the surrounding cosmic flux, yet the placename is also treasured as a tiny, somewhat unstable anchor in the vast, unintelligible scheme of things. The possibility of treasuring a local identity in the face of an inconceivably huge expanding universe may be absurd, but it is absurdly human and therefore valuable. Kuppner's fascination with the solar system and beyond does not contradict his fascination with tenement rooms.

In *The Intelligent Observation of Naked Women* the tenemental imagination is explicitly to the fore in 'Passing Through Doorways', a beautiful account of visits to various Glasgow tenements with which the speaker has or has had connections. There's a fascination again with the ordinary, with 'How such a banal building could contain her', (13) with both beloved intimacy and exclusion. We're less aware here of language as a distancing medium, and more conscious of Kuppner's lyricism and whimsy which teeteringly skirt the banal and the sentimental.

> xii
> Now, I am fascinated by such, as it were, pauses in life,
> As being closer to what life normally is
> Than the supreme events which documents tend to fill up with,
> As if only spectacular oceans are deep.

Here, democratically, little and large are brought together once more to assert the dignity of the little. This process takes place strikingly in the title poem of *The Intelligent Observation of Naked Women* where personal experience is set beside the unknown bounds of the physical universe, and where we perceive what John Ash has written of in New York's *Village Voice Literary Supplement* as Kuppner's unusual sensitivity to 'the way a city's inhabitants relate to its architecture and public spaces' (quoted in the blurb on the back of *A Very Quiet Street*). The Kuppner who imagines a spacecraft passing his room becomes for a moment a whimsical Edwin Morgan, but maintains surely his own quirky idiom in speaking again of the limits of privacy and insight.

> xxxix
> Nearness is nearness only up to a point;
> Although better by far she should be in the same room
> Than lost unspoken elsewhere in this city,
> It is still a private cosmos whose foot I touched.

Kuppner's preoccupations ('How near to us other, unknown people were' – 98) continue to be prominent throughout this book. He has flirted with what he called in the *Verse* interview the idea that 'intellectual extremism' and being 'unrelenting in pursuit of a line of thought' are strong in the tradition of Scottish writing, whether in Hume or MacDiarmid. For some readers, Kuppner's work proves too obsessively repetitive, tries too hard to show off.

Kuppner so often mocks his own ego that one wonders sometimes if his modesty has some falseness in it. His literary techniques involve both secrecy and self-protection, but also perhaps a sort of jokey ego-guarding. He reviewed his own 'novel, of sorts', *A Very Quiet Street* (Edinburgh: Polygon, 1989) for the *Glasgow Herald*, saying he would be a fool not to recommend it. When invited to be interviewed for *Verse*, he conducted the interview himself. It should be said that the result was extremely useful, funny and revealing, but one wonders about what it may occlude. Kuppner's supposed interviewer was 'AM' – no doubt a relative of the Biblical 'I AM', and of the Kuppner-voiced divine being who narrates 'Lost Work', the first piece in the tripartite knock-out mixture of poetry and prose that is *Ridiculous! Absurd! Disgusting!* This being has again Kuppner's tenemental imagination: 'At night I slipped through their houses (transparent to me)'. (*RAD*, 12) Kuppner's not-so-celestial speaker also shares his Glaswegian maker's interest in the mundane and secret. His thought that 'it remains true no less that other people are books written in language which you sometimes mistake for your own' (*RAD*, 17) gestures back to the translatorese of *A Bad Day for the Sung Dynasty*. But with its slips from first person to third, its jokes against ideas of order, space and time, this prose 'Lost Work' is also a stunning fantasia on ideas of evolution, survival and the apparent biographical randomness of existence in a world where God is dead or (in this case) an apparently omniscient but forgetful Being who is about to snuff it. This divine narrator allows Kuppner to play with ideas of narratorial omniscience; Frank Kuppner is back in the library (*RAD*, 31) and back at his old language games: 'Or rather, to be more accurate, the opposite of all this'. (*RAD*, 20–1).

In a text which plays with register, presents meditations on old photographs of Glasgow University's demolished buildings, and which ponders repeatedly on tiny, lost yet preserved moments of apparent aimlessness, we return to other familiar Kuppner themes. The exploration of them, however, is more arresting than ever. We are presented with a view of the universe and all its productions as clearly material when Kuppner offers us his hilarious description of two well-wined-and-dined turds discussing Poetry. People in this work are meat, are turds, are words. As Peter Reading does, though in his own idiosyncratic manner, Kuppner investigates *ad absurdum* not just the materiality of language, but the materiality of all creation. Dead, or undead, the narrator talks 'in a non-existent voice, of unimportant, incoherent things'. (*RAD*, 70) If the presentation of the term 'L=A=N=G=U=A=G=E' is designed to suggest that all signs have equivalent (=) value, then Kuppner confronts with frightful comedy the idea that all value is a precarious construct foisted on the material universe by some of the material in it – us. His metamorphic musings recall at times (*RAD*, 71) the MacDiarmid of 'On A Raised Beach' or of the encyclopedic late poems, but Kuppner has an enjoyment of the fantastic and ludic which MacDiarmid generally eschewed. It's as if the late, information-processing MacDiarmid is being endlessly tickled with a feather.

The comic vastness of space with its unbelievable curios and huge numbers has replaced China. Repeated glimpses into rooms of the past, present and future state and restate the metamorphic power of Kuppner's imagination. Other writers – Lautréamont, MacDiarmid, Gray, Morgan – are converted into Kuppner's science fantasies. Ego jokes ('statues of Shakespeare, Tang Yin, and myself' – *RAD*, 31) recur throughout works where the self dissolves and reforms as frequently as it does in the poems of Ashbery. Kuppner in *Ridiculous! Absurd! Disgusting!* remains the insider-outsider involved with and distant from his subject-matter whose clutter is now the clutter of all the matter that is, has been, will be.

Structurally, Kuppner's pieces seem all tangents, and he writes in the *Verse* interview that if you refuse to be sidetracked 'you will never be a poet'. Alerting us to the constructed, arbitrary nature of texts, he likes to make his works appear endlessly digressive. But there are in them recurring pre-occupations, some of which have been outlined above. As Kuppner's career develops, a question for his readers has to be whether or not his pieces repeat themselves too much, whether or not technical devices become handy, over-used mannerisms. Kuppner's liking for absurdly long numbers, for instance, is probably over-indulged in *Ridiculous! Absurd! Disgusting!*. 'Let us say, for 14,963 years – that way it will sound more convincing' (*RAD*, 143) is well nigh a repetition of a joke already made on p. 34, and one could catalogue other examples of Kuppner's over-recycling of material which has stood him in good stead previously. His trick of going back over a previous sentence and pointing out various alternative word choices (or slips of the pen he almost made) comes up rather too often. His reviews of scientific books in the *Glasgow Herald* have sometimes a samey feeling to them. Kuppner needs to avoid repeating his earlier successes. Yet one is prepared to forgive a good deal in a writer for whom 'the niggling old question reasserts itself: am I or am I not the President of Finland?'. (*RAD*, 147)

A Very Quiet Street has at its centre issues of secrecy and revelation again, but one also senses in it a certain moral passion, an investigative sense of justice that is present, sometimes fleetingly, in the poetry. The

book is 'about' one of the most famous Scottish murder cases – the Oscar
Slater trial. This trial resulted in the wrongful conviction of Oscar Slater
for the murder of a Glasgow lady. Evidence seems to have been rigged,
mistakes covered up, the real murderer was never found. Kuppner levels
incisive criticisms against the Scottish legal system; like language, it seems
a system bound up with misinterpretation. *A Very Quiet Street* is linked to
The Quincunx (some of which Kuppner read in typescript) as an urban
novel preoccupied with law and with how we interpret the past, how we
recreate it. But since Kuppner grew up close to the scene of this early-
twentieth-century crime, his book is also about its author's childhood. He
mixes and remixes reminiscences of his own early years in the tenements
of West Princes Street, Glasgow with his investigations into the
falsifications and obscurities of the Slater trial. These investigations are
conducted by Kuppner in the Mitchell Library where he pores over books
about the case and other accounts of the proceedings.

There are many links with Kuppner's poetry. Again he is an outsider-
insider: the crime took place before he was born, yet he knows its location
and details intimately. The apparent ordinariness of this 'very quiet street',
an ordinariness to which various witnesses testify, grips Kuppner; and it
was in the midst of this that the large, catastrophic act of murder erupted.
Like *A Bad Day*, this is another book about inscrutability and interpreta-
tion, about the investigation of secrets. In his novel's fifty-eight prose
sections, Kuppner opens and reopens the same tenement doors, speculates
on documents, goes over and over the evidence as if it were an alien text
which he is trying to decode or interpret. The murder is seen as a random
act that governs who survived, who was jailed, who went undiscovered,
and the text confronts us again with a writing that is also a reading, a way
of bringing into communion Kuppner and his audience in the act of
investigation ('On the reading that I adhere to, the murder was acciden-
tal' – 24). Pieces of evidence that are innocent in themselves come to bear
the signs of guilt. The word 'murderer', like a floating signifier, hovers
over various persons; the killer seems, like the referent of a
deconstructionist's sign, to be endlessly elusive. The 'outside world' and
the world of the text become, however, enmeshed ('the killer may have
visited the library ... to consult the transcript of the trial ...' – 280). Vivid
recollections of his own childhood along with the moral fervour of the
detective story seem to ground the text in the actual at the same time as
Kuppner is sucked into an expanding textscape of reported claims and
counter-claims, hidden signs, old telephone directories and imagined
secret movements all of which, like a good policeman or translator, he
tries to interpret, battling against other, corrupt policemen and phoney
translators of the evidence, against the resistance of the texts he confronts.

Text is sieved through text; tangents and unstable hypotheses abound, and Kuppner's own personal associations are unsuppressed. This produces a writing ridden with brackets – a typesetter's nightmare in which parenthesis interrupts parenthesis so that sometimes at the end of a sentence we realise from the number of brackets just how enmeshed we have become: '(I suppose this is more probably Miss Burrell than A.B.)))))'. (105) Some readers will be annoyed by this 'deep text' technique, but it is not a gratuitous mannerism. For *A Very Quiet Street* is another Kuppner text about secrecy, and the author-detective is trying to prove what is hidden, what is bracketed within brackets within brackets. We're aware of the shiftiness of evidence and signs, and the fallibility of a narrator unable to be omniscient: '(G. being an abbreviation for either Glasgow or Gilchrist, I forget which)'. (107) This awareness of possible alternatives between signs is familiar to the reader of Kuppner's verse, as is Kuppner's alertness to the accidental, to slips of the pen, vagaries of the author – 'It was a long wait. (The manuscript here, by the way, reads 'a long weight')'. (119) Kuppner the poet has a daftly pedantic wit. The blurb writer for *Ridiculous! Absurd! Disgusting!* is acute in quoting as indicative of the flavour of Kuppner's work the opening of part VIII of 'The Autobiography of a Non-Existent Person':

> It was morning. I was standing by the window
> admiring the charming combination of
>
> passers-by and absences of passers-by
> on the street far below – more accurately
> a small square – even more accurately
>
> an irregular heptagon.
>
> (*RAD*, 154)

This concern for accuracy is seen in *A Very Quiet Street* but affects us there differently because it goes along with a sense of urgency and of dealing with persons who did and in some cases still do exist. In attempting to investigate and solve the murder, the author is like a translator who is constantly being faced with barely-decipherable or ambiguous signs: 'Managing to locate my Street Atlas of Glasgow, I discover that there are *two* Windsor Streets nowadays'. (126) But the reader who might be earnestly suspicious of Kuppner's more playful signage in his other works is likely to sense the admirable, dogged, obsessive fervour with which texts are interrogated in the novel. For Kuppner here (unlike some other postmoderns) there remains a stress on the importance of an approachable truth, though that truth may turn out to be surprising and elusive. Rifling through signs, aliases, clues, here he concludes, on one level at least, that the killer was probably 'A.B., alias Dr Frank Charteris, late of St. Andrew's (sic) University'. (132)

Tenementally-minded, Kuppner is extremely far-removed from the writers of the Kailyard, but he is throughout his works a linguistic experimenter *and* a writer interested (like so many of his Scottish predecessors) in the theme of community, its restrictions and its strengths. What intrigues him in *A Very Quiet Street* is what concerns him in much of the rest of his output – 'the mutual independence of contemporary lives'. (180) Law and language, both systems in which Kuppner is passionately interested in *A Very Quiet Street*, permit as well as regulate this 'mutual independence'. The last words of the book are worth pondering with regard to all that has gone before in Kuppner's published writing: 'I open the volume at random, genuinely at random, and point a blind finger into it. Clarence Street, Kingston. No. 38, the Scottish Co-operative Society. No, that won't do for the murderer, will it? Just above, at No. 50, "Burgess A." Perhaps him? Three steps above, at No. 108, "Gray, A." Can all these people be innocent? What do we know about these people?'

Here again we're brought up against uneasily floating signs. Could 'Burgess A.' and 'Gray A.' be meant to refer to Anthony Burgess and the Alasdair Gray whom Burgess admires? But this is impossible in the 1870 Post Office directory Kuppner is quoting from. Or has his imagination made it possible? How scrutable is this text Kuppner is dealing with, and how scrutable is the text he has produced for us? What do we know of all the people in the court cases or all of the texts about them? Kuppner's novel offers us a small model of the world and of philosophical problems about knowledge of the self and other persons. But it's also a joke book, a compulsive entertainment. The author takes leave of us with vertiginous humour. He departs from us as both literary joker and honest seeker for justice, at once a co-operative and an unco-operative Scottish writer. Kuppner is the most idiosyncratic of the younger Glasgow poets. His work, like Alasdair Gray's, carries its obsessions from poetry to prose and back again. *A Very Quiet Street*, the last of his four 1980s books, may form the most approachable introduction to the writing with which in that decade he has courageously maintained the open-ness of Scottish literature both to its own Carlylean, genre-busting traditions and to the experimentalism of the international avant-garde.

Yet Kuppner appears to have less affection for *A Very Quiet Street* than he has for his other works. Perhaps it is rather more conventional and explicit than much of his writing. Though it resists hard, eventually it can be dragooned into the brigade of 'Glasgow novels'. Kuppner is a writer who dislikes such pigeon-holing. So it may seem all the more strange to consider him as one of those 'identifying poets' who construct for themselves an identity which links them to a particular territory. I hope, however, that this chapter has demonstrated that in several of his literary affinities, in many of the details of his writing and in some of his central preoccupations, Kuppner is well worth viewing in a Scottish context, as a writer who is articulating an identity at once postmodern and Scottish. The complexity and potential of such an endeavour emerges only cumulatively in the reading of his work, but it may be clearest in the 1990 prose volume, *A Concussed History of Scotland*.

Subtitled with Kuppnerian jokiness 'A Novel of Another Sort', this work, like *Ridiculous! Absurd! Disgusting!*, is poised between poetry and prose. Perhaps it is best read as a series of often linked prose poems. Its division into 500 chapters provides a parody of exact structuring. As in the chapters of *A Very Quiet Street*, Kuppner doubles back in one chapter over the ground covered in another; he skims away into apparent irrelevance, the text becomes a palimpsest of second and third thoughts added to still visible first drafts. Unlike *A Very Quiet Street*, however, *A Concussed History of Scotland* lacks a clear narrative framework and subject-matter.

Or does it? The title encourages us to view this volume as a history book, and sure enough the volume opens with an arresting, comical and anxious postmodern creation myth; it ends with an uneasy open-endedness. The structure of the volume, then, mirrors what we know of history. But 'History' conventionally excludes most of what happens – sweeping away the bulk of the occurrences of the universe as belonging either to other areas of knowledge (cosmology, geology, astronomy, 'prehistory', etc.) or else belonging to the huge, unarticulated category of the 'unimportant'. The book's blurb prepares us for a confrontation with conventional notions of history: 'Kuppner poses questions which even the great historians have failed to note the relevance of. This is the history of people failing to be reunited with their luggage at the airport, of occasional sharp pains in the chest (which always seem to go away).'

Kuppner the sophisticate knows that in a world which is postmodern, deconstructed and overloaded with information as well as with cultural theories, the old epistemological categories are in flux; disciplines have become interdisciplines; there is no longer any simple, single, supposedly omniscient historical 'point of view'. Kuppner the often disarmingly honest tenement dweller knows also that from one point of view and point in time pains in the chest may be more important than the Middle Ages. 'History' in this book is seen from shifting and telescoped points of view. The man looking at his lover asleep is also aware of physical laws about the circulation of the blood and is a speaker saturated by his own memories and knowledge. Constantly the text delivers to us as readers a point of view or amalgam of points of view which we might call the 'trivial-cosmic':

Chapter 159

Both of our brains contained enormously subtle assemblages of thousands of millions of interconnected neurons. Neither of us knows what a neuron is, of course, although *I* think I do. Nor did we even, either of us, begin to grasp intuitively the immensity of time which was necessary before such things could contrive to develop from the witless entities which accidentally started replicating in the sea. Oh, ignoble fornicators! That such should be the ancestors of us, who can sit looking at each other's eyes for hours!

Chapter 160

Such anyway was pretty much what I said to her, leaving out a few hints and witticisms and mildly flirtatious exaggerations which may even have required her eyes. Although she at first favoured one with the sort of glance which one might well choose (for whatever reason) to bestow on the only mammal so far developed – as far as I know anything to the contrary – capable of throwing an English literary magazine out of the window of a moving train somewhere before Kilwinning, she eventually became restive. It will not surprise you to learn, however, that we have also developed techniques for dealing with such minor and transient emergencies.

This, then, is concussed history. The text has about it a MacDiarmidian penchant for bringing together the scientific, cosmological, evolutionary and personal, but (as in *Ridiculous! Absurd! Disgusting!*) it is as if MacDiarmid is being entertainingly transformed from a Langholm autodidact and cosmologue into a self-mocking, self-taught Glaswegian punter. Where drink in *A Drunk Man* permitted abrupt shifts and juxtapositions, concussion may 'explain' the liberties taken in Kuppner's text. Drink and concussion, though, are mere 'decoy-explanations'. *A Drunk Man* takes its form from modernism, *A Concussed History* takes its from postmodernism. The intellectual climate of two different eras lies behind the compositional method of these two Scottish works. Drink and concussion are merely hints extended to perhaps bemused readers. Apparently Kuppner had intended to call his book *A Concise History of Scotland*, but his publisher was worried that this would have confused or annoyed bookshops too much.[8]

The rejected title *A Concise History of Scotland* also stimulates useful reflections on the book. For this volume seems to suggest that to explain any one aspect of human existence (for example, the existence and state of Scotland) necessitates accounting for and recounting the entire previous evolutionary history of the universe, not to mention that of its putative Creator. 'Concision' in such circumstances is a joke, since to explain

Scotland or to recount its history produces a text that teeters on the brink of infinity, constantly hinting at unspoken and even unspeakable immensities beyond its mere 500 chapters. Again, the book's blurb is helpful, drawing attention to the book's spoof-MacDiarmidian question 'What? Scotland Small? Is it small *enough*?' If MacDiarmid (like the Morgan of *Sonnets from Scotland*) maintained that

> He canna Scotland see wha yet
> Canna see the Infinite
> And Scotland in true scale to it.[9]

then this is what, in our postmodern world, Kuppner does in his *Concussed History*. Infinity in its daft, apparently random immensities stretches away on all sides, yet Kilwinning persists. Scotland's literary totems, Burns, Stevenson, Carlyle and others crop up in Kuppner's *History*, but their words have become garbled, caught up in a crazy, often enjoyable postmodern *mélange*. So we read of 'the truth of Carlyle's apercu that to be fully human is to be obsessed by little tits'. (*CH*, 119) Other luminaries of Scottish history seem to have fallen victim to similar historical concussions: 'Might it not perhaps indeed by true, as I think John Knox so memorably put it, that they also serve the general purpose who only sit about in a relative's bedroom with the curtains drawn, fighting the temptation to masturbate?' (*CH*, 163)

Personal, literary, political and galactic history assemble and reassemble here – 'The past is a previous cloud formation'. (*CH*, 112) The text is irresponsible; it is, after all, a text produced by one of those '"poets", who are nothing if not the frilly panties of History'. (*CH*, 144) Yet as one reads through the book, it becomes apparent that there are certain enduring themes to it, including desire, identity, time and the pathetically misguided rage for order (in religion and in science and in historiography) which is both innate and constantly parodied throughout the neat sum of the book's 500 chapters.

Another of these themes, oblique, present most often in detail and aside, is the subject signalled most clearly by the book's title: Scotland. This is not the Scotland of travel-guides or conventional histories. It is more like the Scotland glimpsed while spinning a globe or, better still, while flicking through an atlas of the known universe. This Scotland may be as MacDiarmid put it, a 'flea' in relation to the cosmic Great Wheel; nonetheless, it persists in references throughout Kuppner's text, and Kuppner's title means that for the reader the book's explorations of the physical and personal universes take place against the background of 'Scotland'. So Scotland is both peripheral and central to this *History* which considers all sorts of apparently unrelated matters. Peripheral and central, absurdly random yet returned to, intimately inhabited yet a cosmic joke, the Scotland which Kuppner has articulated is very much a postmodern Scotland.

Such an achievement may not endear Kuppner to those whose Scotland is an essentialist Scotland, an unproblematic 'given'. It seems as unlikely that Kuppner will become a widely popular poet as it seems improbable that MacDiarmid's later work will achieve widespread popularity. Furthermore, it would be ridiculous to contend that the only subject of Kuppner's experimental postmodern writing is Scotland. For all that, the uncertain, awkward and wayward position of Scotland clearly interests this writer who is so often preoccupied with the uncertain, awkward, plural and wayward. Like many of his writings, the 'First General Druidical Service' shows Kuppner's interest in religion as one of the major systems which humans use to make sense of the universe.[10] For Kuppner religion is a frequently crazy and oppressive, all too human phenomenon, and as such a fascinating one. Kuppner's Hieromach, Acolyte and Chorus (X) speak in front of an indentifiably Scottish 'Congregation' and their discourse plays with Scottish chauvinisms and heretical anxieties which may be typical of the precarious relativity of all chauvinisms and anxieties about identity.

H: Oh, Lord! Some say that Ben Nevis is not in fact so very large.
A: Strike them dead, O Lord: it's an absolutely *huge* mountain.
X: I was going to say something here, but I've thought better of it.
H: And could you not have made the Gaelic a little easier?

Kuppner's dissection of Scottish troubles is comically and uncomfortably accurate:

H: And, Lord – about England. A word in your divine shelllike.
     I am troubled at how best to enunciate these feelings,
     uneager as I am to be called *simplificateur*.
     But, could you not have put it somewhere else? After all,
     You are the fount of mercy, and the Atlantic
     looked conspicuously underoccupied, to me at least.
A: And why do you play such cruel games with Edinburgh?
H: Indeed. It is clearly the capital of somewhere.
     All that we ask of you, in thy great mercy,
     is, simply, to tell us: of *what*?

Oblique, witty, and wide-ranging, Kuppner is alert to the question of cultural persistence. His first book may have been made up of mildly concussed dynastic songs that were ostensibly about a remote civilization in which a MacPherson dynasty is thinkable only in terms of ludicrous anachronism. Yet some of his other writings remind us that awkward questions of cultural persistence and of ludicrous anachronism are also familiar much closer to Kuppner's home. Frank Kuppner has his own, readily identifiable style. At first sight it may appear very surprising that he might be seen meaningfully as a Scottish writer or as an 'identifying poet', the countryman of MacDiarmid or Morgan; but only at first sight.

7

Home

Consideration of the ways in which such very different poets as MacLean and Ashbery, Murray and Kuppner might be considered as 'identifying poets' prompts the further speculation that the poet who constructs an identity which allows that poet to identify with a particular territory is the paradigmatic modern poet, in the Anglophone world at any rate. Thankfully, poets are sufficiently individual that the term 'paradigmatic' is of limited help. Yet the phrase 'identifying poet' may be of use in any reconsideration of twentieth-century poetry. Not least it allows us to see ways in which poets from cultures too easily regarded as marginal – Scotland, say, or Australia – may be re-viewed as crucial to modern traditions. The phrase 'identifying poet' has about it none of the covert cultural imperialism that too easily attends words like 'regional', 'provincial', or even 'national', all of which can be used in implicit marginalization or relegation, when defined against assumed metropolitan norms. Much of my own writing has involved a challenging of such assumed norms, and I am aware that the assumptions come from both outside and inside the metropolitan zone. In contending that the 'identifying poet' may be an important model for the interpretation of modern verse, I shall consider in this concluding chapter a range of contemporary writers, at first sight quite dissimilar, all of whom have constructed for themselves identities which allow them to be identified with particular territories. My aim is to suggest that the 'identifying poet' is becoming more rather than less important as the century concludes. Having pressed that point home, I want to give some thought to ways in which the position of poets in Scotland is typical of this situation, and to suggest that though the increase in identifying poets may be related to international concerns with nationalism, nonetheless the Scottish situation may be both typical and valuable in suggesting that subtle identifying poets may help prevent any too crude or racist, 'purist' versions of national identity.

In *Devolving English Literature* I have written about such poets as

Seamus Heaney, Tony Harrison, Les Murray and Douglas Dunn as developing certain 'provincial' strains in modernism as part of a widespread celebration of home territory and non-metropolitan values. In this connection, one could as easily point to some of these poets' older contemporaries, such as Edwin Muir or Norman MacCaig, two poets particularly admired by Dunn, Heaney and Murray. In each of these cases, though, it is crucial to bear in mind that the identifying voice of the poet is consciously chosen or constructed. This is signalled by the way in which each 'remade' his poetic self after an initial, very different beginning. While one may tend to think of Muir's as in many ways a mystical and quintessentially Orcadian voice, Muir's first book *We Moderns* (1918) contained work of a very different, Nietzschian and modernist cast. Only after this did he reconstruct his poetic self as the one with which we are now familiar. Perhaps because MacCaig is so well-known to living audiences, and because he has been a cunning self-fashioner, his complex reconstruction of a poetic self is less clearly perceived. Since MacCaig is increasingly viewed as a powerful and beautiful poet (one acute Irish poet and critic speculated in the *Times Literary Supplement* in 1991 that MacCaig might be the late twentieth century's Robert Frost), it is worth spending a little time on this point.[1]

The very names of MacCaig's first two collections, the acutely-titled *Far Cry* (1943) and *The Inward Eye* (1946) signal preoccupations which recur throughout his *Collected Poems* which includes work from *Riding Lights* (1955) to *Voice-Over* (1988) and beyond, yet which excludes all work from his first two volumes of poetry. The poem from *Riding Lights* with which the *Collected Poems* opens is a poem, like so much of MacCaig's verse, about perception. 'Instrument and Agent' is concerned with the way in which even the most distant stimulus (a 'far cry') may be altered, reshaped, given a new identity by entering the few 'inches' of the consciousness of a perceiver ('The inward eye'). That poem ends with the question 'And which is star – what's come a million / Miles or gone those inches farther?' That last word returns us again to the first element of the title of MacCaig's first book, but 'Instrument and Agent' also looks towards another of MacCaig's obsessions: difference. The poem asks how different the world out there may be from our perception of it. The title *Far Cry* alerts us to that too, since it relies on the colloquial phrase 'It's a far cry from *x*'. MacCaig's 1983 book title *A World of Difference* is in some ways a later version of the title *Far Cry*, and reminds us (if we need to be reminded) that MacCaig is our great poet of 'difference', that theme which has obsessed many of the literary theorists of the late twentieth-century. It is his preoccupation with difference which is part of his fascination with metaphor, and part of his worries about solipsism. Those obsessions are there from his avant-garde beginnings as a New Apocalyptic. He is a poet whose music is much closer to that of W. S. Graham than we might think, and whose work may yet demand fruitful consideration beside that of his apparently more 'experimental' Scottish contemporaries.

A superb poet of self-consciousness, MacCaig likes to keep close control of his own image as a poet, which is why he has sanctioned no reprinting of his first two books, preferring to make his apparent 'beginning' in these *Collected Poems* the work which was produced at the mature age of forty-five. This gives us an intimidating MacCaig, who seems to be born fully-formed, like Minerva. It is an act of profound self-fashioning. The magnificence, attractiveness and difficulty of that mature achievement are not in doubt. MacCaig is in Seamus Heaney's accurate phrase a poet whose work has a lovable 'mixture of strictness and susceptibility'. I hope, though, that we will have one day a *Collected Poems* which lets us read those very-hard-to-get first two collections as part of this poet's ouevre. Once this happens, we shall be able to appreciate all the better the ways in which MacCaig is not only a poet constantly identifying with territory (something to which I shall return briefly later in this chapter), but is also a poet whose identifying voice has complex and carefully managed roots.

MacCaig, like MacLean, is a poet born before the First World War. As I write, Dunn, Harrison, Heaney and Murray are all poets in their fifties. Lest the identifying poet is thought of as a peculiarly mid-century phenomenon, one should bear in mind not only such earlier examples as Yeats, MacDiarmid and Frost, but also the way in which the celebration of home ground has made itself a, perhaps even the, crucial topic of late twentieth-century verse.

'Where do you come from?' is one of the most important questions in contemporary poetry – where's home? Answering the pulls and torsions of that question certainly produces much of the verse of Heaney, Harrison, Murray and Dunn, but it also produces very different kinds of poetry. Martianism had nothing to do with Mars, everything to do with home, the place where Craig Raine (like Murray or Dunn) feels richest. Surely Martianism comes from the 'Ithaca' section of *Ulysses*, that quintessence of home seen from abroad. The Joycean epigraph to *A Martian Sends a Postcard Home*, not to mention the blurb's emphasis on 'home' as a word that 'sounds ... throughout the collection' reinforces such contentions.[2] Home can be a bit smug, though; and sometimes constricting. The poetic celebrants of home at the moment tend not to be women. But if it was once fashionable to see home as a 'provincial' bore, there have been poets around for some time, such as Edwin Morgan and Roy Fisher, who give the lie to that. Home is no longer 'so sad.'

At home few people speak 'Proper English' all the time. Home-based poetry may be in dialect, which is present in nearly all the writers considered here; but it may also fuel itself with a hyper-articulate, decorous Queen's English that deliberately celebrates the sort of cultures where dialect is spoken. Harrison does this when he harnesses his classical learning and tones to write about working-class Leeds (he also uses straight dialect); Dunn does it when he writes in *Northlight* with Marvellian decorum about Tayport; Murray when he writes about Bunyah. Use of proper names (where's Tayport? where's Bunyah? where's Glanmore?), confidently deployed local allusions, the belief that as Larkin put it prefacing Dunn's *New Poets from Hull* anthology, 'poetry, like prose, happens anywhere' – all these factors function as a sort of 'silent dialect' which reminds us that the text's origins matter and that they are part of what the poem is about.[3] Dialect is crucial to much contemporary poetry of sometimes happy, sometimes disturbing home and homing. The verse of our time is Ithacan in its orientation.

Like Murray's collection, *The Daylight Moon*, Dunn's *Northlight* is also an Ithacan book. Its opening lines, 'Innermost dialect / Describes Fife's lyric hills', set the tone for much of what follows. One of the strongest poems in the volume, 'Winkie', is about a pigeon homing to the Firth of Tay where Dunn now lives. A good deal of the book celebrates his homemaking there, but Dunn is also aware of the pressures on such a home. These pressures are not just physical (the local military airport), they are also intellectual as the two voices of 'Here and There' make clear in their argument over the word 'provincial'. The Tayport speaker in this poem may be an understated version of the Dunn who asked in the *Glasgow Herald* 'What did London ever do for a Scottish writer apart from patronise or condescend with the vicious tactic of patting work on the back as "legitimate?"'[4] Dunn's work (discussed most fully in the recent volume, *Reading Douglas Dunn*) is technically splendid; his stance commands admiration, and he is willing to take the risk of being a man of independent mind not only vis à vis London but also towards Scotland, both in and out of his poetry.[5] In verse, the form of Dunn's risk-taking is unusual. He dares to write of the domestic with immense decorum, and a scrupulous attention which makes him the finest Scottish poet of his generation. In so doing, what he risks is Becoming Great Literature. There were occasional moments in *Elegies* when something went wrong. The line 'How well my lady used her knife and fork!' was awkward because too Literary.[6] And Dunn in *Northlight* celebrating his '*Moon-puddled water, mystic Firth*' again treads dangerously close to Higher Things.[7] *Northlight*'s scope is admirable, reaching to Australia and Europe as well as to the pain of foreign wars and the way that pain is brought home. The book's daring (that long poem about a stuffed pigeon) shows a poet inscribing himself in his cultural home, and championing it with skill. Yet also in this splendid book are moments when the focus on the hinterlands of Dundee seems too archaically soft-focused.

> Air-psalters and pages of stone
> Inscribed and Caledonian
> Under these leaf-libraries where
> Melodious lost literature
> Remembers itself![8]

There's a whiff here of the loftily musing Poet; there's something a little stagey about that exclamation mark, but such worries vanish with

> I do not like the big brave boasts of war.
> GIVE ME GOOD PIGEONS! –
> A very large number of Great Commoners
> Built like Nye Bevan or Gambetta.[9]

Strong, rather than prettily melodious, clear and confident, this is the voice of Dunn at his best, homing in on subject-matter that is both universal and domestic.

Though distinguished by its style, Dunn's book was far from alone in its attention to home in the later 1980s. Charles Causley's collection, *A Field of Vision*, was full of poems in which as its blurb stresses, 'he comes home again and again'. The much younger Scottish poets John Burnside and W. N. Herbert developed the theme of home in complex, but related ways, as is suggested in a published conversation which they had in 1991, discussing the real or unreal existence of such entities as 'Palestine' and 'Scotland'.[10] Burnside's first collection, *The Hoop*, appeared in 1988, when the Dunfermline-born poet was thirty-three. His family moved to England when he was almost eleven, and he now lives in Surrey. Whether for this or other reasons, one of the themes that runs through *The Hoop* is an awareness of the uncertain construction of identity, a topic occasionally given specifically Scottish resonances, as in 'Exile's Return':

> Hard to imagine it, lying intact,
> folded into books: identity
> to be assumed like tartan

This poem moves on to ask 'Do we know / where we are in these tourist hills?' before concluding with how

> we remember the legends of giant fish
> that no one believed and everybody told
> as we drove south that morning, years ago,
> pretending we could find our own way home.[11]

The poem uses the pronoun 'we', but it is not called 'Exiles' Return'. Its actual title may refer both to the return of an exiled person and to the return of the sensation of exile. In its honest refusal to simplify what 'home' means and how it is invented and developed, this poem is worth setting beside the conclusion of W. N. Herbert's 'Mariposa Pibroch', where Burnside's younger contemporary, another East coast Scottish poet living in southern England, refuses to simplify his perception of

> airs
>
> that are built into the childhood
> but aren't genuine, and the drone
>
> that alone demarks this foreign
> music I feel kin to, salutes
>
> or seems to the offerings I cannot
> make: only the hearing is authentic.[12]

Such a juxtaposition indicates that it does make sense to include John Burnside's work in the context of contemporary Scottish poetry. The working title of his second collection, *Home* (eventually the book was published as *Common Knowledge* in 1991), suggests that the concerns about the uncertainties of identity and homing glimpsed in an explicitly Scottish context in 'Exile's Return' are central to Burnside's imagination.

But 'home' and the often complex identity which goes with it is far from the prerogative of recent Scottish poetry. It is a topic which pervades contemporary verse – so much so that people who write a poetry of home have become aware of its dangers, though they may not always avoid them. David Dabydeen's 'Coolie Odyssey', dedicated 'for Ma', opens,

> Now that peasantry is in vogue,
> Poetry bubbles from peat bogs,
> People strain for the old folk's fatal gobs
> Coughed up in grates North or North East
> 'Tween bouts o' livin dialect,
> It should be time to hymn your own wreck,
> Your house the source of ancient song ...

Like Edwin Morgan, Dabydeen is a poet-academic whose careers are interlinked and who cares deeply about his particular community. His language doesn't reach flashpoint often enough, and sometimes his tone is uncertain – how ironic is he being in that Ossianic line 'Your house the source of ancient song'? But I respect and admire the way he both perceives his black ancestors as lying 'like texts / Waiting to be written by the children', while he also knows that in writing these texts he may risk becoming an ethnic performer who will see himself reading

> To congregations of the educated
> Sipping wine, attentive between courses –
> See the applause fluttering from their white hands
> Like so many messy table napkins.[13]

In some ways Dabydeen stands in the position of the Dunn of *Barbarians*; certainly some of the writers anthologized by Fred D'Aguiar as representatives of 'Black British Poetry' in the 1988 anthology *The New British Poetry* make interesting links with other analogous predicaments. D'Aguiar, the celebrant of his own home ground in *Mama Dot* and *Airy Hall*, takes as the epigraph to his introduction Stephen Dedalus's description of Irish art from *Ulysses* – 'The cracked lookingglass of a servant' – a turn of phrase which Stephen immediately realizes may be both apt and marketable.

Dabydeen and all other poets who sometimes use dialect might relish John Agard's 'Listen Mr Oxford Don' ('mugging de Queen's English / is the story of my life'). This poem is intelligent and funny, yet it risks boxing itself in by marketing a stereotypical speaker who is a sort of licensed clown:

> Me not no Oxford don
> me a simple immigrant
> from Clapham Common
> I didn't graduate
> I immigrate[14]

The cadence and wit of those last two lines convinces me and makes me smile. Yet at the back of my mind I start to think of stage Scotsmen, impersonating themselves, and about why MacDiarmid hated Harry Lauder. Maybe Merle Collins's poem about a popular soup 'Callaloo' avoids such worries better, coming with balletic line-breaks out of an oral tradition, a home that nurtures but does not imprison:

> Mix up
> like callaloo
> Not no watery callaloo
> But
> a thick, hot, sweet
> callaloo
> burnin' you tongue
> Wid dem chunk o' dumplin'
> goin' down nice

an' wid coconut
wid o' widdout deaders
as de case may be
as de taste may be
as de pocket may be
but sweet
an' hot[15]

Merle Collins is not content to stay in an area some might condemn as 'local colour'. She pushes 'Callaloo' towards a wider consideration of what home means, and writes about the need to throw off a feeling of shame 'when de man ask / "whey you from?"' Investigation of history and the compiling of anthologies are always essential to the provision of confident answers to that question, though for some people, literature still cuts free of questions of home and origin, so that writing is like stepping into the fridge.

Home is a place with a dialect and tradition. Sometimes writers, whether James Macpherson or T. S. Eliot, attempt to make up a tradition which stands in lieu of home. A tradition isn't just an academic's card index, it can also be a writer's life-support-system; writing is usually a solitary activity, but encouragement and stimulation often come from knowing oneself part of a historical or geographical community of voices. Gillian Allnutt was aware of this in her 1988 selection of 'Quote Feminist Unquote Poetry' in *The New British Poetry*. Her introduction steers clear of claiming that there is yet any discernible 'tradition' in this area, yet she feels at least that 'It is now beginning to be possible to construct the "line" in retrospect'. The use of various kinds of 'silent dialect' which make the reader aware that the speaker is a woman often helps achieve some sort of communal solidarity, melding a tradition. Certainly a sense of isolation and the corresponding need for some such common cultural home seems evident in many of the themes and titles of the poems selected, such as Gillian Allnutt's 'Alien', Eavan Boland's 'The Oral Tradition', Carol Ann Duffy's 'Telephoning Home' and 'Foreign', Selima Hill's 'Crossing the Desert in a Pram', Maria Jastrzebska's 'Bi-lingual', and Evangeline Paterson's 'Dispossessed'.[16] A sense of dispossession, not simply restricted to gender issues, is often bound up with the topic of home in the work of such poets as Boland, Duffy and Kathleen Jamie. Yet the question 'Whey you from?' is just as important in the work of the quite different male poet, Mick Imlah, whose first collection, *Birthmarks* (1988), deliberately hinted in its title and contents at origins which cannot be rubbed off.

Several times in *Birthmarks* underneath the cosmetic voice-surgery of social climbing lies the Ur-accent of home. In 'Cockney' an aspiring cosmopolite showing off to 'the Previns' at a party which

                                                    seemed an
                        acceptable social *milieu*
            If only because it was something like six million light years
                        away from the planet of Millwall

finds himself reclaimed in mock-Eliotic tones by 'the ghost of me mum'
identifying him as 'the same little boy that I sent out in winter with
Cockney inscribed on your satchel!' After that, the socialite is struck by a
vengeful personal vowel-shift ('ALL ROYT MOY SAHN! HA'S YOR
FARVAH?') and, his cover blown, takes to destroying the party around
him. A quiet afterlude reveals that

        Sometimes, there's a song in my head as I sit down at tea,
                    and I know what the tune is
        But can't catch the words. And when I get tired of the
                    humming, it's off down to Terry's or Tony's,
        A couple of pints, then across to the club till it closes, for
                    snooker with Pakistanis.

Other betrayals of home and aborted escapes from it dominate the poems
of Imlah's first collection. In 'Goldilocks' an upwardly-mobile Oxford
donlet who has just spoken on "Systems of Adult-to-Infant Regression"
expels from his guest-room a red-haired Scottish tramp, mentally de-
nouncing him as an imposter. Imlah's version of donspeak may be a little
over the top. Hard to imagine even the most confirmed don coming out
with the words 'A little ginger chap, / Of the sort anthropologists group
in the genus of *tramp*', but throughout the book the verbal caricatures are
constantly funny. After the geneticist of 'Goldilocks' has elbowed out the
wheedling tramp, he confides to the reader '(Och, if he'd known *I* was
Scottish! Then I'd have got it.)' That 'Och', the verbal birthmark, is again
the revenge of home, the insistent inner 'Whey you from?'[17]

    It is that question which links Imlah's work to Caribbean, Australian
and New Zealand writing, as well as to the work of many of the other
Scottish poets which Douglas Dunn presented alongside Imlah's
'Goldilocks' in the *Faber Book of Twentieth-Century Scottish Poetry* (1992).
The number of poets in that anthology whose work is in some sense
'identifying' may stress once again how important Scottish verse is in this
area of writing, yet it is worth emphasizing that it may be seen as norma-
tive rather than unique.

    As if to prove this, we may turn to the different heritage of the Caribbean
poet Derek Walcott to see how out of a complex cultural and linguistic
background he produced in 1990 a massive poem which must rank as one
of the major books of verse about 'home' in the late twentieth century.

Walcott's work has always circled round this theme, and his may be seen as a genius presiding over (but also learning from) some of his younger international contemporaries, including Murray and Heaney. One of Walcott's early poems, 'As John to Patmos' envisages his own Caribbean island home in terms of the Greek islands, while Homeric and Greek motifs are present in the long poem *Another Life* (1973). 'Penelope' and 'Troy' feature in the poem 'Origins' from Walcott's 1964 *Selected Poems*, a poem whose speaker is seen as situated 'Between the Greek and African pantheon'.[18] If the search for origins and homecoming had always featured in Walcott's poetry alongside the machinery of the Greek world and its literature, then *Omeros* marks the culmination of this fusion in Walcott's work and constitutes a major landmark in the late twentieth century's identifying poetry of home.

Though *Omeros* looks to the work and world of Homer, it relates most of all to the *Odyssey*, that great adventure story of homecoming. It's with a version of lines from the *Odyssey* that Pound opens the huge voyage of his *Cantos*, his enormous 'tale of the tribe'; it's the *Odyssey* that underpins *Ulysses*, that great examination of home by the exiled Irishman whom Walcott's long poem calls 'our age's Omeros'; it's the *Odyssey* to which Nikos Kazantzakis wrote the poem published in English as *The Odyssey: A Modern Sequel*, adding rather too much of a sensuous lushness not present in the original; it's the *Odyssey* that the Hebridean John MacLean (Sorley MacLean's brother) translated into Gaelic – as if to remind us that it is the epic of an islander.

Walcott's *Omeros*, at over 300 pages, might be related to all of these modern *Odysseys*. *Omeros* is a tale of the tribe, an exile's examination of home and displacement, a repeatedly sensuous (but not lush) epic of Caribbean islanders. The poem offers us a necessary sense of universal humanity bonded to a sometimes hurt local pride. This risk-taking epic of Tennysonian amplitude has a clear narrative line with principal characters whose names come from the *Iliad* – Achille, Hector, Helen – and from Greek myth (Philoctete). Yet as the island fisherman Achille and the fisherman-turned-taxi-driver Hector quarrel over a Helen who is a little too easily emblematic of island culture, we are made more aware of the *Odyssey* than the *Iliad* as a governing structure. For this is a poem of voyages, the slave voyages to the Caribbean, the spiritual voyage of the modern Caribbean islander in search of an African past, the voyages of the island poet who is also Professor of English at Boston University in the 'new empire' of America. Walcott is writing the biography of a culture, interweaving his own autobiography with it. Not least among the risks he takes is his use of names such as 'Achille'. The danger is that the whole poem takes on too much library dragweight, that the characters become heroic stereotypes, and their habitat with its kind-hearted innkeeper, retired British military couple and comic politician drifts towards *Under Milk Wood*. This book doesn't fully avoid stereotyping: its intellectuals tend to be male, its women are creatures of instinct. Yet Walcott navigates around most of the dangers. What saves him and makes his poem so sharply beautiful is his apparently inexhaustible gift for vivid physical particulars whose description ties into the larger intellectual geometry of *Omeros*. A seemingly effortless flow of long sentences is typical of the poem, but it avoids being trapped by the sort of postcard beauty that Walcott worries about elsewhere. For the constant suggestions of endless, intense circulations of weather, and particularly of water, tie in with the greater design of a poem much given over to the sea, opening with the making of canoes and closing with the words 'the sea was still going on.' Constantly repeated details provide not the mere and dangerous local colour of the exotic colour-calendar, but the structural reinforcement of pertinent motifs, like the migrating swift whose repeated but unobtrusive present rhymes thematically with the migratory movements of this poet and his poem. Attempting to blend his voice with an ancient and ageless bardic Voice, Walcott suggests that such a method of motifs is also that of the *Odyssey* – 'the Homeric repetition / Of details'.[19] But perhaps this is a description less of Homer's formulaic phrases than of the more consciously-structured 'luminous details' of a modern epic such as Pound's, or Les Murray's quite different epic of homing, *The Boys Who Stole the Funeral*.

If Pound aimed at a poem containing history, then Walcott's epic narrative of a postmodern age is aware not so much of an older, unitary concept of history as of a postmodern plurality of histories. 'History', its construction, dissemination and manipulation is one of the major themes of *Omeros*, which offers us such various histories as that constructed by the white British ex-pat naval historian Plunkett and that envisioned by the black Caribbean Achille seeking the suppressed story of his African ancestors. History, like narrative and like literature, is seen as something re-made, retold over and over, each time with different inclusions and exclusions. Walcott's generous plurality of histories in this poem sympathetic both to white and black represents, like Murray's work, an effort at reconciling inclusiveness.

Maybe, sometimes, inclusiveness can go too far. A word Pound used of the *Cantos* was 'rag-bag'; Robert Lowell thought that history and his own notebook were roughly coterminous. There's a strain in American thought going back at least to Emerson which sees all history as contained in the self and which can lead to megalomania and one-man imperialism. For the most part the majestically awkward blend of humanity and assertion and the anti-imperialist current of *Omeros* avoid this dangerous aggrandizement, though there may be those who are troubled by a latent *hubris* in the way Homer and Walcott are blent. This is a necessary *hubris*, present in Joyce, for example. But it puts one on one's guard.

What wins the reader over, despite occasional worries about grandiosity, is the marvellous richness of the detail and the fluidity of Walcott's loosely-deployed *terza rima* that often sounds very close to the Heaney of the 'Station Island' sequence. Probably Walcott replays too often Heaney's version of the Eliotic meeting with a familiar compound ghost. Yet Walcott achieves a fluidity most easily perceived if one reads a long stretch of his poem, but certainly glimpsed in short sections also. Heaney's cadences surface often in *Omeros*. A line such as 'and the shining drops of the drizzle's aftermath' seems very Heaneyesque; while lines like 'In the grey vertical forest of the hurricane season' are very close to the cadences and diction of Les Murray.[20] Such echoes don't trap or spoil Walcott's epic which, though it's a little too long, does have a physical scale substantially different from that of any individual piece by Heaney or even by the Murray of *The Boys Who Stole the Funeral*, that verse novel that shares elements with *Omeros*. These echoes don't trap, but they do suggest rich affinities.

For if home was one of the great themes of the poetry of the 1980s – of Dunn, Harrison, Heaney, Murray and Walcott – then the Ithacan orientation of *Omeros* continues this theme in a powerful and expansive way. Moreover, the themes of provincialism, of being marginalized by History and Literature, which are so strong in the work of these poets remain Walcott's themes also. His poetry, like theirs, is both locally-grounded and potent in universal appeal. Ultimately, it is the strength of its language which makes *Omeros* so impressive, and the strength of that language is bonded to an impulse common in much of the most important modern verse, a homing impulse which ensures that, however far a poet voyages as sophisticated contemporary intellectual, he also returns with fidelity to his roots. Such poets are both Ulysses and Penelope. Their *Odyssey* is different from that of Pound because one of their fundamental motivations is, in Murray's words, 'to speak the names of all the humble'. Walcott's poem is at one with this desire, in its wish for an epic of humility when it lets us hear the voice of the poet's father, presenting the nature of the poet's task in terms of those barefoot, staggering Caribbean women carrying coal, whom the poet saw in his childhood, years before he had the skill and opportunity 'to give those feet a voice'.[21] The impulse to celebrate the inhabitants of a home territory is central to Walcott's epic. It is an impulse captured in a pun repeated throughout *Omeros*, a pun not possible in Greek but effective in English – the pun that links Homer to homing.

Omeros is a poem of home ground, but it is also the poem of a culture at large, so that for some (though he might not like this) Walcott can be seen as a Caribbean Poet Laureate. *Omeros* is a poem of a territory and its people. In this, it is markedly different from, for instance, the Laureate poems of Ted Hughes, which seem to focus on myth, heraldic beasts and on the past, avoiding looking at the contemporary people of their sovereign territories.[22] Hughes is certainly in several senses an identifying poet involved in the construction and defence of one of those 'Englands of the Mind' of which Heaney has written in his important essay of that title. Yet if one were seeking a contemporary 'identifying poet' of England, one might well turn to another poet whose work has been less discussed than the accomplished poetry of Hughes, yet who has been identified recently and rightly by an acute and provocative critic as 'the unoffical laureate of a decaying nation'.[23] That poet is Peter Reading.

Reading's work is postmodern with a vengeance, and he could be seen as a darling of the metropolitan scene. Yet he has maintained a fierce integrity as a writer in whose poetry heteroglossia proliferates spikily, an obsessively self-reflective aestheticism (*'but am I Art?'*) going hand in hand with a despairingly apocalyptic politics.[24] From almost the start of his development he investigated how to make verse out of texts that (often explicitly) comment on themselves and on other texts. An early poem, 'Plague Graves', signals a debt to Hughes and speaks of litter being destroyed when 'Sheep maul / beyond recognition alarmingly quickly / the sandwich-paper memorials left / by charabanc trippers, dissolving all tangible / trace of us'. Very soon in Reading's development we get other bits of paper, ones we can read, supposedly copied into the text in fragment form, eroding yet tangible traces which are commented on – 'Quite nice' says a voice in 'Early Stuff', ironically deflating some lines of cemetery poetry which rhetorically assert the triumph of love.[25] Reviews of his own writing come to be incorporated into his verse. He attacks what he sees as pseudo-poetry encouraged by the 'Plashy Fen School' whose Grasmeraholic, off-Georgian members send him notes for which they are so excoriated that one begins to sympathize with them, wishing they might write to him, 'Dear Mr Reading / FUCK OFF / yrs / The Plashy Fen School'. But they don't.

Like the independent Ian Hamilton Finlay, and like Geoffrey Hill to whom the early Reading of such phrasing as 'congregations / are still here mulched into the cider orchard' pays its dues, this is a poet who likes to maintain and investigate the strains and alliances between violence and the language of art.[26] It often seems that Reading's main concern is with physical decay and aggression, but at least as important is his preoccupation with style. What fascinates him is mixtures of discourse, how they

control and manipulate their subject-matter, their readers and their writ-
ers. If literary theorists were more alert to contemporary poetry, they
would swoop on Reading with glee. He delights in playing with fantasies
about the Death of the Author. Throughout his writing, he loves posing
as an editor who is mixing up a heteroglossic brew of clashing styles, a
brew in which style itself is often at odds with or awkwardly bonded to its
subject. The start of the poem 'Editorial' from *Diplopic*, with its finely-
tuned use of the verb 'compose', might serve as a model for his mode:

> Being both *Uncle Chummy's Letter Box*
> *of Kiddies' Column* and *Supa Scoop* besides
> (*Your Headlines as They Happen*), and having the shakes
> uncellophaning fags this crapulous morning,
> I compose: BOY (13) CLUBS DAD TO DEATH,
> CHILD (10) SCALDS GRANNY (87) TO DEATH,
> SKINHEAD (14) STONES KITTIWAKES TO DEATH
> AS RSPCA ASKS 'WHERE'S THE SENSE?'.[27]

Sometimes critics see Reading as a kind of social-worker (or social-
worker-*manqué*) revealing the underside of our dole-full, opulent society.
It would be possible to write interestingly about him as bard of a society in
cancerous decline, harkening to the Muse of Death like the George
MacBeth who saw England as *The Cleaver Garden* or the Blake Morrison
who heard *The Ballad of the Yorkshire Ripper*. Yet what sets Reading apart
is that he has constantly signalled that he is fascinated as much with cut-
ups of the text as of the body, as much by style-victimization as by
atrocity. It is this postmodern display of design-consciousness as crucially
as his display of social inequalities and batterings which gives his verse its
powerfully individual bite and which made him such an arresting, self-
aware artist, and an authentic voice from the England that generated
Thatcherism.

Perduta Gente, following hard on the heels of *Final Demands*, con-
firmed that Reading, fascinated all along by a polyphony of sometimes
interacting, sometimes clashing voices of commentators and critics, has
now moved nearer to an art of visual collage. The voices have become
distinct graphics. Bits of newspaper stories, handwritten sheets from a
tear-off pad, leaks from a typewritten report on nuclear contamination, are
photographically reproduced as part of the 'edited' text. Where earlier
Reading poems like 'Fiction' played with how writing structured and
produced 'fact', now the poet graphically enacts what he previously dis-
cussed.[28] Style remains his vital preoccupation. He is as interested in the
texture and symptoms of tabloid journalism as he is in the subject-matter
which is reported. Ads for and accounts of London apartments make up

the left-hand page of 'Parallel Texts' (to borrow a title from an earlier
Reading poem) the other half of which is an account of a 'lone hag
gippo'.[29] But each half of the text also invades the other. At the end of
newspaper cut-ups detailing the sale of barns for six-figure sums to 'buyers
seeking a quiet country life', the reprocessor of the text has stuck the cut-
out letters of the word 'doss', while whoever it is produces the text of the
right-hand page mixes the 'gippo' vocabulary of 'pisspot', 'turd', and
'skedaddled' with the academic polysyllables of 'fenestration' and 'etio-
lated'.[30] The society's own linguistic mix is used to present its tensions and
fissures. On these pages in this poem-album, as so often before, Reading is
mixing textures of discourse, juxtaposing them, modulating one theme
rapidly into another, compressing and overlaying motifs and forms of
expression like Sibelius in his Fifth Symphony. At his mixer's console,
Reading revels in virtuosity. His poem begins with an end, the provocative
word 'bray' tripping us forward from Culture to culture, the words
'tenebrous concert' glancing back eerily from culture to Culture as Read-
ing the Anti-Laureate demonstrates his skill as an identifying poet of the
late twentieth-century England presented in this brutal vignette:

> South Bank: Sibelius 5's
> incontrovertible end –
> five exhalations, bray of expiry,
> absolute silence ...
>
> *Under* the Festival Hall is a foetid
> tenebrous concert
> strobed by blue ambulance light.
> PVC/newspapers/rags[31]

Since Reading on the first and last pages of this book imitates these 'five
exhalations', it's curious that there are actually six in Sibelius's original.
Yet, usually, as one would expect of a writer so intent on discourse-
blending, Reading has a splendid ear and eye. He hears, transmits the
contemporary through his diction. So he writes the word 'strobed' and
chooses 'Sibelius 5's' rather than 'Sibelius Fifth's' or even 'Sibelius Five's'.
In its novelized diction and construction this poetry is formally consonant
with the scratch-video; simultaneously, it is aware of having access to the
whole poignant, often useless bank of Great Literature,

> Some on em masturbates, loud.
> *Let us not speak of them, merely observe and*
> *silently pass by.*[32]

Peter Reading is not concerned with pity but with style and accuracy. The maximum of energy comes not from setting a rose or a pocket-calculator beside the formal notation of a verse structure – all are bathed in human ideas of sophistication, elegance, and civilized values. Far more power comes from setting the formal notation of a verse structure beside (even the photograph of) a piece of shit.

This was the technique of Reading's *C* where poetic formalism met cancer. Reading is relentlessly literary in his obsessions. His fascination with painful and offensive subjects is an empowering disguise. How else could he get away with writing a book with such a literary, even academic title as *Stet*? This poet is an aesthete who saves himself by picking up a lump of dirt. Dirt allows him to escape the fatal (Plashy Fen) wound of literariness in his poetry at the same time as he obsessively investigates how poetry works, and where it may fail to work.

Serious imitation of this technique would be futile. Any imitator would be submerged in Reading's constructed voice. This poet is only just succeeding in avoiding imitation of his own earlier writing as he produces a plethora of books. But that 'only just' is enough. Bleak, similar, each volume is as yet a technical advance on its predecessors. Poet, medium and readers are being pushed to their limits. In saying this, I can pay no higher tribute to a writer.

Reading's is a postmodern technique developed from the modernism which reminded its readers of the needs for merds as well as Titians. To put it another way, where Duchamp and his followers brought a toilet bowl into an art gallery, Reading asks us to contemplate oil paintings hung in public toilets. He reminds us that art, fascinating and inescapable, depends on a biology that is eroding fast. He sees the end of the world through the words of Dante and *The Sun*. *Perduta Gente* ends with the cut-up newspaper versions of the syllables 'dis tress' and 'con tam', one overprinted imperfectly on the other. 'Exegi monumentum aere perennius...' – for Reading, a religious poet without God, monuments are a load of crap. Obsessively, he continues to make and unmake them.

The lost people of *Perduta Gente* are very identifiably English. Yet Reading has gone from this to expatiate in *Evagatory* on the global, and even galactic human predicament as our planet faces environmental catastrophe.[33] In so doing he demonstrates that the identifying poet is also the universal commentator. No more than Frost, MacDiarmid, or Murray is Reading a mere local curiosity. His collages of dialects and discourses invite a Bakhtinian perspective, yet, along with his typographical play, they also invite comparison with the work of another art-school trained writer whose work articulates a particular political identity and speaks of home at the same time as engaging with topics of universal importance. Reading admires Gray's most experimental writing in *1982, Janine* whose technical *brio* and much of whose subject-matter parallel Reading's poetry of the 1980s. That such a comparison can be made may remind us both of the variety of recent Scottish literature (the poetry of MacCaig and the composition of *Lanark* are contemporary with each other), but also of the pervasiveness of the theme of home in this polymorphous body of writing. In its articulation of this theme, Scottish writing, rather than provincializing itself, is very much at the heart of what is happening in international literature. A fuller understanding of this, and of the way in which Scotland's plural linguistic heritage is a strength in the resources of identifying poets ought to make for greater confidence in Scottish writing, and greater readiness to see this writing in an international context.

We have seen already in this book that Scottish identifying poets in our century have been as different as Sorley MacLean and Frank Kuppner, but it is worth surveying briefly a number of other poets to emphasize that the pervasiveness of the urge to construct a voice which might be identified with home territory goes far beyond the work of these poets and beyond that of Hugh MacDiarmid. Having pointed out early in this chapter that MacCaig's identifying poetic voice was carefully refurbished, and constructed, it is time to glance more closely at the way that voice repeatedly celebrates bonds between home territory and language. So, for instance, MacCaig walks where

> The edge of the green sea
> Crumples. Bees are in clover.
> I part the grasses and there –
> *Angus MacLeod, drowned. Mary his wife*. Together.[34]

Elsewhere he celebrates gamekeepers who, as scholars, 'read a landscape as / I read a book' and who 'spoke like a native / The language they walked in'.[35] This landscape is hardly unique to MacCaig. What Douglas Dunn has called 'Ground's secret lexicon' is gleefully metamorphosed in Edwin Morgan's 'off-concrete Scotch fantasia', 'Canedolia'.[36] Intoxicated and intoxicatingly juggled placenames appear to let the land speak for itself, celebrating its own shibboleths. Yet just as 'Canedolia', teasing new meanings from old names, celebrates a certain fluidity or slipperiness of language, making it at once foreign and familiar, so MacCaig is aware that the 'ground-lexicon' can be richly elusive. He remembers being unable to answer the incomprehensible Gaelic of 'Aunt Julia', whose voice has become for him a land-language 'with so many questions / unanswered'.[37] The impressive bilingual (Gaelic/English) poet Iain Crichton Smith finds how in 'Australia'

> Sometimes I hear graves singing
> their Gaelic songs to the dingos[38]

Language here seems both bound to the land and lost to it, at once native and translated. Physical translation (exile being a key element in Scottish history and myth) accompanies linguistic translation. In Sorley MacLean's Gaelic (widely available in parallel text only since the mid-Seventies) there is also a cutting awareness of those cleared from the land, men and women whose language seems to have passed into the places they were forced to abandon, as in 'Coilltean Ratharsair' ('The Woods of Raasay').

In such linguistic circumstances, the uncertain survival and fluidity of the native languages can encourage the poet to act as a bardic memory-repository or noble hoarder, like the 'Old Highland Woman' of whom MacCaig writes 'Her people / are assembled in her bones'.[39] Those words are typical of the clarity of MacCaig's work, translucid but deep. The simple words 'Her people' mean family, but also something wider – her tribe. The verb 'assembled' points to the structuring of the skeleton, but also carries an ecclesiastical charge in the country of the General Assembly. The whole image has a slight absurdity – a big crowd of people inside a skeleton; yet it also has a colloquial naturalness, like the phrase 'I feel it in my bones'. The image, making the woman for an instant skeletal, enforces the idea of age and allows the poet to stress the identity of a cultural tradition.

The linguistic fluidity of Scotland was much bewailed by Edwin Muir earlier this century, and can intensify in Scottish poets an almost despairingly strong wish to be able through language to identify firmly with territory. As Dunn once put it 'If I could sleep standing, I would wait here .../ An example of being part of a place'.[40] The wish to be part of place permeates Dunn's work. He too has a 'Vision of Live Maps', and writes beautifully about Scottish soil, but has also a feeling of exile, of being sometimes a 'visitor / To a place of relatives, / A place of names'.[41] Yet in recent years Dunn seems more at ease with Scotland, not least with its languages. Gaelic, Scots and English appear side by side as a matter of course in his *Faber Book of Twentieth-Century Scottish Poetry* – as they should in any anthology of Scottish verse. Linguistic fluidity is to the fore in modern poetry – from Reading to Walcott and from Kuppner to Murray; no longer need it be seen as a drawback; indeed linguistic fluidity may be the stuff of literature, as Bakhtin recognized. In Scotland it may well be that uncertainty over the status of native languages has encouraged linguistic experiments such as those of Edwin Morgan. Certainly stress on bonding between language and place, with words as both a medium of exploration and a territory to be explored is something Morgan shares with his earliest mentor, the late W. S. Graham, some of whose finest work appeared since 1970. However different, Graham's work in its fascination with language and powerful attachment to place parallels the poetry of MacDiarmid. For Graham language itself may be physical – an icescape that is dangerous to negotiate, and that traps. 'What is the language using us for?' asks Graham, whose polar wordscape has its own modern, striking imagery which is not whimsical, but accurate.

> I am in a telephoneless, blue
> Green crevasse and I can't get out.[42]

Anyone who has ever been in a crevasse will tell you how ice absorbs sound. Language in Graham is 'the frozen tundra / Of the lexicon and the dictionary'. It's tempting to relate such white-out conditions partly to Graham's Scottish experience when, as a young man he spent three days and nights out of doors in snowcovered Glencoe before passing out, hallucinating, and being rescued.[43] Graham's late poems deal with language as presence, muse, and obstruction; but they also link this theme to those of self and place – 'loud Greenock long ropeworking / Hide and seeking rivetting town of my child / Hood'.[44] Graham deals with language as a kind of algebra into which writer and reader may be translated. Language is a place where living and dead intersect; its infinite variables, in Graham's poetry, are frequently assigned the values of his Greenock youth.

It might be hard to *prove* that the fluidity of Scotland's linguistic position has encouraged the wealth of linguistic experiment in modern Scottish poetry from Finlay and Graham to Kuppner and MacDiarmid, yet certainly such a fluidity is consonant with some of the stranger developments. 'We Scots are Oriental' wrote MacDiarmid, and recent years have certainly seen an upsurge in Scottish Orientalism, encouraged by elements in the work of Morgan and novelist Alasdair Gray, but encompassing also Kuppner's verse, Iain Bamforth's 'Letters from the T'ang' and 'Walking Back to China' in *The Modern Copernicus* (1984) and some of Ron Butlin's lyrics in *Ragtime in Unfamiliar Bars* (1985).[45] For some this chinoiserie may seem merely flippant, or an effort to escape from having to be as Scottish as a shortbread tin, but again the interest in bridging cultures and examining the areas where cultures don't match as well as the places where they jigsaw is at the heart of the Scottish tradition. In these young writers too it is frequently accompanied by a fascination with linguistic differences and a sense of place. Bamforth ends 'In an Etruscan Dialect'

> Forgive me for speaking
> In this Etruscan dialect,
> For the useless dressing of the dead
> And this indecipherable stone,
> Left for the journey.[46]

Among a number of the younger Scottish poets there seems a worry about Scotland as an empty place, unable to assert its identity, undevolved and unevolved. Butlin ends 'Claiming My Inheritance' with the lines

> The older I become the more
> I am aware of exile, of longing for –
>
> I clench my fist on nothing and hold on. [47]

Yet there is also a general and increasing confidence in the multilinguistic resources of Scotland, and a growing perception that these resources may be seen as rich and productive, aligning Scotland with the many cultures around the world from Ireland to the Caribbean and from Wales to New Zealand in which the choice of native speeches is wider than it once appeared to be in England. This is not the same as saying simply that Scotland should be viewed as 'post-colonial'. It would be smallmindedly chauvinistic to pretend that Scotland was other than a strong participant in the furthering of British Imperial ambitions. Nonetheless, in the century of such identifying poets as MacDiarmid and Murray, Walcott and Reading, and in the century of Bakhtin's liberating criticism, it is surely time for Scots to be at ease with, and even to rejoice in their home's linguistic differences and diversity.

In Scotland we live between and across languages. Anyone who stays here and is interested in the spoken or the written word is constantly aware of being on the edge of another tongue – of being a speaker of English who understands a bit of Scots, but knows no Gaelic; of being a speaker of Scots in the pub or with friends, but a speaker of English in more formal situations, a speaker who knows no Gaelic; of being a Gaelic speaker who knows English, but no Scots; even in a small number of cases of knowing all three tongues. Few Scottish people are totally monolingual, and the variety of languages between and across which we live is increasing, not simply as a result of education but also as a result of population movements that have given us Scottish people who are trilingual in English, Gaelic and Urdu or Glaswegians one of whose languages is Cantonese. Many of our major writers have acknowledged and exploited the multicultural and multilingual nature of the Scottish tradition, crossing and recrossing linguistic boundaries, showing a consciousness of other tongues. That phenomenon is important in Burns and Scott, in Carlyle and MacDiarmid, and is crucial to the cultural amalgam which is modern Scotland.

To maintain this position is not to deny that some writers have found it a curse. Iain Crichton Smith has written of the agonizing predicament of the writer who is torn between languages, unable to commit himself fully to either.[48] Such a description of the writer in Scotland is in some ways similar to that of Edwin Muir in his notorious, stimulating and damaging 1936 study, *Scott and Scotland*, in which he sees post-Reformation Scotland as ruined by 'a confusion of tongues' and sees 'a homogeneous language' as 'The prerequisite of an autonomous literature' which will be required by any putative independent Scotland.[49] Muir's whole position is based on ideas of monoculturalism and linguistic purity which seem unhelpful and even offensive to many people today. Was the language of Shakespeare or Joyce pure and homogeneous? Enlightenment Scotland may have been preoccupied with purifying its language, but we're not. We know that impurity of language matters as much as purity; because in impurity lies richness, imagination and the seeds of new growth. Homogeneity – who needs it? Dictators, racists, *Scots Style-sheeters*, prescriptivists who want us all the same. Where is the homogeneity in MacDiarmid's synthetic Scots, or Burns's synthetic Scots for that matter? Homogeneity is the enemy of Scottish culture, which is and has been for centuries fundamentally, linguistically pluralist.

Those whom we might call the tenured avant-garde of recent times have produced for us artworks in which pluralism and its problems are central. Ashbery's 1979 poem 'Litany' presents us with two ongoing parallel columns which, the poet tells us, 'are meant to be read as simultaneous but independent monologues'.[50] Derrida's 1974 book *Glas*, translated into English in 1986, gives us again parallel columns of text (occasionally three columns) which are placed before us in a split-screen effect, moving in apparently disjunctive simultaneity. Charles Ives and Elliot Carter do that in their music, having several distinct and (it would seem) opposing tunes playing at once. We are familiar with such experiences not just in 'high culture' but in other parts of our everyday lives: the split-screen phenomenon on a television or video, or the act of listening to music while holding a conversation while driving a car. We are used to having our attention divided, to being swamped by systems of signs, to living among what might at first seem impossible simultaneities. For some our lives are enriched, for others demeaned by these activities. They may not be absolutely new, but they are essential to our time. Perhaps as Scots, living like many another people, and many another literary community, between and across languages, we are well placed to respond to, to write about and out of this contemporary condition. Of his two columns, or his split 'screens' Derrida writes: 'Let us space. The art of this text is the air it causes to circulate between its screens. The chainings are invisible, everything seems improvised or juxtaposed. This text induces by agglutinating rather than demonstrating, by coupling and decoupling, gluing and ungluing....[51]

Allowing these words to resonate for a time, I would like to juxtapose with them the condition of poetry in Scots, which does not and has not for centuries existed in any pure, undefiled, single column, but has shown a continuing awareness of its co-existence with English poetry. Constantly it has asserted its otherness, its independence; but those very gestures come about as a result of an awareness of the sprawling parallel text of the English language. Scots as a literary language has constantly to assert that it is alive, to beat loudly the drum of its own heart. You hear that in Allan Ramsay as in MacDiarmid, and critics tediously assert from the eighteenth century to our own day that the language is on the point of expiry; that it is being defiled, made impure by the power of the parallel, English-language column; that Scots is becoming a franglais.

To a degree it is. For English and Scots don't just run in parallel columns, they cross over, merge, and retreat from one another, they couple and decouple, glue and unglue. When, around 1930, Muriel Spark as a book-hungry Edinburgh schoolgirl writes a poem in which the inhabitants of other planets 'Look up to the sky and say / "The Earth twinkles clearly tonight"', then she is surely carrying over into English an effect found in the Scots verse of Robert Louis Stevenson and Hugh MacDiarmid, who likes to see the earth from outer space giving off an 'unearthly licht' as it 'twinkles like a star the night' in his poem 'The Innumerable Christ'.[52]

When MacDiarmid in *A Drunk Man Looks at the Thistle* accuses many people of being 'nocht but zoologically men' or writes with regard to Burns that 'The whisky that aince moved your lyre's become / A laxative for a' loquacity', are those terms 'zoologically', 'laxative' and 'loquacity' good, broad Scots? Doesn't their English, polysyllabic quality heighten the dismissive effect? These crossovers are examples of the sustaining impurity within the amalgam of Scottish culture which does not simply run in separate parallel columns, but also sparks between them, with an energy Bakhtin would have admired.

Modern poetry in Scots is rich because it exploits its impurity, because it utilizes its own uncertain status. A great deal of time can be wasted by engaging in the argument about whether Scots is a language or a dialect or a group of dialects. Much more interesting is the fact that there is such an argument, because it suggests the prevailing uncertainty about what exactly Scots *is*. It suggests that within Scots there is room for free-play, that Scots is not easily fixed and defined, that its boundaries are mobile. This may or may not be because Scots is in decline. Comparing the poetry in Scots written in our century with that written in the nineteenth century surely suggests that Scots is in the ascendant, not because it is fixed but because it is fluid; not because it conforms to the *Scots Style Sheet* or to any one system, but because it frolics and astounds, because frequently 'everything seems improvised or juxtaposed' filled with 'coupling and decoupling ..., gluing and ungluing'. In the introduction to his anthology of contemporary poetry in Scots, *The New Makars* – the first such anthology for thirteen years – Tom Hubbard argues that 'Poets exemplify *homo ludens*. We delight in wordplay, in guddling about in a language. We can have a grand guddle in Scots.'[53] Hubbard's emphasis on the ludic, playful quality of Scots seems to me exemplary, and I would argue that this is enhanced by the free 'play', the uncertainties of just where the borders of Scots lie, uncertainties that cannot be annulled by academic or lexicographical decree, but which may in fact be welcomed both by poets and by those sympathetic to the work of Bakhtin.

In order to develop such contentions, and to argue for greater confidence in Scotland's linguistic resources, I turn now to the verse of four 'identifying poets' who use Scots yet three of whom are excluded from Hubbard's anthology. These poets' work exhibits the keenest awareness of being at home in late twentieth-century Scotland, that cultural amalgam with its enriching simultaneities. These poets are among the most vital carriers of our tradition in Scots simply because they have learned to exploit the uneasy, shifting ground which Scots occupies. They live not just beside the parallel column of English, but also between the gutter and the dictionary, both of which they can see as fruitful resources. These are the writers whose Scots has the most daring imaginative *virr*. Like the heteroglot Murray, Walcott and Reading, they are among the poets in whom language lives, and their language is the language of home.

When Edwin Morgan returned to publishing work after coming home at the end of World War Two, his first published piece was a letter to the *Glasgow Herald* in 1946 which appeared under the heading 'Plastic Scots'.[54] An uncertain Morgan was urging that we should at least suspend judgement on the sort of 'plastic' or 'aggrandised' or 'synthetic' Scots which had been used by MacDiarmid. Later, in the 1950s, it is the very plasticity of the medium which excites Morgan in his best Scots work. Though a delay in book publication meant that they did not appear until 1972, Morgan's translations of the Russian modernist poet Mayakovsky collected in *Wi the Haill Voice* date from the 1950s and 60s and must rank as one of the striking achievements of modern Scots verse. The achievement was conducted under the sign of Hugh MacDiarmid.[55] Morgan's introduction to the book concludes by saying that in making the translations he had 'hoped Hugh MacDiarmid might be right' when he claimed in 'Gairmscoile' that

> ...there's forgotten shibboleths of the Scots
> Hae keys to senses lockit to us yet

– Coorse words that shamble thro oor minds like stots
Syne turn on's muckle een wi doonsin emerauds lit.[56]

In one of those finely incestuous gestures so characteristic of Scottish culture, MacDiarmid himself wrote about the book in the *Cambridge Review*, describing its introduction as 'itself the most valuable article on Mayakovsky yet published in English', and congratulated Morgan on his success.[57]

Morgan's translations certainly descend from and harness MacDiarmid's synthetic Scots, but this eclecticism of diction is quickened by the linguistic experimentalism of his Russian original. Morgan quotes Mayakovsky's 1926 statement that 'Innovation, innovation in materials and methods, is obligatory for every poetical composition', and points out that Mayakovsky had been a signatory to the 1912 futurist manifesto, 'A Slap in the Face of Public Taste', which determined 'to enlarge vocabulary in its *scope* with arbitrary and derivative words (creation of new words)'.[58] Mayakovsky, Bakhtin's contemporary, with his interest in neologism, in mixing registers, and in the sound of poetry of *zaum*, nourished various aspects of Morgan's work, and certainly fuelled the energy of his Scots. In an interview with W. N. Herbert, Morgan recalled 'I started using Scots in translations in the late 1940s and through the 1950s – perhaps this was sparked off by the Lallans controversies of that post-war period'.[59] Morgan, then, was translating Mayakovsky, who controversially extended the boundaries of his Russian language, at a period when a linguistic controversy raged in Scotland about the range, boundaries, and validity of the so-called 'Lallans' or synthetic Scots.

'Ay, but can ye', the first poem in *Wi the Haill Voice*, throws out a challenge:

But you
wi denty thrapple
can ye wheeple
nocturnes fae a rone-pipe flute?
(*WHV*, 19)

Acknowledging that the city is the principal home of modern people, these poems wage war on 'denty' (dainty) taste, and campaign for a poetry that is clearly of the modern age and is urban, of the world of rone-pipes, yet at the same time instinct with lyrical and other possibilities. That word 'rone' is Scots enough to find it in the *Concise Scots Dictionary*, yet also sufficiently familiar in English to find its way into *The Concise Oxford Dictionary of Current English*. The genesis of Morgan's translations shows an awareness of living in the polyphony of Scotland. Morgan translated the poems from Russian into English verse first of all, and then carried

them over once again into Scots. Peter McCarey sees this in part as a
making strange – an *ostranenie* that recaptured something of the oddness
of Mayakovsky's work for its original Russian audience;[60] but Morgan's
translation from English into Scots is also an exploitation of the linguistic
flexibility, the free-play of synthetic Scots in which it is much more
acceptable to steal, invent, and glue together words that it is in 'correct'
English. So the English of 'With ice for shoe-leather' becomes the Scots
of 'wi ice-shoggly bauchles' where the term 'ice-shoggly' is Morgan's
brand-new coinage. The word 'presto' in the English becomes the more
idiomatically energetic Scots 'wheech'.[61] But the poems are not simply
grown out of English seeds which flower in Scots. They also enact a
circulation between English and Scots as is obvious in 'Mandment No. 2
to the Army o the Arts':

> That means you –
> cooerin wi the mystical leafletfuls,
> yir broos aa runklt like plewland –
> futuristicos
> imaginisticos
> acmeisticos
> trachlt in moosewabs o crambo-doodlin.
>
> (*WHV*, 39)

The heteroglot language here is inventive and lively, but is it English or
Scots – is it both or neither? 'Mystical leafletfuls' is English surely – but
'leafletful' is not a word to be found in the *OED*. Are those terms
'futuristicos / imaginisticos / acmeisticos' English or Scots? Perhaps only
a linguistic Spanish Inquisition would demand firm answers to these
questions. What the questions show up is the way Morgan is able to
exploit the disputed frontier, the uneasy boundary between English and
Scots. It is not a problem for him. It is a source of creative energy.

The Scots of *Wi the Haill Voice* does not just extend to neologisms and
dictionary terms like 'crambo-doodlin' which surely were not to be heard
on the lips of Scots speakers in the Fifties, Sixties, or Seventies. It also
extends to the use of Glaswegian registers, the registers of Morgan's home
city. The admired translation of 'Mayakonferensky's Anectidote' (first
published in 1954) includes, for instance, the lines

> I stummle up a hunner sterrs.
> The licht's kinna dim.
>
> (*WHV*, 42)

'Kinna' – is that a Scots word? No, some might reply. It is a phonetic
transcription of a pronunciation of English speech. But 'kinna' in

Morgan's poem is a word, and it is clearly not an English word. Equally clearly, it is being deployed to strengthen the Scottish quality of the diction. 'Kinna' is there, surely, as a locution Morgan knows from Glasgow, just like the line in his translation, 'Versailles',

> Bygode thae deid-yins done theirsels weel!
> (*WHV*, 49)

Rather than squabbling over how exactly we might define that single word 'bygode', it is more fruitful to see that it, like the invented vocabulary of 'comblasticastraflocate sans avizandum', (*WHV*, 44) constitutes an expansion of the range of Scots, extending it in the direction of the language of the Glasgow populace as well as of the professional Russian translator's dictionary. *Wi the Haill Voice* is written in a Scots that is aware of, steals from, veers towards and away from standard English. It is aware not just of the 'other tongue' but also of the freedom which it possesses and the other tongue does not. It is aware of the hard-to-pin-down whittrick fluidity of Scots which can be a Joycean quality. It's no accident that MacDiarmid looked to Joyce in his 1923 'Theory of Scots Letters', nor is it an accident that Morgan has a Scots-speaking MacDiarmid converse with Joyce in the first dialogue of the 1961 sequence *The Whittrick*.[62] But the fluidity of Morgan's Scots extends not just to English and into the Scots dictionary. It also extends in a direction in which MacDiarmid's speech did not go. It breaks away from the dangerous archaizing temptations of a writer like Sydney Goodsir Smith, and begins to explore the possibility of using Glaswegian vernacular in 'serious' Scots poetry. The range of Morgan's Scots is even wider than MacDiarmid's, even more 'improvised or juxtaposed … coupling and decoupling, gluing and ungluing.' It is impure. And that is its strength.

Morgan's work gestured towards the Glasgow streets of his home ground but Morgan himself seems unsure whether or not to call their language Scots. In interviews he seems to regard Glaswegian as a dialect of Scots, yet one might recall Tom Hubbard's assertion that 'Glaswegian dialect is less "Scots" than other dialects.'[63] All this simply emphasizes the way Morgan saw the possibilities afforded by the loose boundaries that go with Scots; it also signposts us towards the work of Tom Leonard.

Leonard's work, like Morgan's exploits our awareness of the Bakhtinian parallel presence of various kinds of language, 'proper' and 'improper': language that is English, that is Scots, and language that operates in border territory.

> right inuff
> ma language is disgraceful
> ma maw tellt mi

> ma teacher tellt mi
> thi doactir tellt mi
> thi priest tellt mi
>
> ...
>
> jist aboot ivry book ah oapnd tellt mi
> even thi introduction tay thi Scottish National Dictionary tellt mi
> ach well
> all livin language is sacred
> fuck thi lohta thim[64]

Clearly Leonard is not writing in English, and the poem relies on us being aware that the people who tell the speaker that his language is disgraceful are probably 'correct' English speakers. But the poem also makes us aware that Leonard's language is likely to be spurned by those who wish to have a pure Scots of the sort found in the *Scottish National Dictionary* – his language is likely to be rejected by some of those whom one might suppose his 'ain folk'. In practice, such is the case, since Scots anthologists such as Alexander Scott and Tom Hubbard exclude him. This seems to be unhelpful, as if purism and pedantry were getting the better of poetry. As a working-class Glaswegian Leonard has complained that 'I turn off when people say "Is it dialect or is it patois?" because inevitably behind that there's a hierarchy going on' and has pointed out that his poetic language 'wasn't just considered bad English, but bad Scots as well, and I thought that was pretty desperate'. While he thinks that it is 'a real possibility for a poet to be using Scots words which you may find in the Scots dictionary', nonetheless, 'One of the things I've found offputting about the Lallans movement on the other hand is that it is extremely conservative as far as poetic form and philosophy is concerned ...': 'I used to get a bit of stick from some of the people who were very strong on it, that I was one of these patter merchants or whatever. I could sense a real class bourgeois trait going on there. I always felt that a lot of these people had been to a fee paying school and then had to go and learn how to speak 'Scottish'. I had more Scottish words in my mouth in five minutes than they would have in a year, you know. These would be the same people who would be wagging their finger and telling me how to be Scottish and so on.'[65]

Leonard's attitude towards many of the Scots language activists is summed up by his drawing of a poster which says

MAKARS' SOCIETY

GRAN' MEETIN'
THE NICHT

> TAE DECIDE THE
> SPELLIN'
> O' THIS POSTER.
> ADMISSION: THRITTY PEE
> (A HEID).
> (*IV*, 53)

Other twentieth-century Scottish poets, for all their interest in what language does to us, have complained about similar phenomena. W. S. Graham recalled the language activist who refused to use the word 'telephone' and urged callers to contact him on 'Farspeak 7638'.[66] MacDiarmid blasted that sort of thing apart, and so in his way does Tom Leonard. This makes some sections of the Scots poetic community keen to exclude his work, but I think it's time we included it as an adventurous and valid broadening of the fluid palette of Scots.

If MacDiarmid's early Scots work was written at a deliberate Scottish angle to the English language, then so is Leonard's. It is a language intensely aware of its own difference. His best Scots poems are always aware of the other tongue or tongues that exist in competition. Morgan has championed the first of the 'Unrelated Incidents' series in which like MacDiarmid in 'Gairmscoile' and like many another Scots poet, Leonard writes not only *in* his language but also *about* it.[67] This poem also relies on the unspoken simultaneous awareness of standard English for its full effect. Its language makes it identifiably local, a poem of home. It is also written clearly out of that Scottish (though far from uniquely Scottish) experience of living across or between as well as in languages. Like the poem about reading 'thi / six a clock / news ... / wia / BBC accent', (*IV*, 88) this poem depends on a heteroglot awareness of parallel languages and on the politically-charged air that circulates in the space between them. But the poem's engagement with the politics of language, and with wider politics beyond that, makes it very much a poem of international appeal, an intellectually lively poem about what Seamus Heaney has called 'the government of the tongue'.[68] Leonard's poetry deals with issues of power which would have been recognized by Burns and MacDiarmid, but he does so in a vocabulary that is an urban Scots handled by neither writer. He has extended and invigorated the language. His work draws on one of the two most exciting linguistic resources open to the contemporary Scots poet: what too many purists wish to dismiss scornfully as 'thi lang-/wij a thi/guhtr'.

Leonard's sharp sense of his home-ground's spoken urban Scots is something he shares with Liz Lochhead, with whom he has collaborated in such projects as the 1982 revue *Tickly Mince*. Certainly the Scots note is sounded only very rarely among the poems in Lochhead's *Dreaming Frankenstein & Collected Poems*, but it is there:

> This some kinnuffa Huntigowk for Hogmany?
> Hell-mend-ye, ye're
> a bad penny, Jimmy –
> Mister Ne'erdy Ne'er-do-Weel
> sae chitterin' ill-clad for the caul'
> sae drawn an' pale,
> oh, wi' the black bun burnin' a hole
> in yir poackit an' the coal
> a Live Coal.[69]

In these lines from 'Fetch On the First of January', 'Huntigowk' is the sort of word that would content the purists, but 'kinnuffa' is probably not. Urban, Glaswegian Scots meets more respectable dictionary language. The familiar and the slightly alien mix in this poem whose last line is close to being in standard English. It is a poem about one self confronting another, so all these shifts in diction and register play their part as self and other graze against one another. Here is a further example of a writer alert to the heteroglossic possibilities of writing in Scots, and, wider than that, of writing in a Scottish linguistic and cultural context.

Though this present book is not about the theatre, I think I would be foolish not to touch on Liz Lochhead's dramatic Scots poetry as exemplified in her version of Molière's *Tartuffe*, an achievement followed more recently by Morgan's *Cyrano de Bergerac*. As Lochhead's Introduction explains, the Scots that she uses is 'a totally invented and, I hope, theatrical Scots, full of anachronisms, demotic speech from various eras and areas; it's proverbial, slangy, couthy, clichéd, catch-phrasey, and vulgar ... – most of the characters are at least bilingual and consequently more or less 'two-faced'.'[70] This 'bi-lingualism' which Lochhead exploits is again made possible by the way we Scots live across languages. Lochhead's language darts between the columns of the parallel text available to her – by which I mean not the parallel columns of French and English, but the columns of English and Scots. Each colours and invigorates the other, and we pass constantly backwards and forwards across the linguistic spectrum that moves from English to Scots.

> MARIANNE: Oh don't do it Valère! D'you think I'd enjoy to see
> Two grown men fighting, and all over me?
> Forget Tartuffe! I'd never marry him anyway.
> Dorine'll tell you I refused point blank. No way!
> DORINE: But yir stepmither! Gently does it baith o' ye –

She'll soart Tartuffe, and yir faither tae!
Tartuffe's aye sookin' in wi her and it's ma theory
He's got an awfy soft spot for Elmire. Eh?
You've never noticed? Mibbe Ah read too much intae
The slaiverin' pee-hereness that you're blin' tae ...
At ony rate: Missis somehow discovered
Orgon's daft scheme and how yir lover'd
Jist get the bum's rush, wi' nae by-yir-leave
So ye'd mairry Tartuffe – well she couldnae believe
It! How could it come up Orgon's humph
To abandon his dochter tae yon big sumph?

(*T*, 29)

It might seem here we pass from Marianne's English to Dorine's Scots, but the abrupt two-word exclamation 'No way!' at the end of Marianne's speech already has an idiomatically Glaswegian ring. We hear that ring throughout, as characters ask, for instance, 'Am I right or am I wrong?' or talk about getting 'the bum's rush'. But this is combined with more respectably, dictionaried Scots like 'bletheranskite'. (*T*, 18) Low and high, gutter and dictionary flow torrentially together to create a diction of kaleidoscopic pace and liveliness, a Scots which manages to bring Tartuffe in touch with Holy Willie while preserving an alertness to the polyphonies of Lochhead's contemporary Scottish homeland. Far too much Scots verse written today sounds as if it might have been written fifty (or sometimes even a hundred) years ago. Liz Lochhead's Scots does not. It is that awareness of the liveliest and most adventurous possibilities in con-temporary Scots which links her to the other writers whose work I am discussing. The very uncertainty of the boundaries of Scots works to her advantage, enlivening her hybrid, heterogeneous language in *Tartuffe* and in sections of the Scots / English play, *Mary Queen of Scots Got Her Head Chopped Off* (Penguin, 1989).

It could be argued that as a translator, Lochhead, like the Morgan of *Wi the Haill Voice* and *Cyrano,* is provided with a given content, and so can devote most of her energy to the formal play of her Scots. While it is true that translation may have encouraged strong concentration on the wordgames possible in an adventurously-deployed Scots, it would be hard to contest with conviction that the witty, at times fierce and physical content of *Tartuffe* was being sacrificed to intellectual game-playing. Translation may encourage a particularly close attention to the formal properties of language, but (as a wide variety of audiences have testified), Lochhead's Scots, like Morgan's, is eminently successful in the theatre.

Along with Tom Leonard, Liz Lochhead belongs to that middle

generation of Scots poets who were born in the 1940s, while Edwin
Morgan (b. 1920) belongs to the distinguished senior generation which
directly inherited the achievements and possibilities of Scots as developed
by MacDiarmid. If we move to the younger generation, it seems to me the
most exciting voice in Scots poetry is that of the Dundonian W. N.
Herbert. Incest is a phenomenon one soon encounters in Scotland as in
many other cultures, so it is only fair that I should declare immediately
that I have collaborated with Herbert on several projects, and have even
shared *Sharawaggi*, a 1990 book of poems with him. Yet it seems right to
include his work here because he is surely a strong inheritor of the
imaginatively adventurous line in contemporary Scottish poetry of home
which I have been outlining.

Herbert was born in Dundee in 1961 and schooled (like a number of
other young Dundonian writers including the novelist James Meek and
the young poet Matthew Fitt) at the Grove Academy where he was taught
by Forbes Browne, now Business Editor for the magazine *Gairfish* of
which Herbert is founder editor. Though he lives in Oxford, where he
read English at university, Herbert floods his poetry with the sight and
sounds of his home town of Dundee. It is clearly Dundonian in accent,
using the form 'Eh' for the 'I' pronoun, and drawing on various elements
of local vocabulary. It is an urban Scots, alert to the 'language of the
gutter' as well as to the dictionary. Herbert wrote his doctorate on Hugh
MacDiarmid, whom he has described in an interview as 'Papa', and on
whom he has published a book.[71] Arguably his own Scots in its love of the
dictionary owes a good deal to MacDiarmid, but also to the streets of his
home city. It is a Scots that is wider-ranging than that of Leonard or
Lochhead, a Scots that is lyrical and intellectually ambitious in its hetero-
dox assembly. Herbert's 1986 manifesto piece, 'Radical Scots' gestures
towards Ashbery's 'Litany' and the music of Elliot Carter, while contend-
ing that 'unavoidably, Scots exists *with reference* to English, that is its
present strength'. In a sparky piece of flyting, Herbert savages the 'Scot-
tish Languageites' whom he pictures as 'a thin grey line of bespectacled
beetles, ex-eighteenth-grammarians, pseudo-autodidacts, and refugees
from the sacking of the Academie Francaise, all carting the Anchises of the
Scots Style Sheet, all lightly twittering "we must have one Scots and one
Scots only ..."'

Herbert celebrates and deploys what he sees as the 'insatiably heteroge-
neous faculty' in the most exciting contemporary Scots.[72] He particularly
admires the work of Morgan, and one can sense Morgan's urbanizing of
Scots, as well as the voice of Whitman in Herbert's impressive prentice-
work the 'Dundee Doldrums', a number of which were published by
Duncan Glen in the final issue of *Akros* magazine in October 1983 and

then republished by Galliard in volume form with an introduction in 1991:

> Ghaist o Thurties, Dundee whan thi Daith cam doon,
> Grey sinders descendin, meldit wi claiths an dreams,
> Dundee whan Amerika fell,
> Dundee whan thi Depreshun cam owerseas
> An bided, an restit in our faithers braces –
> Oor flatbunnits! Bandylegs! Oor rickets!
> – Waulkin uppa street, a deid, a ghostie,
> A passedby, a damnit, a wurkir;
> Ghaist restless an nivir kennin green.

In publishing the first 'Dundee Doldrums', Duncan Glen hailed 'a young man (only twenty-one) not afraid to be risk-taker in the service (and joy) of language and poetry'.[73] Herbert's later work in Scots has been praised by a variety of commentators, including Douglas Dunn, Edwin Morgan, and Iain Crichton Smith. His Scots has also been blasted by critics including Alasdair Macrae and Maurice Lindsay. Herbert is certainly the most controversial of the younger Scots poets; my treatment of him here is partisan. But his heterogeneous language as well as the reach of his imagination and intellect are outstandingly exciting. His most recent poetry in Scots uses a simpler, more colloquial diction, but some of his most controversial pieces use an impasto Scots; the poems come with their own glossaries, are presented as plunges into the 'other' of the language which is both native and foreign. They guddle with words, achieving strange effects, as in the part-surreal lyrical ending of 'The Socialist Manifesto for East Balgillo' in which the 'Eh' of the poem revisits in sleep the landscape and language contours of his upbringing 'whaur Dundee dovirs oan thi rink / o ma frore-thicht lyk a Michael- / angelo oan skates', and achieves a vision of the dignity of Scotland:

> Eh pense o naethin, lat naethin be,
> see thi mense of Scoatlan lyk Mozart's
> gartillin conert, hiz piana spaldit
> assa smokie, and innuts paums
> a gaitherin o chestnuts lyk shut een.[74]

That surreal process by which a Mozartian piano splits open to become an Arbroath smokie is characteristic of Herbert's at times lyrically destructive imagination. The poem ends ambiguously, offering chestnuts from which the future may grow, but which are also severed, asleep and blind. Herbert's relations with Dundee are problematical and often bitter, and the city's cultural establishment has tended to give him the cold shoulder.

But, as an extract from *The Testament of Piers Parallax* in Tom Hubbard's *New Makars* anthology makes clear, Herbert is well aware that his home town of 'Dundee' and 'Duende' (that quality of 'deep song' celebrated by Lorca) are anagrams of one another.

> Cam doon *Duende, Duende* cam doon:
> Dundee is yir pit and anerly toon ...[75]

I have quoted liberally from the work of W. N. Herbert because he is the least well-known of these four contemporary Scots poets of home. His work combines, like that of the others, simultaneous awareness of the gutter and the dictionary. It has a Dundonian voice which moves easily back and fro between the Hilltown and Renaissance art. It is often a difficult voice, but that difficulty is part of its powerful and heterogeneous life, which is the strong, heteroglot life both of Herbert's home town and of his home country. Herbert is as much a poet of his home city of Dundee as Morgan, Leonard and Lochhead are poets of Glasgow. Yet none is restricted by his or her home ground, any more than Les Murray is restricted by Bunyah or Peter Reading by his home in Shropshire. All these poets, like the others considered in this book, are 'identifying poets', yet their identities are no more 'pure' than their language. Their identities, rather, are fruitfully impure, in keeping with the ideas of Bakhtin. These are identities developed out of contact with, and sometimes by partaking of, a 'significant other', another language, *Anither Music* (to use the title of a 1991 collection by Herbert), or another culture or another self.[76] For the poet in a culture such as Scotland or Australia or America, there are internal as well as external 'significant others'. So, for instance, the poet who writes in Scots in Scotland is likely to have to engage with the 'other' of English; equally the poet who writes in English in Scotland is likely to be subtly aware of Gaelic and Scots identities which are Scottish also. Identity for the Scottish identifying poets, and for identifying poets generally, is not a matter of purity but of an amalgam of resources. To pretend differently in this postmodern age is to be guilty of something analogous to racism.

It may be that in future poets will grow weary of, and may wish to elude the heritage bequeathed to them by the twentieth century's identifying poets. No poet wishes to feel obliged simply to be a spokesperson for his or her community. One sees the signs of discomfort with that role in the work of Murray and Heaney, for instance. For Scottish poetry as I write the prospects seem exciting. Work by younger writers such as Kathleen Jamie, Don Paterson, John Burnside, Meg Bateman and Angela McSeveney is beginning to command attention. Though there are signs that several of these writers are already 'identifying poets', it is impossible to predict what will happen, and I have no wish to try to do so. The logic of a good poet's development is often apparent in retrospect, but never in prospect. This book is not designed to function as a crystal ball, but is intended to support the contention that, whatever happens to poetry in the third millenium, it is increasingly evident as the twentieth century nears its close that it has been, and continues to be a century of 'identifying poets'. The more fully we realize this fact, the less ready we shall be to accept the hierarchy of taste which subtly downgrades the poetry of home as 'regionalist'. Once that begins to happen, the century's critics will have started to catch up with its poets and a subtly different, more accurate and generous map of modern verse may emerge, one with which the identifying poets are at home.

Notes

INTRODUCTION

1. Les Murray, 'The Suspect Captivity of the Fisher King', in *Blocks and Tackles: Articles and Essays 1982 to 1990* (North Ryde, NSW: Angus & Robertson, 1990), 151–8; Dana Gioia, 'Can Poetry Matter?', *The Atlantic Monthly*, May 1991, 94–106; in Britain Gioia's article was reprinted in *Poetry Review*, Vol. 81, No. 4 (Winter 1991/92), 36–46; Dana Gioia interviewed by Robert McPhillips, *Verse*, Vol. 9, No. 2 (Summer, 1992), 9–27.
2. Anthony Elliot, 'Finding One's Self in a Self–less World', review of S. Lash and J. Friedman, eds, *Modernity and Identity*; A. J. Cascardi, *The Subject of Modernity*; Seyla Benhabib, *Situating the Self*, *Times Higher Education Supplement*, 10 July 1992, 19 and 22.
3. William Wordsworth, *The Prelude, or Growth of a Poet's Mind (Text of 1805)*, ed. Ernest de Selincourt, revised impression (London: Oxford University Press, 1960), 197.
4. Wordsworth cited in René Wellek, *A History of Modern Criticism 1750–1950, Vol. 2. The Romantic Age* (1955; rpt. Cambridge: Cambridge University Press, 1981), 138.
5. See Arthur Rimbaud, *Complete Works*, translated by Paul Schmidt (New York: Harper & Row, 1976), 102 (letter to Paul Demeny, 15 May 1871).
6. S. I. Lockerbie, 'Introduction' to Guillaume Apollinaire, *Calligrammes*, translated by Anne Hyde Greet (Berkeley: University of California Press, 1980), 8.
7. See Fernando Pessoa, *Selected Poems*, second edition, translated by Jonathan Griffin (Harmondsworth: Penguin Books, 1982).
8. Robert Louis Stevenson, *Dr Jekyll and Mr Hyde and Other Stories*, ed. Jenni Calder (Harmondsworth: Penguin Books, 1979), 81.
9. *Ibid.*, 84, 87, 93.
10. *Ibid.*, 97.
11. C. S. Peirce, cited in David K. Danow, *The Thought of Mikhail Bakhtin: From Word to Culture* (Basingstoke: Macmillan, 1991), 23.
12. On Bakhtin and the Marburg School see Katerina Clark and Michael Holquist, *Mikhail Bakhtin* (Cambridge, Mass. : Harvard University Press, 1984), 54–62; Eliot's interest in the Marburg School has yet to be explored fully, but see Lyndall Gordon, *Eliot's Early Years* (Oxford: Oxford University Press, 1977), 65.
13. M. M. Bakhtin, *Art and Answerability*, ed. Michael Holquist and Vadim Liapunov, translated by Vadim Liapunov (Austin: University of Texas Press, 1990), 65–6 ('Author and Hero in Aesthetic Activity').
14. See John C. Pope's articles 'Prufrock and Raskolnikov', *American Literature*, 17 (November 1945), 213–30, and 'Prufrock and Raskolnikov Again: A Letter from Eliot', *American Literature*, 18 (January, 1947), 319–21.

15. Robert Burns, 'To a Louse', in *Poems and Songs*, ed. James Kinsley (Oxford: Oxford University Press, 1969), 157. While there is obviously much that separates Bakhtin from this Burns poem and from the Smith of the *Theory of Moral Sentiments*, it is worth juxtaposing those Scottish works with the Bakhtin who writes in *Art and Answerability* that 'we are constantly and intently on the watch for reflections of our own life on the plane of other people's consciousness, and, moreover, not just reflections of particular moments of our life, but even reflections of the whole of it. ' ('Author and Hero in Aesthetic Activity', 16).

16. David McCrone, *Understanding Scotland: The Sociology of a Stateless Nation* (London: Routledge, 1992), 1.

17. Robert Crawford, *Devolving English Literature* (Oxford: Clarendon Press, 1992).

18. See, for example Katie Wales, *The Language of James Joyce* (Basingstoke: Macmillan, 1992) and Steve Ellis, *The English Eliot: Design, Language and Landscape in 'Four Quartets'* (London: Routledge, 1991), 54–76.

19. M. M. Bakhtin, *The Dialogic Imagination: Four Essays*, ed. Michael Holquist, translated by Caryl Emerson and Michael Holquist (Austin: University of Texas Press, 1981), 12 ('Epic and Novel').

20. W. N. Herbert, draft of 'Carrying MacDiarmid On', published in revised form in *Chapman* No. 69–70, Autumn 1992, 20.

21. Bakhtin, *The Dialogic Imagination*, 61 ('From the Prehistory of Novelistic Discourse').

22. Bakhtin cited in Tzvetan Todorov, *Mikhail Bakhtin: The Dialogic Principle* (Manchester: Manchester University Press, 1984), 66.

23. Bakhtin, *The Dialogic Imagination*, 66 ('From the Prehistory of Novelistic Discourse').

24. Tony Crowley, 'Bakhtin and the History of the Language' in Ken Hirschkop and David Shepherd eds, *Bakhtin and Cultural Theory* (Manchester: Manchester University Press, 1989), 70.

25. *Ibid.*, 85.

26. *Ibid.*

27. Bakhtin, *The Dialogic Imagination*, 272 ('Discourse in the Novel').

28. Clark and Holquist, *Mikhail Bakhtin*, 22.

29. 'Art and Answerability' occupies pp. 1–3 of the book of that title (see note 13 above); 'From the Prehistory of Novelistic Discourse' occupies pp. 41–83 of *The Dialogic Imagination* (see note 19 above); M. M. Bakhtin, 'Response to a Question from the *Novy Mir* Editorial Staff' in *Speech Genres and Other Late Essays*, ed. Caryl Emerson and Michael Holquist, translated by Vern W. McGee (Austin: University of Texas Press, 1986), 1–9; Mikhail Bakhtin, *Rabelais and His World*, translated by Hélène Iswolsky (Bloomington: Indiana University Press, 1984).

30. For Clark and Holquist see note 12 above; for Danow see note 11 above; David Lodge, *After Bakhtin: Essays on Fiction and Criticism* (London: Routledge, 1990). Michael Holquist's *Dialogism: Bakhtin and his World* in the New Accents series (London: Routledge, 1990) seems to me less 'student-friendly' than one might expect.

31. Bakhtin, *The Dialogic Imagination*, 49 ('From the Prehistory of Novelistic Discourse').

32 Michael Palmer edited *Code of Signals: Recent Writing in Poetics* (Berkeley: North Atlantic, 1983) which contains Michael Davidson's essay 'Discourse in Poetry: Bakhtin and Extensions of the Dialogical'; Ian Gregson makes use of Bakhtin's work in his essay, '"There are many worlds": The "Dialogic" in *Terry Street* and After' in Robert Crawford and David Kinloch, eds, *Reading Douglas Dunn* (Edinburgh: Edinburgh University Press, 1992), 17–31.

33. Edwin Morgan, conversation with the present writer, Edinburgh, 9 July 1992; questioned in a later phone call (16 July 1992), Morgan recalled knowing about Bakhtin's ideas in the 1970s – 'maybe early Seventies' –

before he read some of Bakhtin's work in English translation in the later Seventies. He found the ideas very attractive since they 'chimed in' with his own interests. 'Apart from references and quotations I think the first extended things I came across were his [Bakhtin's] book on Rabelais (published in America, MIT, 1968) and the essay "Discourse Typology in Prose" (from his book on Dostoyevsky) included in *Readings in Russian Poetics*, ed. Matejka and Pomorska (also from MIT, 1971). ' (Postcard to the present writer, 17 July 92).

34. Gary Saul Morson and Caryl Emerson, *Mikhail Bakhtin: Creation of a Prosaics* (Stanford: Stanford University Press, 1990).

35. Julia Kristeva, 'Word, Dialogue and Novel' (originally written in French in 1966 and published in 1969) in Toril Moi, ed., *The Kristeva Reader* (Oxford: Blackwell, 1986), 34–61; Tzvetan Todorov, *op. cit.* (see note 22 above).

36. Don H. Bialostosky, *Wordsworth, Dialogics, and the Practice of Criticism* (Cambridge: Cambridge University Press, 1992); John Carey, *The Intellectuals and the Masses: Pride and Prejudice among the Literary Intelligentsia, 1880–1939* (London: Faber and Faber, 1992), 215.

37. Clark and Holquist, *Mikhail Bakhtin*, 327.

38. Morson and Emerson, *Creation of a Prosaics*, 50–1; the abbreviation *TRDB* refers to Appendix I of *Problems of Dostoevsky's Poetics* (see following note).

39. Mikhail Bakhtin, *Problems of Dostoevsky's Poetics*, ed. and translated by Caryl Emerson (Minneapolis: University of Minnesota Press, 1984), 301, note 7.

40. M. M. Bakhtin, *Speech Genres*, 6–7 ('Response to a Question from the *Novy Mir* Editorial Staff').

CHAPTER 1

1. William H. Pritchard, *Frost, A Literary Life Reconsidered* (New York: Oxford University Press, 1984), 36.

2. *Selected Letters of Robert Frost*, ed. Lawrance Thompson (London: Jonathan Cape, 1965), 514. Further references to this book will be found in the text under the abbreviation, *SL.*

3. William R. Evans, *Robert Frost and Sidney Cox, Forty Years of Friendship* (Hanover, New Hampshire: University Press of New England, 1981), 258. Further references to this book will be found in the text under the abbreviation, *Cox.*

4. John C. Kemp, *Robert Frost and New England, The Poet as Regionalist* (Princeton: Princeton University Press, 1979), 97. Further references to this book in the text will be found under the abbreviation, *Kemp.*

5. Lawrance Thompson, *Robert Frost, The Early Years 1874–1915* (London: Jonathan Cape, 1967), 37–8. Further references to this book will be found in the text under the abbreviation, *EY.*

6. *Newdick's Season of Frost: An Interrupted Biography of Robert Frost*, ed. William A. Sutton (Albany: State University of New York Press, 1976), 23. Further references to this book will be found in the text under the abbreviation, *Newdick.*

7. *Interviews with Robert Frost*, ed. Edward Connery Lathem (London: Jonathan Cape, 1967), 165. Further references to this book will be found in the text under the abbreviation, *Interviews.*

8. See John St C. Crane, *Robert Frost, A Descriptive Catalogue of Books and Manuscripts in the Clifton Waller Barrett Library, University of Virginia* (London: Dawson, 1974), 61.

9. Frost, 'The Figure a Poem Makes,' reprinted (from US editions of the *Complete Poems*) in James Scully, ed., *Modern Poets on Modern Poetry* (London: Collins, 1966), 57; cp. *EY*, 55.

10. Though the two men disagreed on many points, it is interesting to compare this with Eliot's stress on 'auditory imagination', *The Use of Poetry and The Use of Criticism* (1933; rpt. London: Faber and Faber, 1964), 118.

11. A good idea of the nature of Mrs Frost's story can be got from extracts reprinted in *EY*, 493–6.
12. Interestingly, the narrator of the poem perceives what the neighbour says to be his father's saying. The neighbour never tells us this.
13. George MacDonald, *Phantastes: A Faerie Romance for Men and Women* (London: Smith, Elder and Co., 1858), 13.
14. George MacDonald, *At the Back of the North Wind* (London: Strahan and Co., 1871), 345.
15. *Ibid.*, 349–50.
16. *Phantastes, ed. cit.*, 275.
17. Richard Poirier, *Robert Frost, The Work of Knowing* (New York: Oxford University Press, 1977), 303–13.
18. *At the Back of the North Wind, ed. cit.*, 373.
19. *Ibid.*, 237.
20. 'He [Frost] cut a strip about two inches wide down to the scalp from Richardson's forehead over the top of his head and down the back to the nape of the neck. He then cut a corresponding strip from one ear up over the head and down to the other ear. About this time Richardson [a fellow student] realized that something was wrong. . . '. (*Newdick*, 35)
21. Tom Paulin, 'Poetry and Power: Robert Frost' in *Minotaur: Poetry and the Nation State* (London: Faber and Faber, 1992), 171–89.

CHAPTER 2

1. Robert Crawford, *Devolving English Literature* (Oxford: Clarendon Press, 1992), Chapter V.
2. Peter McCarey, *Hugh MacDiarmid and the Russians* (Edinburgh: Scottish Academic Press, 1987), 15.
3. Kenneth Buthlay, ed., *A Drunk Man Looks at the Thistle* by Hugh MacDiarmid, (Edinburgh: Scottish Academic Press, 1987) 'Introduction,' l–li.
4. All the biographical information in this chapter is drawn from Alan Bold, *MacDiarmid* (London: John Murray, 1988).
5. Alan Bold, ed., *The Letters of Hugh MacDiarmid* (London: Hamish Hamilton, 1984), 10–11 (20 August 1916). Hereafter this work is referred to in the text using the abbreviation *L*.
6. Emma Letley, *From Galt to Douglas Brown: Nineteenth Century Fiction and Scots Language* (Edinburgh: Scottish Academic Press, 1988), 244–58.
7. Buthlay, *ed. cit.* in note 3 above, 21.
8. *Ibid.*
9. W. S. Graham, *Collected Poems* (London: Faber and Faber, 1979), 191.
10. C. M. Grieve, *Annals of the Five Senses* (1923; rpt. Edinburgh: Polygon Books, 1983), 28.
11. Hugh MacDiarmid, *The Complete Poems*, ed. Michael Grieve and W. R. Aitken (2 vols; London: Martin Brian & O'Keeffe, 1978), 240. Hereafter references to this work are given in the text of this chapter using the abbreviation *MCP*.
12. See John Davidson, *A Selection of His Poems*, ed. M. Lindsay, with Preface by T. S. Eliot, and Essay by Hugh MacDiarmid (London: Hutchinson, 1961); and Robert Crawford, *The Savage and the City in the Work of T. S. Eliot* (Oxford: Clarendon Press, 1987), 36–60.
13. See note 1 above.
14. T. S. Eliot, *The Complete Poems and Plays* (London: Faber and Faber, 1969), 98. Hereafter references to this work are given in the text of this chapter using the abbreviation *ECP*.
15. T. S. Eliot, *The Use of Poetry and the Use of Criticism* (1933; rpt. London: Faber and Faber, 1964), 148.
16. See James Joyce, *Ulysses*, (1922; rpt. Harmondsworth: Penguin, 1971), 591.

17. Hugh MacDiarmid, 'A Theory of Scots Letters' (1923), rpt. in Alan Bold, ed., *The Thistle Rises, An Anthology of Poetry and Prose by Hugh MacDiarmid* (London: Hamish Hamilton, 1984), 129–30. Hereafter references to this work are given in the text of this chapter using the abbreviation *TR*.
18. I am grateful to W. N. Herbert for informing me that this is where the poem first appeared.
19. See note 1 above.
20. Hugh MacDiarmid, *The Company I've Kept* (London: Hutchinson, 1966), 77.
21. Buthlay, *ed. cit.* in note 3 above, 109.

CHAPTER 3

1. Sorley MacLean, Letter to Hugh MacDiarmid, 8 March 1941 (Edinburgh University Library), cited in Joy Hendry, 'Sorley MacLean: the Man and his Work' in Raymond J. Ross and Joy Hendry, eds, *Sorley MacLean: Critical Essays* (Edinburgh: Scottish Academic Press, 1986), 27.
2. See Tomás Mac Síomóin, 'Poet of Conscience: The Old and the New in the Poetry of Somhairle MacGill–Eain', in Ross and Hendry, *op. cit.*, 112.
3. Somhairle MacGill-Eain, *Ris a' Bhruthaich: The Criticism and Prose Writings of Sorley MacLean*, ed. William Gillies (Stornoway: Acair, 1985), 117.
4. Sorley MacLean, 'Edinburgh Impressions,' *Alumni Bulletin: University of Edinburgh Alumni Magazine*, 1990, 5; Sorley MacLean in conversation with the present writer, St Andrews, 16 October 1991 – other information not specifically footnoted is drawn from my notes on this conversation. All quotations from MacLean's verse in this essay are taken from his *O Choille gu Bearradh/ From Wood to Ridge: Collected Poems in Gaelic and English* (Manchester: Carcanet, 1989), hereafter abbreviated in the text as *CPGE*.
5. The text of this poem, 'East Wind', is reproduced by Joy Hendry on p. 14 of her very useful article, cited in note 1 above. I am grateful to Wendy Aprilchild of Edinburgh University Library's Department of Special Collections for confirming that MacLean used the English forms of his name in David Daiches, ed., *Private Business* (Edinburgh: Edinburgh University English Literature Society, 1933).
6. *Ris a' Bhruthaich*, 10.
7. *Ris a' Bhruthaich*, 38–9; T. S. Eliot, 'The Metaphysical Poets', (1921) in *Selected Essays,* third enlarged edition (London: Faber and Faber, 1951), 288.
8. *Ris a' Bhruthaich*, 20, 38–39, 35, 42, 39.
9. *Ris a' Bhruthaich*, 115; T. S. Eliot, *The Use of Poetry and the Use of Criticism* (1933; rpt. London: Faber and Faber, 1964), 118.
10. Zbigniew Herbert, *Report from the Besieged City*, translated by John and Bogdana Carpenter (Oxford: Oxford University Press, 1987), 77.
11. Norman MacCaig, *Collected Poems*, new edition (London: Chatto & Windus, 1990), 15.
12. *Ibid.*, 189.
13. Particularly interesting on MacCaig and Gaelic culture is John MacInnes, 'MacCaig and Gaeldom' in Joy Hendry and Raymond Ross, eds, *Norman MacCaig: Critical Essays* (Edinburgh: Edinburgh University Press, 1990), 22–37.

CHAPTER 4

1. The following abbreviations are used in this piece to refer to works by Les Murray:

AY   *The Australian Year: The Chronicle of our Seasons and Celebrations* (North Ryde: Angus & Robertson, 1985).

BT   *Blocks and Tackles: Articles and Essays 1982 to 1990* (North Ryde, NSW: Angus & Robertson, 1990).

Boys   *The Boys Who Stole the Funeral* (North Ryde, NSW: Angus &

Robertson, 1980; Manchester: Carcanet, 1989); numerals in my text refer to sonnet numbers.

CP   *Collected Poems* (Manchester: Carcanet, 1991).

DFF   *Dog Fox Field* (North Ryde, NSW: Angus & Robertson, 1990; Manchester: Carcanet, 1991).

DM   *The Daylight Moon* (North Ryde, NSW: Angus & Robertson, 1990; Manchester: Carcanet, 1991).

NOB   *The New Oxford Book of Australian Verse*, Expanded Edition (Melbourne: Oxford University Press, 1991).

PF   *Persistence in Folly* (North Ryde, NSW: Angus & Robertson, 1984).

PM   *The Peasant Mandarin: Prose Pieces* (St Lucia: University of Queensland Press, 1978).

PO   *The People's Otherworld* (North Ryde, NSW: Angus & Robertson, 1983).

PT   *The Paperbark Tree* (Manchester: Carcanet, 1992).

Oles   Interview with Carole Oles, *American Poetry Review*, March/April 1986, 28–36.

Porter Interview with Peter Porter, *Australian Studies*, Number 4 (December 1990), 77–87.

SP   *Selected Poems* (Manchester: Carcanet, 1986).

TNY   *Translations from the Natural World* (Paddington, NSW: Isabella Press, 1992; Manchester: Carcanet, 1992).

VR   *The Vernacular Republic: Poems 1961–1981* (Edinburgh: Canongate, 1982).

Verse Interview with Robert Crawford, *Verse* issue 5, (1986), 21–32.

Many, but not all, of the Murray essays quoted in this piece are now available in Britain in *The Paperbark Tree*.

2. Paul Kane's study of Murray is forthcoming from Oxford University Press (Australia).

3. Judith Wright, *A Human Pattern: Selected Poems* (North Ryde, NSW: Angus & Robertson, 1990), 30; all the other Wright poems cited in the present piece are to be found in *A Human Pattern*, now also published by Carcanet in Britain.

4. Vincent Buckley, 'Introduction' to *The Faber Book of Modern Australian Verse* (London: Faber and Faber, 1991), xxv.

5. Chris Wallace–Crabbe, 'Hiccups' in *Falling into Language* (Melbourne: Oxford University Press, 1990), 181.

6. *The Poetry of Robert Frost*, ed. Edward Connery Lathem (London: Jonathan Cape, 1971), 348; A. D. Hope, *Selected Poems*, ed. Ruth Morse (Manchester: Carcanet, 1986), 17.

7. John Barnie, 'Dodging the National Parks' (Interview with Murray), *Planet, The Welsh Internationalist*, No. 54, December/January 1985-6, 17–18.

8. Geoffrey Hill, 'Genesis' in *For the Unfallen* (London: André Deutsch, 1959), 17.

9. See especially "On Sitting Back and Thinking About Porter's Boeotia", *PM*, 172–84.

10. *Les Murray: The Vernacular Republic*, directed by Richard Tipping, 1984 (video produced and distributed by Third Millenium Pictures in the series 'Writers Talking'; made under the auspices of the Australia Council's Literature Board and Archival Film Program). For Blake Morrison on Murray, see 'Platonic Justice, Poems from the Colonial Fringe', *The Age Monthly Review*, Vol. 5, No. 5, September 1985, 4–5. Some other stimulating pieces on Murray are Peter Porter, 'Les Murray: An Appreciation', *Journal of Commonwealth Literature*, XVII, 1, 1982, 45–52; Bruce Clunies Ross, 'Les Murray's Vernacular Republic' in Peter Quartermaine, ed., *Diversity Itself, Essays in Australian Art and Culture*, Exeter: University of Exeter Press, 1986, 21–37; Iain Bamforth, 'Physiognomy of a Maximalist – The Poetry of Les Murray', *Verse*, Vol. 6, No. 2 (June 1989), 31–40; and Kevin Hart, '"Inter-

est" in Les A. Murray', *Australian Literary Studies*, Vol. 14 No. 2, October 1989, 147–59.

11. Anecdote told on R. Tipping's film (see preceding note).
12. Private communication with the present writer.
13. See Iain Crichton Smith, *Collected Poems* (Manchester: Carcanet, 1992), 74–91 ('Ben Dorain'), 35–44 ('Deer on the High Hills').

CHAPTER 5

1. The following abbreviations are used for Ashbery's works to which reference is made in this chapter.

   AG   *April Galleons* (Manchester: Carcanet, 1987).
   AWK *As We Know* (1979; rpt. Manchester: Carcanet New Press, 1981).
   FC   *Flow Chart* (Manchester: Carcanet, 1991).
   HD   *Houseboat Days* (New York: Viking Penguin, 1977).
   HL   *Hotel Lautréamont* (Manchester: Carcanet, 1992).
   SHT *Shadow Train* (1981; rpt. Manchester: Carcanet New Press, 1982).
   SP   *Self-Portrait in a Convex Mirror* (1975; rpt. Manchester: Carcanet New Press, 1977).
   ST   *Some Trees* (1956; rpt. New York: Corinth Books, 1970).
   TC   *The Tennis Court Oath* (Middletown, Ct: Wesleyan University Press, 1962).
   TP   *Three Poems* (New York: Viking, 1972).
   SHT *Shadow Train* (1981; rpt. Manchester: Carcanet New Press, 1982).
   W   *A Wave* (Manchester: Carcanet, 1984).

2. John Ashbery, 'An Interview with John Murphy', *Poetry Review* (Vol. 75, No. 2), August, 1985, 23; hereafter this interview is cited as *Murphy*.
3. See Mark Ford, 'John Ashbery and Raymond Roussel,', *Verse*, Vol. 3, No. 3 (November 1986), 13–23.
4. Marjorie Perloff, '"Fragments of a Buried Life": John Ashbery's Dream Songs,' in David Lehman, ed., *Beyond Amazement, New Essays on John Ashbery* (Ithaca: Cornell University Press, 1980), 74–6.
5. 'John Ashbery in conversation with John Ash', *PN Review* (Vol. 12, No. 2), June 1985, 33; hereafter cited as *Ash*.
6. Walter Pater, 'Conclusion' to *The Renaissance, Studies in Art and Poetry* (1873; rpt. Glasgow: Fontana, 1961), 220, 222, 224.
7. Pater, *Plato and Platonism* (London: Macmillan, 1893), 129, 12, 102; *Ash*, 32. Pater's discussions of Plato on 'the non–experienced' (114) seem relevant also. The passage about flashing light within comes from p. 108.
8. Robert Crawford, 'Ashbery and the Nineteenth Century', *Verse* No. 6 (1986), 33–43; J. D. McClatchy, *White Paper: On Contemporary American Poetry* (New York: Columbia University Press, 1989), 55
9. Interview with David Lehman, 17 October 1977, cited in David Lehman, 'The Shield of a Greeting: The Function of Irony in John Ashbery's Poetry', in *Beyond Amazement*, 111.
10. John Ashbery, 'Neglected Fictions', *Times Literary Supplement*, 18 October 1985, 1179.
11. *SP*, 69, quoted in James Fenton, 'Getting Rid of the Burden of Sense', *New York Times Book Review*, 29 December 1985, 10.
12. Ashbery's remarks on Tennyson are taken from an account given me by Dr R. M. Cummings of Glasgow University, referring to Ashbery's answers to questions after a reading at the University of Strathclyde, Glasgow, in June 1985. I am grateful to Dr Cummings for this information, and to John Ashbery for confirming his strong liking for 'The Lady of Shalott'.
13. Sue Gangel, 'An Interview with John Ashbery', *San Francisco Review of Books* 3, No. 7 (November 1977), 12; cited by Perloff, art. cit., 66.
14. Ashbery's remarks on Smith are taken from his conversation with the present writer, 13 June 1985. On Smith as urban poet see Robert Crawford, 'Alexan-

der Smith, James Macfarlan, and City Poetry', *Scottish Literary Journal*, November 1985, 35–52.

15. On Ashbery's humour and avoidance of value–judgements see Thomas A. Fink, 'The Comic Thrust of Ashbery's Poetry', *Twentieth Century Literature*. Vol. 30, No. 1., Spring 1984, 1–14. A Marxist reading is provided by Keith Cohen, 'Ashbery's Dismantling of Bourgeois Discourse', in *Beyond Amazement*, 128–149.

16. See Marjorie Perloff, 'The Word as Such: L=A=N=G=U=A=G=E Poetry in The Eighties', *American Poetry Review*, May/June 1984, 15–22.

17. Michael Palmer, 'Sun', *Sun* (San Francisco: North Point Press, 1988), 83–6.

18. John Shoptaw, 'Investigating *The Tennis Court Oath*', *Verse*, Vol. 8, No. 1 (Spring 1991), 61–72.

19. Charles Altieri, 'Ashbery as Love–Poet', *Verse*, Vol. 8, No. 1 (Spring 1991), 8–15.

20. Noted by Fenton, art. cit. in note 11 above.

21. Fenton, *ibid*. Edwin Morgan '"In a Convex Mirror", Etc.' in *Seven Poets* (Glasgow: Third Eye Centre, 1981), 85.

22. T. S. Eliot, 'Swinburne as Poet', in *Selected Essays*, Third Enlarged Edition (London: Faber and Faber, 1951), 327.

CHAPTER 6

1. Interview, *Verse*, Vol. 6, No. 2, June 1989, 45.

2. This Kelman story was first published in 1978 and is reprinted in Moira Burgess and Hamish Whyte, eds, *Streets of Stone: An Anthology of Glasgow Short Stories* (Edinburgh: Salamander Press, 1985), 75.

3 In John Linklater, Dorothy Porter and JoAnne Robertson, eds, The *Red Hog of Colima: Scottish Short Stories 1989* (London: Collins, 1989), 87–92.

4. Frank Kuppner, 'A laugh to break the silence of space', *Glasgow Herald*, 30 December 1989, 20.

5. See Edwin Morgan, *Language, Poetry, and Language Poetry*, The Kenneth Allott Lectures, No. 5 (Liverpool: Liverpool Classical Monthly, 1990).

6. 'Notes for Echo Lake 2', *Notes for Echo Lake* (San Francisco: North Point Press, 1981), 4.

7. *Verse*, Vol. 6 No. 1, March 1989, 16–17.

8. I am indebted to Ms Marion Sinclair of Polygon for this information.

9. Hugh MacDiarmid, *Complete Poems 1920–1976*, 2 Vols., ed. Michael Grieve and W. R. Aitken (London: Martin Brian & O'Keeffe, 1978), I, 162 (*A Drunk Man Looks at the Thistle*); when asking if Scotland is small enough, Kuppner is alluding to MacDiarmid's well-known question, 'Scotland small?' and the lines which follow it – see *Complete Poems*, II, 1170–1.

10. This work was published in *Verse*, Vol. 9, No. 3 (Winter 1992), 60–1.

CHAPTER 7

1. Bernard O'Donoghue, 'Coming with the Territory', review of Norman MacCaig's *Collected Poems*, *TLS*, 5 April 1991, 25; all MacCaig poems quoted are from this 1990 *Collected Poems* (London: Chatto and Windus).

2. Craig Raine, *A Martian Sends a Postcard Home* (Oxford: Oxford University Press, 1979).

3. Philip Larkin, Foreword to *A Rumoured City: New Poets from Hull*, ed. Douglas Dunn (Newcastle: Bloodaxe Books, 1982), 9.

4. Douglas Dunn, 'England Sunk', review of Hugh Kenner's *A Sinking Island*, *Glasgow Herald*, Weekender, 8 October 1988, 2.

5. Robert Crawford and David Kinloch, eds, *Reading Douglas Dunn* (Edinburgh: Edinburgh University Press, 1992).

6. Douglas Dunn, *Elegies* (London: Faber and Faber, 1985), 27 ('Dining').

7. Douglas Dunn, *Northlight* (London: Faber and Faber, 1988), 19 ('75°').

8. *Ibid.*, 4 ('Abernethy').

9. *Ibid.*, 35 ('Winkie').

10. John Burnside, interviewed by W. N. Herbert, *Verse*, Vol. 9, No. 2, Summer 1992, p. 74.

11. John Burnside, *The Hoop* (Manchester: Carcanet, 1988), 50 ('Exile's Return').

12. Robert Crawford, ed., *Other Tongues: Younger Scottish Poets in English, Scots and Gaelic* (St Andrews: Verse, 1990), 40 ('Mariposa Pibroch').

13. David Dabydeen, *Coolie Odyssey* (London and Coventry: Hansib and Dangaroo, 1988), 12, 9. ('Coolie Odyssey').

14. Gillian Allnutt, Fred D'Aguiar, Ken Edwards, Eric Mottram, eds, *The New British Poetry* (London: Paladin, 1988), 5 ('Listen Mr Oxford Don').

15. *Ibid.*, 23 ('Callaloo').

16. *Ibid.*, 80, 84, 91, 92, 103, 108, 118.

17. The quotations from Mick Imlah's *Birthmarks* (London: Chatto and Windus, 1988) are from pp. 36, 37, 17, 18.

18. Derek Walcott, *Collected Poems 1948–1984* (New York: The Noonday Press, Farrar Straus & Giroux, 1986), 12; apart from *Omeros*, the other Walcott poems mentioned here can be found in this volume.

19. Derek Walcott, *Omeros* (London: Faber and Faber, 1990), 96.

20. *Ibid.*, 306, 52.

21. *Ibid.*, 76.

22. Ted Hughes, *Rain-Charm for the Duchy and other Laureate Poems* (London: Faber and Faber, 1992).

23. Seamus Heaney, 'Englands of the Mind', in *Preoccupations: Selected Prose 1968–1978* (London: Faber and Faber, 1980), 150–69; Tom Paulin, 'Junk Britain: Peter Reading' in *Minotaur: Poetry and the Nation State* (London: Faber and Faber, 1992), 287.

24. Peter Reading, *Essential Reading* (London: Secker & Warburg, 1986), 89 ('Opinions of the Press').

25. *Ibid.*, 2 ('Plague Graves') and 16 ('Early Stuff').

26. *Ibid.*, 6 ('Easter Letter').

27. Peter Reading, *3 in 1* (London: Chatto & Windus, 1992), 7.

28. Peter Reading, *Essential Reading*, 65.

29. *Ibid.*, 79 ('Parallel Texts'); Peter Reading, *Perduta Gente* (London: Secker & Warburg, 1989) (the pages of this book are not numbered).

30. *Ibid.*

31. *Ibid.*

32. *Ibid.*

33. Peter Reading, *Evagatory* (London: Chatto & Windus, 1992).

34. Norman MacCaig, *Collected Poems*, New Edition (London: Chatto & Windus, 1990), 126 ('Neglected Graveyard, Luskentyre').

35. *Ibid.*, 168 ('Among scholars').

36. Douglas Dunn, *St. Kilda's Parliament* (London: Faber and Faber, 1981), 30 ('The Harp of Renfrewshire'); Edwin Morgan, *Collected Poems* (Manchester: Carcanet, 1990), 156 ('Canedolia').

37. Norman MacCaig, *Collected Poems, ed. cit.*, 189 ('Aunt Julia').

38. Iain Crichton Smith, *Collected Poems* (Manchester: Carcanet, 1992), 229('Australia').

39. Norman MacCaig, *Collected Poems, ed. cit.*, 417 ('Old Highland Woman').

40. Douglas Dunn, *Terry Street* (London: Faber and Faber, 1969), 55 ('Landscape with One Figure').

41. Douglas Dunn, *Love or Nothing* (London: Faber and Faber, 1974), 28 ('Port Logan and a Vision of Live Maps'), 23 ('Renfrewshire Traveller').

42. W. S. Graham, *Collected Poems 1942–1977* (London: Faber and Faber, 1979), 191.

43. Robert Frame, 'W. S. Graham at Sandyford Place', *Edinburgh Review*, No. 75, November 1987, 63.

44. W. S. Graham, *Collected Poems*, 213.
45. Hugh MacDiarmid, 'A Theory of Scots Letters' (1923), rpt. in *The Thistle Rises*, ed. Alan Bold (London: Hamish Hamilton, 1984), 136; Iain Bamforth, *The Modern Copernicus* (Edinburgh: Salamander Press, 1984), 27–37; Ron Butlin, *Ragtime in Unfamiliar Bars* (London: Secker & Warburg, 1985), 13 ('This Embroidery').
46. Iain Bamforth, *The Modern Copernicus* (see preceding note), 41.
47. Ron Butlin, *Ragtime in Unfamiliar Bars*, 45.
48. See Iain Crichton Smith, 'The Double Man' in R. P. Draper, ed., *The Literature of Region and Nation* (Basingstoke: Macmillan, 1989), 136–46.
49. Edwin Muir, *Scott and Scotland: The Predicament of the Scottish Writer* (1936: rpt. Edinburgh: Polygon Books, 1982), 6 and 7.
50. John Ashbery, 'Author's Note' to 'Litany' in *As We Know* (Manchester: Carcanet New Press, 1981), 2.
51. Jacques Derrida, *Glas*, translated by John P. Leavey, Jr, and Richard Rand (Lincoln, Nebraska: University of Nebraska Press, 1986), 75.
52. Muriel Spark quotes these lines from her poem in 'Personal History: The School on the Links', *New Yorker*, 25 March 1991, 81. The MacDiarmid poems quoted in this chapter are from *Complete Poems 1920–1976*, ed. Michael Grieve and W. R. Aitken (2 vols, London: Martin Brian & O'Keeffe, 1978).
53. Tom Hubbard, ed., *The New Makars: The Mercat Anthology of Contemporary Poetry in Scots* (Edinburgh: Mercat Press, 1991), 'Introduction'.
54. Edwin Morgan, 'Plastic Scots' (letter), *Glasgow Herald*, 15 November 1946, 4. I am grateful to Hamish Whyte of the Mitchell Library, Glasgow for supplying me with a text of this piece.
55. For the dates of these pieces see the appropriate entries in Hamish Whyte's 'Edwin Morgan: A Checklist' in Robert Crawford and Hamish Whyte, eds, *About Edwin Morgan* (Edinburgh: Edinburgh University Press, 1990), 140–255.
56. Edwin Morgan 'Introduction' to Vladimir Mayakovsky, *Wi the Haill Voice, 25 Poems*, translated into Scots with a Glossary by Edwin Morgan (South Hinksey, Oxford: Carcanet Press, 1972), 17; hereafter the title of this book is abbreviated in the present text as *WHV*.
57. Hugh MacDiarmid, review of *Wi the Haill Voice*, *Cambridge Review*, 17 November 1972, quoted on rear jacket of Edwin Morgan, *Rites of Passage: Selected Translations* (Manchester: Carcanet New Press, 1976).
58. Morgan, 'Introduction' (see note 56 above), 10–11.
59. Edwin Morgan, *Nothing Not Giving Messages: Reflections on his Work and Life*, ed. Hamish Whyte (Edinburgh: Polygon, 1990), 117.
60. Peter McCarey, 'Edwin Morgan the Translator' in Crawford and Whyte, *op. cit.* in note 55 above, 101–2.
61. *Ibid.*, 102.
62. Hugh MacDiarmid 'A Theory of Scots Letters' (1923), rpt. in *The Thistle Rises: An Anthology of Poetry and Prose*, ed. Alan Bold (London: Hamish Hamilton, 1984), p. 129; Edwin Morgan, *Collected Poems* (Manchester: Carcanet, 1990), 79–82.
63. Morgan, *op. cit.* in note 59 above, 105 and 42; Hubbard, *art. cit.* in note 53 above, 182.
64. Tom Leonard, *Intimate Voices: Selected Work 1965–1983* (Newcastle upon Tyne: Galloping Dog Press, 1984), p. 120 (untitled). Hereafter the title of this book is abbreviated in the present text as *IV*.
65. Tom Leonard, interview with Barry Wood, *Edinburgh Review*, No. 77, May 1987, 68–9.
66. W. S. Graham, 1979 article quoted in Tony Lopez, *The Poetry of W. S. Graham* (Edinburgh: Edinburgh University Press, 1989), 11.
67. Edwin Morgan, 'The Sea, the Desert, the City : Environment and Language in W. S. Graham, Hamish Henderson, and Tom Leonard', *Yearbook of English Studies*, Vol. 17, 1987, 42.

68. Seamus Heaney, *The Government of the Tongue: The 1986 T. S. Eliot Memorial Lectures and Other Critical Writings* (London: Faber and Faber, 1988).

69. Liz Lochhead, *Dreaming Frankenstein & Collected Poems* (Edinburgh: Polygon Books, 1984), 66. For much fuller discussions of Lochhead's language, including her language in the theatre, see Robert Crawford and Anne Varty, eds, *Liz Lochhead's Voices* (Edinburgh: Edinburgh University Press, 1993).

70. Liz Lochhead, *Tartuffe: A Translation into Scots from the Original by Molière* (Edinburgh and Glasgow: Polygon and Third Eye Centre, 1985), 'Introduction'. Hereafter the title of this book is abbreviated in the present text as *T*.

71. 'W. N. Herbert Talking with Richard Price', *Verse*, Vol. 7, No. 3, 93; W. N. Herbert, *To Circumjack MacDiarmid* (Oxford: Clarendon Press, 1992).

72. W. N. Herbert, 'Radical Scots,' *Verse*, Issue 6 (1986), 55–6.

73. W. N. Herbert, '2nd Doldrum (Elephant's graveyard)' and Duncan Glen 'Editorial', *Akros*, Vol. 17, Nos 51, 58 and 7 respectively; see also W. N. Herbert, *Dundee Doldrums* (Edinburgh: Galliard, 1991).

74. Robert Crawford and W. N. Herbert, *Sharawaggi* (Edinburgh: Polygon, 1990), 135.

75. W. N. Herbert, 'From The Testament of Piers Parallax' in *The New Makars* (see note 53 above).

76. W. N. Herbert, *Anither Music* (London: Vennel Press, 1991).

Index

Index

191